# Pulitzer Prize Editorials

AMERICA'S BEST WRITING
1917-2003

*Third Edition*

Wm. David Sloan
Laird B. Anderson

Blackwell
Publishing

WM. DAVID SLOAN is professor of journalism in the College of Communication at the University of Alabama.

LAIRD B. ANDERSON is professor emeritus of journalism at the American University School of Communication in Washington, D.C.

©1980, 1994 Iowa State University Press
©2003 Iowa State Press
A Blackwell Publishing Company
All rights reserved

Blackwell Publishing Professional
2121 State Avenue, Ames, Iowa 50014

Orders:     1-800-862-6657
Office:      1-515-292-0140
Fax:         1-515-292-3348
Web site:   www.blackwellprofessional.com

Printed on acid-free paper in the United States of America

First edition, 1980
Second edition, 1994
Third edition, 2003

International Standard Book Number: 0-8138-2544-X

Library of congress Cataloging-in-Publication Data

Pulitzer prize editorials : America's best writing, 1917–2003 / [compiled by] Wm. David Sloan, Laird B. Anderson.—3rd ed.
     p. cm.
   ISBN 978-0-8138-2544-1          (alk. paper)
   1. Editorials. 2. Pulitzer prizes. I. Sloan, W. David (William David), 1947- II. Anderson, Laird B.
   PN4726.P8 2003
   070.44 2—dc21

                              2003009427

The last digit is the print number:  9  8  7  6  5  4  3  2

# Contents

# Preface

Awork of the nature of this anthology would be impossible without the help of numerous individuals. We are grateful to the following for the time and consideration they gave us during work on the first and second editions of this book.

Pulitzer Prize winners who assisted, always kindly, include J.D. Maurice, Warren L. Lerude, Paul Greenberg, John S. Knight, Virginius Dabney, Hazel Brannon Smith, John Strohmeyer, William Dorvillier, Ed Yoder, Meg Greenfield, Robert L. Bartley, Jack Rosenthal, Jim Hampton, Albert Scardino, Richard Aregood, Jack Fuller, Jonathan Freedman, Jane Healy, Lois Wille, Thomas J. Hylton, Ron Casey, Harold Jackson, Maria Henson, Michael Gartner, R. Bruce Dold, John C. Bersia, Bernard L. Stein, Michael Goodwin, Jeffrey Good, Robert B. Semple, Jr., Alex Raksin, Bob Sipchen and Cornelia Grumman.

Others who provided editorials or information, often only after time-consuming efforts of searching old newspaper files and corresponding with other sources, were Edward G. Hawkins, editor of the editorial page, the *Trentonian* (Trenton, N.J.); F.T. Weaver, manager, *Jackson* (Mich.) *Citizen Patriot*; Joseph R. L. Sterne, editor of the editorial pages, *Baltimore Sun*; Anthony Day, editor of the editorial pages, *Los Angeles Times*; Joe H. Stroud, editor, *Detroit Free Press*; John Springer, librarian, *Kansas City* (Mo.) *Star and Times*; Don Benson, director of public events, *Des Moines Register and Tribune*; James B. Boone, Jr., president, Boone Newspapers; Harry W. Baehr, editorial writer, *New York Herald Tribune*; James H. Wagner, Scripps-Howard Newspapers; Hal Gulliver, editor, *Atlanta Constitution*; Kevin Parrish, managing editor, *Fremont* (Neb.) *Tribune*; John Ball, executive editor, *Santa Barbara* (Calif.) *News-Press*; Ray Jenkins, editor, *Montgomery Advertiser* and *Alabama Journal*; Charles Scarritt, University of Alabama; Edward Grimsley, editor of the editorial page, *Richmond* (Va.) *Times-Dispatch*; John H. Metcalfe, assistant to the editor, *New York Daily News*; John O. Wynne, vice-president, Landmark Communications, Inc.; William F. Woo, editor of the editorial page, *St. Louis Post-Dispatch*; Martin L. Duggan, editorial page editor, *St. Louis Globe-Democrat*; and Walter G. Cowan, editor, *New*

*Orleans States-Item.* Of special help at the Pulitzer Prize office at
Columbia University were Richard T. Baker, Rose Valenstein,
Robin Kuzen, and Bud Klement.

Permission to reprint editorials in this anthology has been
given by the following institutions and individuals: *International
Herald Tribune*; *Louisville Courier-Journal*; *Omaha Evening
World-Herald*; Mrs. William L. (Katharine) White, *Emporia
Gazette*; *Boston Herald*; *Charleston News & Courier*; *New York
Times*; *Montgomery Advertiser* and *Alabama Journal*; Landmark
Communications, Inc. (owner of the *Norfolk Virginian-Pilot*);
*Fremont Tribune*; *Kansas City Star and Times*; *Atlantic* (Iowa)
*News-Telegraph*; *Washington Post*; Scripps-Howard Newspapers;
*Baltimore Sun*; Des Moines Register and Tribune Co.; *Portland
Oregonian*; *St. Louis Post-Dispatch*; Edward Fay and *The Daily
News*, New York City; *Providence* (R.I.) *Journal-Bulletin*;
Greenville (Miss.) *Delta Democrat Times*; *Wall Street Journal,* Dow
Jones & Co.; Virginius Dabney, *Richmond Times-Dispatch*; *Jackson
Citizen Patriot*; The Times-Picayune Publishing Co.; *St. Louis
Globe-Democrat*; *Detroit Free Press*; *Tuscaloosa* (Ala.) *News*;
*Arkansas Gazette*; *Atlanta Constitution*; William J. Dorvillier and
*San Juan* (Puerto Rico) *Star*; *Santa Barbara News-Press*; Ira B.
Harkey, Jr., *Pascagoula Chronicle*; Hazel Brannon Smith,
*Lexington* (Miss.) *Advertiser*; *Gainesville* (Fla.) *Sun*; John S.
Knight, Knight Newspapers; Paul Greenberg, *Pine Bluff* (Ark.)
*Commercial*; John Strohmeyer, *Bethlehem* (Pa.) *Globe-Times*; Roger
B. Linscott, *Berkshire Eagle*; *The Trentonian* (Trenton, N.J.); J.D.
Maurice, *Charleston* (W.V.) *Daily Mail*; *Los Angeles Times*; Warren
Lerude, *Nevada State Journal* and *Reno Evening Gazette*; Ed Yoder,
*Washington Star*; Robert L. Bartley, *Wall Street Journal*; Jack
Rosenthal, *New York Times*; Jim Hampton, *Miami Herald*; Albert
Scardino, *Georgia Gazette*; Richard Aregood, *Philadelphia Daily
News*; Jack Fuller, *Chicago Tribune*; Jonathan Freedman, *San
Diego Tribune*; Jane Healy, *Orlando Sentinel*; Sentinel
Communications Co.; Lois Wille, *Chicago Tribune*; Thomas J.
Hylton, *Pottstown* (Pa.) *Mercury*; Ron Casey, *Birmingham* (Ala.)
*News*; Maria Henson, *Lexington* (Ky.) *Herald-Leader*; Sandra
Spikes, *Chicago Tribune*; Phil Gailey and Barbara Oliver, *St.
Petersburg Times*; Dave Kraemer, *Ames* (Iowa) *Tribune*; Bernard L.
Stein, *The Riverdale* (N.Y.) *Press*; David Moats and Robert B.
Miller, *Rutland* (Vt.) *Herald*.

We appreciate the assistance of Robert M. Gravely, a graduate fellow at American University, in preparing the manuscript for
the second edition of this book.

# The Pulitzer Prize for Editorial Writing

The April announcement from Columbia University heralds the fourteen Pulitzer Prize winners in journalism, the six in letters and drama, and one for music with stock descriptions recognizing the work. The description for editorial writing is one of the longest. It outlines the general standards evaluators use in assessing entries and specifies the financial reward to the winner:

> *For distinguished editorial writing, the test of excellence being clearness of style, moral purpose, sound reasoning, and power to influence public opinion in what the writer conceives to be the right direction, due account being taken of the whole volume of the editorial writer's work during the year, seven thousand five hundred dollars ($7,500).*

The announcement briefly describes the winner's topics, sometimes with a comment, followed by a listing of those nominated as finalists, usually two, and their subjects. In 1993, when there was no award for editorial writing, the three finalists were listed beneath a glaring No Award notice.

What goes into selecting the winner, or determining there is no winner, is veiled in secrecy. Only the chairman and the prize administrator are authorized to speak for the all-powerful eighteen-member Pulitzer board that makes the final decisions based on recommendations from nominating juries. In recent years, the selection process—the board has great flexibility in its decision making and can, for instance, move nominees from one category to another, or dip into entries that had not been nominated—has angered and bruised the feelings of some jurors and finalists. But the board quietly maintains its ultimate authority, and excitement runs deep at many news organizations when announcement time rolls around every year.

## BACKGROUND OF THE AWARDS

There was probably no contention when Joseph Pulitzer established the initial awards in 1917 that editorial writing would be one of them. Opinion writing was his passion, and Pulitzer's chief concern in his *New York World* centered on its editorial page. It is not surprising, then, that his will establishing awards for journalism and letters included a prize for "the best editorial article written during the previous year."

In announcing his plans for a journalism school at Columbia University, Pulitzer in 1902 had indicated that he wished "the college to pay from the large income I am providing, a sum of —— in annual prizes to particular journalists and writers for various accomplishments. For instance, they might offer an annual prize of one thousand dollars for the best editorial."

It took a decade or so for the prizes to get the attention of many editors. But their prestige grew steadily, and today they are acknowledged as the most distinguished awards recognizing excellence in journalism.

The intention of the original edition of *Pulitzer Prize Editorials* was to make the winning editorials more easily accessible than they had been. As a group, the editorials were available only in the archives of the Pulitzer Prize administration at Columbia University—inaccessible to most people. In fact, even the archives do not have a copy of every winner. Despite the fact that winning newspapers announce the accomplishment with great fanfare, often running self-serving in-house advertisements in addition to lead news stories, some newspapers, particularly those that won in the early years of the award, do not have their winning editorials on file. Some have even forgotten that a staff writer years earlier had won the award. Only a few news organizations have reprinted the editorials or made them available to journalists and students of editorial writing.

*Pulitzer Prize Editorials* seeks to remedy the situation. This third edition contains the material from the earlier editions, includes some editorials of previous years not available in the first, and updates the collection through 2003.

The key to understanding the main standard on which the
award is based is to understand that the original description of the
editorial writing award has undergone a subtle but major change.
The original read: "For distinguished editorial writing in a United
States newspaper, published daily, Sunday, or at least once a week,
during the year, the test of excellence being clearness of style, moral
purpose, sound reasoning and power to influence public opinion in
the right direction." In 1928 the last phrase was changed to "power
to influence public opinion in what the writer conceives to be the
right direction."

Although Pulitzer had indicated a desire to have the award
based on the best individual editorial during the year, the emphasis is now placed on "the whole volume of the writer's editorial work
during the year," although in fact the prize frequently has been
awarded for a series of editorials on the same subject. Until 1933,
every award except one—Grover Cleveland Hall's in 1928—was
based on an individual editorial. Since then, the award has been
given only four times (1934, 1952, 1955, 1956) for a single editorial, although in a number of years a particular editorial has been cited as exemplary of a writer's work.

Not all editorials included in a winner's entry are reprinted
here because the number submitted has gradually climbed over the
years. When Don Murray of the *Boston Herald* submitted more
than 100 for his winning 1954 exhibit, the Pulitzer administrators
decided it was time for a crackdown and settled on a maximum of
twelve, although in unusual circumstances more would be acceptable. Today, an entry usually consists of about ten editorials for review.

THE SELECTION PROCESS

Our selections for this anthology, featuring one editorial in
most cases, are, we hope, representative of the writer's work, but
that judgment is ours alone. For the years in which the Pulitzer
was given for a single editorial, that editorial is included. For years
in which the Pulitzer committees cited a specific editorial from the
winning entry (1939, 1946, 1957, 1959, 1960), that editorial is used
in this anthology. When no specific editorial was cited, we have chosen an editorial that either seems outstanding or has been frequently cited by other writers. When no editorial stands out, we
have chosen one that seems typical of the work of the winning

writer. When the committee named more than one writer from the staff of a newspaper (1977, 1991), we have included one editorial by each writer.

There is no question that the prize brings winners new professional attention and adds some luster to their résumés. On a practical level, the original $500 prize today brings $7,500.

Many people may think that every editorial written in a given year in the United States is considered for the Pulitzer Prize. The Pulitzer for Editorial Writing is, however, awarded like most other journalism prizes. It goes to those who make the effort to enter. The author—or someone acting in the author's behalf—must apply for it. Many of the larger newspapers today have personnel devoted to packaging entries in dozens of award competitions and, when it comes to the Pulitzer, for many of the categories. That attention frequently pays dividends. In 1993, for instance, reporters for the *Los Angeles Times* and the *Philadelphia Inquirer* were nominated as the two finalists in the Beat Reporting and National Reporting categories. The *Times* also won the Spot News Reporting award and was nominated as a finalist in the International Reporting category. The *Miami Herald* that year won in two categories, Public Service and Commentary, and was a finalist in two others: Criticism and Spot News Photography, while the *Wall Street Journal* was a winner in one category, Beat Reporting, and a finalist in two others, Explanatory Journalism and Feature Writing. In 2002, the *New York Times* won in seven categories based mainly on its reporting on the 9/11 terrorist attacks of 2001, an extraordinary accomplishment even considering its location and resources in place. The categories in which it won were Public Service, Explanatory Reporting, Beat Reporting, International Reporting, Commentary, Breaking News Photography, and Feature Photography—but not Editorial Writing.

The deadline for entries, known as "exhibits," is February 1. The entries are reviewed by a five-member jury of journalism professionals, many of them prior Pulitzer winners or finalists. Their recommendations are forwarded to the board, which decides the winners, who are announced in the spring, usually in April.

Until the mid-1970s an Advisory Board reviewed the nominations made by the jurors and sent its suggestions to the Columbia University trustees. The trustees then normally ratified the suggested winners. Following several instances, however, in which the final choices were criticized because they were not the ones the jurors had recommended, the procedures were changed to have the board make the final decisions on winners. Despite the change, the name Advisory Board was retained until 1979. Changes in terminology had been contemplated for some time, and controversies over the 1978 awards spurred the action. The jurors who submit nominations for winners are now designated the *nominating* jurors. The Advisory Board became the Pulitzer Prize Board. One reason for the change was to indicate that jury nominations are only recommendations to the board and are not binding.

Another change requires the jury to make three nominations or to recommend that no one be awarded the prize. In years past, the jury could propose that either one entry or several entries or no entry at all was worthy. The jury now must list its recommendations in alphabetical order with descriptive material, rather than in order of preference. The jury does have some leeway in signaling a special recommendation to the board, but that practice is strongly discouraged.

In most years, the winner of the Pulitzer Prize has been the writer preferred by the jury, but this has not always been the case. In 1978, for example, the Pulitzer Prize Board (then the Advisory Board) chose Meg Greenfield of the *Washington Post* over Paul Greenberg of the *Pine Bluff* (Ark.) *Commercial*, winner of the editorial writing prize in 1969, whom the jury had recommended. In 1979, the jury's choice of Philip Goldsmith of the *Philadelphia Inquirer* was bypassed in favor of Edwin Yoder of the *Washington Star*. In 1993, the board raised eyebrows when it decided not to make an award in the editorial writing category despite the fact that the jury had submitted three nominations. In another category, international reporting, the board the same year stirred controversy by elevating a *New York Times* correspondent who was not one of the final nominees to dual award status with a *Newsday* reporter.

Although one recipient of the editorial writing award normally is chosen, there have been exceptions. Twice, in 1936 and 1949, two winners were named. In 1983 the entire editorial board of the *Miami Herald*, including the cartoonist, was cited. In 1999 the editorial board of the *New York Daily News* won.

There are at least two years from which no records of winning editorials are officially available. Files in the Pulitzer Prize office do not include the exhibit of George B. Parker (1936), and Scripps-Howard Newspapers has not kept a file of his entry. Virginius

Dabney of the *Richmond* (Va.) *Times-Dispatch* received the 1948 award without submitting an entry. For this anthology, we have included a Dabney editorial for which he won the 1948 Sigma Delta Chi editorial writing award.

## WRITING CONCERNS

The failure of editorial writing to snare a prize in 1993 and what that might mean for the future is vexing in editorial writing circles. Since 1917, editorial writing has failed to win an award seven times, the most of any journalism category.

The word repeated by many writers in describing editorials today is that many lack "passion." John Haile, editor of the *Orlando* (Fla.) *Sentinel* and chair of the 1993 editorial writing jury that nominated three finalists, none of whom won, acknowledged that many of the editorials reviewed by the panel seemed squeezed dry and "were void of passion." None of the exhibits reviewed were explosive, he said. "Nothing jumped to the top of the stack." Editorials, he opined, need a "greater sense of spontaneity, conviction and moral purpose."

Rob Elder, editor of the *San Jose* (Calif.) *Mercury News*, wrote in a column, "Notwithstanding the failure of editorial campaigns to win a Pulitzer this year, some hard-driving journalists insist that editorial pages can be revived only by more vigorous crusades. Stop intellectualizing, they argue. Give us more passion." But then he reflected, "Well, newspapers *were* more passionate when they spoke for ambitious, egomaniacal publishers like Joseph Pulitzer or William Randolph Hearst. They also were frequently wrong."

The founder of the Pulitzer Prize likely would have rejected the appraisal that he was frequently wrong, although he would have gloried in the assessment being leveled at Hearst, his chief competitor in the circulation wars.

Lack of passion may be an appropriate criticism in judging editorials today, but it is probably overworked. Each of us has a personal definition of what passion means in writing. Words that spur a gut reaction. Words that raise the heartbeat and blood pressure. Words that make readers leap to their feet in joy or anger. Passion, of course, has to do with the tone of the editorial voice. But the voice can get out of control and lose readers, while a more reasoned yet less impassioned tone can invoke a powerful response. Passion, however it is defined and used, should be carefully considered. Not every editorial can or necessarily should be a barn-burner. Stephen S. Rosenfeld, former editorial page editor of the *Washington Post*, put it this way:

> The best editorials show a command of context. They indicate what earlier choices led to the particular event in the news and what further options exist now. Very few events lend themselves to clear pronouncements of yes or no, good or bad. For those editorials one does not really need research, only a powerful impulse welling up from within. There is a place for them, but our more common kind—the kind that sets out to deal with events and issues in their true complexity—requires something else.

Still, in explaining how he sets himself up for writing, he hopes "that I have done enough preparation to create a critical mass." Explosion or passion? Or are they the same?

The importance of tone in reaching the ears as well as the eyes of the reader cannot be minimized. Harry D. Marsh, writing in 1985 about Pulitzer Prize editorialist Hodding Carter (1946), mused that his

> editorials were written in the rhetoric of the South. Carter's macho personality came through like a Rebel yell. They were not coldly impersonal as the vast majority of editorials were then and are now. The comments were not the slick analysis that the news magazines provided, nor boorish as were many of the segregationist writings in Mississippi. There is an intimate intensity to them typical of the never-ending arguments within an extended family in the South.

Whatever their attributes, whatever their tone of voice, we would like to be able to say that all the Pulitzer Prize editorials are outstanding, but they are not. One of the most obvious characteristics is their ordinariness. The cause of this problem lies, at least in part, in the low number of entries in the editorial writing category. For the 2002 competition, the number of entries totaled a mere eighty-three from the approximate 1,480 dailies and 7,300 weeklies that produced thousands upon thousands of editorials in 2001. The number of entries submitted from 1994 to 2002 averaged only eighty-eight per year. In all of the fourteen journalism categories in 2002, exhibits totaled 1,339, down from 1,390 the year earlier. Clearly, many editorialists were not interested, did not think their work measured up, were unfamiliar with the entry process, or were discouraged by the amount of work involved in preparing an exhibit and competing with larger newspapers that dedicate people to plan and develop slickly packaged entries. Whatever the reason, the fact is that editorials from only a handful of newspapers enter and are considered. It is fair to assume that more entries could provide stronger candidates for the final nominees, from which one might be an undisputable winner in the view of the judges.

The qualifications of judges also may contribute to the quality of winning editorials. There is no reason to believe that Pulitzer judges are either extraordinarily qualified to determine editorial perfection or omniscient. Jurors are usually respected former or practicing editorial writers who may have won the prize or been a finalist at some point. But nothing necessarily makes Pulitzer jurors and board members more qualified than judges of several other major editorial writing competitions.

The judges also are human and have their particular outlooks and biases. One obvious area in which judges' attitudes appear is subject matter of winning editorials. A typical subject has been press freedom. At least five winning writers have dealt either solely or primarily with the topic, a reflection of the egocentric interests of journalists and Pulitzer judges. Another popular topic has been race relations, treated with a strong emphasis on the rule of law. The first winning editorial on the subject was Harvey Newbranch's "Law and the Jungle" (1920). Several other winners have duplicated Newbranch's approach, but none has done a better job. A judicious editorial writer living in a Southern town experiencing racial difficulties in the 1950s or the 1960s who wrote about obedience to the U.S. Constitution probably had a good shot at the prize.

Winning editorials also have exhibited similar political leanings during specific periods. Every winning editorial writer from 1931 through 1956 who covered a political or economic topic exhibited conservative tendencies and usually sided with the Republican party. Strong nationalism or patriotism was also a hallmark of many winners. In the late 1950s a shift took place. Many editorials since then have been marked by liberalism, strongly supporting civil rights and liberties in the face of prevalent social or governmental attitudes. The change in contest rules adding "power to influence public opinion in what the writer conceives to be the right direction" to the description, laid a heavy responsibility on judges to give the edge to the quality of writing and argumentation in the context of the point of view no matter what the position. Theoretically, judges are forced to swallow their personal beliefs in the interest of the craft, although there is no practical way to judge their actions in this regard. When one notes the similarity of winners' political and social views, it is not difficult to imagine that an important factor in deciding winners is the judges' conception of what the "right direction" is. A writer who takes a stand highly unpopular with journalistic thinking—such as limiting freedom of the press—is not likely to win the Pulitzer any time soon.

Routineness of winning editorials, often coupled with unevenness of the pieces selected for entry, probably has been encouraged somewhat by the change from selecting a single outstanding editorial to basing the prize on a large volume of work by the writer. So a writer today who pens one "great" editorial along with standard fare may have little chance. John Haile, chair of the 1993 jury, noted this when he said his colleagues may have been struck by several editorials in an exhibit, but that others turned out to be flat in tone and overall quality. What we get from some winners is usually a collection of editorials above average in quality but not classic in perfection.

If the Pulitzer administration is looking for ways to improve the system—as it has in developing over time specific categories under the broad "reporting" label (spot news reporting, investigative reporting, explanatory journalism, beat reporting, national reporting, international reporting)—it might consider giving three awards in editorial writing: one (as is now done) for a series of editorials on a specific topic; another for a writer's volume of work throughout the year (as specified in today's description of the award); and a third for an individual editorial (as Pulitzer specified in his will and as was done in the early years of the award).

Although most recent winning editorials have been of acceptable quality, many of them seem to have at least one of two common problems: dull writing and lack of unity. There are exceptions, of course. Some that come to mind since 1979, when the first edition of this anthology concluded, include the work of Albert Scardino of the now-defunct weekly *Georgia Gazette* (1984); Richard Aregood of the *Philadelphia Daily News* (1985); Jane Healy of the *Orlando Sentinel* (1988); Lois Wille of the *Chicago Tribune* (1989); R. Bruce Dold of the *Chicago Tribune* (1994); Jeffrey Good of the *St. Petersburg Times* (1995); Michael Gartner of *The Daily Tribune* of Ames, Iowa (1997); and Bernard Stein of the *Riverdale* (N.Y.) *Press* (1998). Their lively, biting, sometimes sarcastic but always reflective editorials rivet attention and keep the readers on track. One has no doubt where they are leading. And yes, some of their work *is* passionate without being bombastic.

Still, the hard-hitting editorial spirit of some of the early winners seems muted in recent years. Compare, for example, the style and tone of such editorials as "Vae Victis!" (1918), "The Unknown Soldier" (1922), "To an Anxious Friend" (1923), "The House of a Hundred Sorrows" (1926), "The Gentleman from Nebraska" (1931), "A Church, A School—" (1959), and the personal and professional courage of William J. Dorvillier (1961) and Hazel Brannon Smith (1964), with many of the editorials in the 1970s. A distinct difference in phrasing, feeling, and flavor is apparent. This is not to say that no editorials since the 1960s are interestingly written. F. Gilman Spencer, for example, winner of the 1974 award, certainly had a distinctive style. And, as noted earlier, there's a lot of spirit in many of those of the 1980s. The change in style is not necessarily an indication of a change in writing ability. Rather, it more accurately reflects the history of the time in which editorials were written and a changing concept of what an editorial should do and be.

The National Conference of Editorial Writers through its quarterly journal, *The Masthead,* and at its annual meetings constantly returns to the state of editorial writing and editorial-page philosophy in rousing critique sessions and panel discussions. Overall, however, in editorial writing circles there is not much reflection on the earlier editorials that relied on the writer's personality and on formal logic to persuade readers. Today the editorial more often bases its attempt to persuade, if indeed it even has persuasion as its purpose, on statement of fact and an apparently unbiased analysis in an attempt to be more balanced and fair. Its writing style is more often intended primarily to communicate and is divorced from any other purpose. Although many early writers tried to be aesthetic, many recent writers often try simply to be informative.

Eugene Patterson, editorial writing prizewinner in 1967, leaned in that direction when he wrote that the longer he lives "the more I believe that the value of the editorial is not so much to comfort the good and convert the evil. To achieve these goals the average editor would have to be a lot smarter than he is. The true and lasting value lies in getting people to think for themselves, to talk and to argue, and finally to decide what they want to decide." Others, however, view editorials as punchy debates that make a clear point and answer major rebuttals in advance.

Breakdown of unity in editorials is as common as tepid writing. Usually this results when the writer has had no clear thematic focus or structural design in the editorial or has attempted to bring in too many aspects of details in too short a space. This problem, which needlessly deflects readers who may promptly stop reading, is apparent in a number of editorials in this anthology. Dullness and lack of clear theme are lethal when it comes to arresting readers.

Despite these shortcomings, the collection of editorials that have won the Pulitzer Prize is an excellent source of illustrations of editorial quality. The large number of editorial winners over the 86 years of the prize offer examples of a wide variety of editorial writing techniques, among them linkage to a clear news peg, argumentation, analysis, interpretation, levity, sarcasm, description, brevity, narration, common sense, metaphor, and symbolism.

It should be noted that more editorials today are making use of visual enhancement, although it is not fully reflected here, using logos, drawings, photographs, and other devices to entice the mind's eye. It is probable, in our view, that this break from tradition will grow, although there will be some resistance.

Finally, it is important that readers of this anthology put each editorial in historical context when comparing writing style and approach. It is an oversimplification, of course, to note that the world has changed in thousands of ways since 1917, but it bears repeating as you reflect on how editorial writing has adjusted and tried to come to grips with the complexity of the times. In short, think about the history of the times when you read these.

THE WINNERS

Following is a list of winners of the Pulitzer Prize for editorial writing and the official citations by Columbia University. In a few instances, winners were officially cited only by name and news organization, and thus "citations" do not exist. A number of errors, primarily in phrasing of editorial titles, have been made in the official citations. Such errors have been corrected in the list here, accounting for differences some readers might notice between this and the citations maintained by the Pulitzer Prize office.

1917 *NEW YORK TRIBUNE* for an editorial article on the first anniversary of the sinking of the *Lusitania.*

1918 *LOUISVILLE COURIER-JOURNAL* for the editorial article "Vae Victis!" and the editorial "War Has Its Compensations."

1919 No award.

1920 HARVEY E. NEWBRANCH, *Omaha Evening World-Herald,* for an editorial entitled "Law and the Jungle."

1921 No award.

1922 FRANK M. O'BRIEN, *New York Herald,* for an article entitled "The Unknown Soldier."

1923 WILLIAM ALLEN WHITE, *Emporia* (Kan.) *Gazette,* for an editorial entitled "To an Anxious Friend."

1924 *BOSTON HERALD* for an editorial entitled "Who Made Coolidge?" A special prize of $1,000 was awarded to the widow of the late FRANK I. COBB, *New York World,* in recognition of the distinction of her husband's editorial writing and service.

1925 *CHARLESTON* (S.C.) *NEWS & COURIER* for the editorial entitled "The Plight of the South."

1926 EDWARD M. KINGSBURY, *New York Times,* for the editorial entitled "The House of a Hundred Sorrows."

1927 F. LAURISTON BULLARD, *Boston Herald,* for the editorial entitled "We Submit."

1928 GROVER CLEVELAND HALL, *Montgomery* (Ala.) *Advertiser,* for his editorials against gangsterism, floggings and racial and religious intolerance.

1929 LOUIS ISAAC JAFFE, *Norfolk Virginian-Pilot,* for his editorial entitled "An Unspeakable Act of Savagery," which is typical of a series of articles written on the lynching evil and in successful advocacy of legislation to prevent it.

1930 No award.

1931 CHARLES S. RYCKMAN, *Fremont* (Neb.) *Tribune,* for the editorial entitled "The Gentleman from Nebraska."

1932 No award.

1933 *KANSAS CITY* (MO.) *STAR* for its series of editorials on national and international topics.

1934 EDWIN P. CHASE, *Atlantic* (Iowa) *News-Telegraph*, for an editorial entitled "Where Is Our Money?"

1935 No award.

1936 FELIX MORLEY, *Washington Post*, and George B. Parker, Scripps-Howard Newspapers, for distinguished editorial writing during the year.

1937 JOHN W. OWENS, *Baltimore Sun*, for distinguished editorial writing during the year.

1938 WILLIAM WESLEY WAYMACK, *Register and Tribune*, Des Moines, Iowa, for his distinguished editorial writing during the year.

1939 RONALD G. CALLVERT, *Portland Oregonian*, for his distinguished editorial writing during the year, as exemplified by the editorial entitled "My Country 'Tis of Thee . . ."

1940 BART HOWARD, *St. Louis Post-Dispatch*, for his distinguished editorial writing during the year.

1941 REUBEN MAURY, *New York Daily News*, for his distinguished editorial writing during the year.

1942 GEOFFREY PARSONS, *New York Herald Tribune*, for his distinguished editorial writing during the year.

1943 FORREST W. SEYMOUR, *Register and Tribune*, Des Moines, Iowa, for his editorials published during the calendar year 1942.

1944 HENRY J. HASKELL, *Kansas City* (Mo.) *Star,* for editorials written during the calendar year 1943.

1945 GEORGE W. PORTER, *Providence* (R.I.) *Journal-Bulletin*, for his editorials published during the calendar year 1944, especially for his editorials on the subject of freedom of the press.

1946 HODDING CARTER, *Delta Democrat-Times* (Greenville, Miss.), for a group of editorials published during the year 1945 on the subject of racial, religious and economic intolerance, as exemplified by the editorial "Go For Broke."

1947 WILLIAM H. GRIMES, *Wall Street Journal*, for distinguished editorial writing during the year.

1948 VIRGINIUS DABNEY, *Richmond* (Va.) *Times-Dispatch*, for distinguished editorial writing during the year.

1949 JOHN H. CRIDER, *Boston Herald*, and Herbert Elliston, *Washington Post*, for distinguished editorial writing during the year.

1950 CARL M. SAUNDERS, *Jackson* (Mich.) *Citizen Patriot*, for distinguished editorial writing during the year.

1951 WILLIAM H. FITZPATRICK, *New Orleans States*, for his series of editorials analyzing and clarifying a very important constitutional issue, which is described by the general heading of the series, "Government by Treaty."

1952 LOUIS LACOSS, *St. Louis Globe-Democrat*, for his editorial entitled "The Low Estate of Public Morals."

1953 VERMONT CONNECTICUT ROYSTER, *Wall Street Journal*, for distinguished editorial writing during the year.

1954 DON MURRAY, *Boston Herald*, for a series of editorials on the "New Look" in national defense, which won wide attention for its analysis of changes in American military policy.

1955 ROYCE HOWES, *Detroit Free Press*, for an editorial on the cause of a strike, impartially and clearly analyzing the responsibility of both labor and management for a local union's unauthorized strike in July 1954 that rendered 45,000 Chrysler Corporation workers idle and unpaid. By pointing out how and why the parent United Automobile Workers' union ordered the local strike called off and stating that management let dissatisfaction get out of hand, the editorial made a notable contribution to public understanding of the whole program of the respective responsibilities and relationships of labor and management in this field.

1956 LAUREN K. SOTH, *Register and Tribune*, Des Moines, Iowa, for the editorial inviting a farm delegation from the Soviet Union to visit Iowa, which led directly to the Russian farm visit to the United States.

1957 BUFORD BOONE, *Tuscaloosa* (Ala.) *News*, for his fearless and reasoned editorials in a community inflamed by a segregation issue, an outstanding example of his work being the editorial entitled "What a Price for Peace," published on February 7, 1956.

1958 HARRY S. ASHMORE, executive editor of the *Arkansas Gazette*, for the forcefulness, dispassionate analysis and clarity of his editorials on the school integration conflict in Little Rock.

1959 RALPH MCGILL, editor of the *Atlanta Constitution*, for distinguished editorial writing during 1958, as exemplified in his editorial "A Church, A School—," and for his long, courageous and effective editorial leadership.

1960 LENOIR CHAMBERS, editor of the *Norfolk Virginian-Pilot*, for his series of editorials on the school segregation problem in Virginia, as exemplified by "The Year Virginia Closed the Schools," published January 1, 1959, and "The Year Virginia Opened the Schools," published December 31, 1959.

1961 WILLIAM J. DORVILLIER, *San Juan* (Puerto Rico) *Star*, for his editorials on clerical interference in the 1960 gubernatorial election in Puerto Rico.

1962 THOMAS M. STORKE of the *Santa Barbara* (Calif.) *News-Press* for his forceful editorials calling public attention to the activities of a semisecret organization known as the John Birch Society.

1963 IRA B. HARKEY, JR., editor and publisher of the *Pascagoula* (Miss.) *Chronicle*, for his courageous editorials devoted to the processes of law and reason during the integration crisis in Mississippi in 1962.

1964 HAZEL BRANNON SMITH of the *Lexington* (Miss.) *Advertiser* for steadfast adherence to her editorial duty in the face of great pressure and opposition.

1965 JOHN R. HARRISON of the *Gainesville* (Fla.) *Sun* for his successful editorial campaign for better housing in his city.

1966 ROBERT LASCH of the *St. Louis Post-Dispatch* for his distinguished editorial writing in 1965.

1967 EUGENE PATTERSON of the *Atlanta Constitution* for his editorials during the year.

1968 JOHN S. KNIGHT of the Knight Newspapers for distinguished editorial writing.

1969 PAUL GREENBERG of the *Pine Bluff* (Ark.) *Commercial* for his editorials during 1968.

1970 PHILIP L. GEYELIN, *Washington Post*, for his editorials during 1969.

1971 HORANCE G. DAVIS, JR., of the *Gainesville* (Fla.) *Sun* for his editorials in support of the peaceful desegregation of Florida's schools.

1972 JOHN STROHMEYER of the *Bethlehem* (Pa.) *Globe-Times* for his editorial campaign to reduce racial tensions in Bethlehem.

1973 ROGER B. LINSCOTT of the *Berkshire Eagle* (Pittsfield, Mass.) for his editorials during 1972.

1974 F. GILMAN SPENCER, editor of the *Trentonian* of Trenton, N.J., for his courageous campaign to focus public attention on scandals in New Jersey's state government.

1975 JOHN DANIELL MAURICE of the *Charleston* (W. Va.) *Daily Mail* for his editorials about the Kanawha County schoolbook controversy.

1976 PHILIP P. KERBY of the *Los Angeles Times* for his editorials against government secrecy and judicial censorship.

1977 WARREN L. LERUDE, FOSTER CHURCH and NORMAN F. CARDOZA of the *Nevada State Journal* and *Reno* (Nev.) *Evening Gazette* for editorials challenging the power of a local brothel keeper.

1978 MEG GREENFIELD, deputy editorial page editor of the *Washington Post*, for selected samples of her work.

1979 EDWIN M. YODER, associate editor of the *Washington Star*.

1980 ROBERT L. BARTLEY of the *Wall Street Journal*.

1981 No award.

1982 JACK ROSENTHAL of the *New York Times*.

1983 THE MIAMI HERALD EDITORIAL BOARD (including its cartoonist) for its campaign against the detention of illegal Haitian immigrants by federal officials.

1984 ALBERT SCARDINO of the *Georgia Gazette*, Savannah, for his series of editorials on various local and state matters.

1985 RICHARD AREGOOD of the *Philadelphia Daily News* for his editorials on a variety of subjects.

1986 JACK FULLER of the *Chicago Tribune* for his editorials on constitutional issues.

1987 JONATHAN FREEDMAN of the *San Diego* (Calif.) *Tribune* for his editorials urging passage of the first major immigration reform act in 34 years.

1988 JANE HEALY of the *Orlando* (Fla.) *Sentinel* for her series of editorials protesting overdevelopment of Florida's Orange County.

1989 LOIS WILLE of the *Chicago Tribune* for her editorials on a variety of local issues.

1990 THOMAS J. HYLTON of the *Pottstown* (Pa.) *Mercury* for his editorials about a local bond issue for the preservation of farmland and other open space in rural Pennsylvania.

1991 RON CASEY, HAROLD JACKSON, and JOEY KENNEDY of the *Birmingham* (Ala.) *News* for their editorial campaign analyzing inequities in Alabama's tax system, and proposing needed reforms.

1992 MARIA HENSON of the *Lexington* (Ky.) *Herald-Leader* for her editorials about battered women in Kentucky, which focused statewide attention on the problem and prompted significant reforms.

1993 No award.

1994 R. BRUCE DOLD of the *Chicago Tribune* for his series of editorials deploring the murder of a 3-year-old boy by his abusive mother and decrying the Illinois child welfare system.

1995 JEFFREY GOOD of the *St. Petersburg* (Fla.) *Times* for his editorial campaign urging reform of Florida's probate system for settling estates.

1996 ROBERT B. SEMPLE, JR. of the *New York Times* for his editorials on environmental issues.

1997 MICHAEL GARTNER of the *The Daily Tribune*, Ames, Iowa, for his common sense editorials about issues deeply affecting the lives of people in his community.

1998 BERNARD L. STEIN of the *Riverdale* (N.Y.) *Press*, a weekly, for his gracefully-written editorials on politics and other issues affecting New York City residents.

1999 EDITORIAL BOARD of the *NEW YORK DAILY NEWS* for its effective campaign to rescue Harlem's Apollo Theater from the financial mismanagement that threatened the landmark's survival.

2000 JOHN C. BERSIA of the *Orlando Sentinel* for his passionate editorial campaign attacking predatory lending practices in the state, which prompted changes in local lending regulations.

2001 DAVID MOATS of the *Rutland* (Vt.) *Herald* for his evenhanded and influential series of editorials commenting on the divisive issues arising from civil unions for same-sex couples.

2002 ALEX RAKSIN and BOB SIPCHEN of the *Los Angeles Times* for their comprehensive and powerfully-written editorials exploring the issues and dilemmas provoked by mentally ill people dwelling on the streets.

2003 CORNELIA GRUMMAN of the *Chicago Tribune* for her freshly challenging editorials against the death penalty.

# Acknowledgments

We gratefully acknowledge the permissions granted to reprint material appearing first in the following publications:

1917—Frank H. Simonds, in the *New York Tribune*; 1918—Henry Watterson, in the *Louisville Courier-Journal*; 1920—Harvey E. Newbranch, in the *Omaha Evening World-Herald*; 1922—Frank M. O'Brien, in the *New York Herald*; 1923—William Allen White, in the *Emporia Gazette*; 1924—Frank Buxton, in the *Boston Herald*; 1925—Robert Lathan, in the *Charleston News & Courier*; 1926—Edward M. Kingsbury, in the *New York Times*; 1927—F. Lauriston Bullard, in the *Boston Herald*; 1928—Grover Cleveland Hall, in the *Montgomery Advertiser*; 1929—Louis Isaac Jaffe, in the *Norfolk Virginian-Pilot*; 1931—Charles S. Ryckman, in the *Fremont Tribune*; 1933—Henry J. Haskell, in the *Kansas City Star*; 1934—Edwin P. Chase, in the *Atlantic News-Telegraph*; 1936—Felix Morley, in the *Washington Post*; 1936—George B. Parker, in the Scripps-Howard Newspapers; 1937—John W. Owens, in the *Baltimore Sun*; 1938—William Wesley Waymack, in the *Des Moines Register*; 1939—Ronald G. Callvert, in the *Portland Oregonian*; 1940—Bart Howard, in the *St. Louis Post-Dispatch*; 1941—Reuben Maury, in the *New York Daily News*; 1942—Geoffrey Parsons, in the *New York Herald Tribune*; 1943—Forrest W. Seymour, in the *Des Moines Register*; 1944—Henry J. Haskell, in the *Kansas City Star*; 1945—George W. Potter, in the *Providence Journal-Bulletin*; 1946—Hodding Carter, in the *Delta Democrat Times*; 1947—William H. Grimes, in the *Wall Street Journal*, © Dow Jones & Co.; 1948—Virginius Dabney, in the *Richmond Times-Dispatch*; 1949—John H. Crider, in the *Boston Herald*; 1949—Herbert Elliston, in the *Washington Post*; 1950—Carl M. Saunders, in the *Jackson Citizen Patriot*; 1951—William H. Fitzpatrick, in the *New Orleans States*; 1952—Louis LaCoss, in the *St. Louis Globe-Democrat*; 1953—Vermont Connecticut Royster, in the *Wall Street Journal*, © Dow Jones & Co.; 1954—Don Murray, in the *Boston Herald*; 1955—Royce Howes, in the *Detroit Free Press*; 1956—Lauren K. Soth, in the *Des Moines Register*, © 1955, Des Moines Register and Tribune Co.; 1957—Buford Boone, in the *Tuscaloosa News*; 1958—Harry S. Ashmore, in the *Arkansas Gazette*; 1959—Ralph McGill, in the *Atlanta Constitution*; 1960—Lenoir Chambers, in the *Norfolk Virginian-Pilot*; 1961—William J. Dorvillier, in the *San Juan Star*; 1962—Thomas M. Storke, in the *Santa Barbara News-Press*; 1963—Ira B. Harkey, Jr., in the *Pascagoula Chronicle*; 1964—Hazel Brannon Smith, in the *Lexington Advertiser* and *Durant News*; 1965—John R. Harrison, in the *Gainesville Sun*; 1966—Robert Lasch, in the *St. Louis Post-Dispatch*; 1967—Eugene Patterson, in the *Atlanta Constitution*; 1968—John S. Knight, in the Knight Newspapers; 1969—Paul Greenberg, in the *Pine Bluff Commercial*; 1970—Philip Geyelin, in the *Washington Post*; 1971—Horance G. Davis, Jr., in the *Gainesville Sun*; 1972—John Strohmeyer, in the *Bethlehem Globe-Times*; 1973—Roger B. Linscott, in the *Berkshire Eagle*; 1974—F. Gilman Spencer, in the *Trentonian*; 1975—John

Daniell Maurice, in the *Charleston Daily Mail*; 1976—Philip P. Kerby, in the *Los Angeles Times*, © 1975, Los Angeles Times; 1977—Foster Church, Norman F. Cardoza, and Warren L. Lerude, in the *Nevada State Journal* and the *Reno Evening Gazette*; 1978—Meg Greenfield, in the *Washington Post*; 1979—Edwin M. Yoder, in the *Washington Star*; 1980—Robert L. Bartley, in the *Wall Street Journal*; 1982—Jack Rosenthal, in the *New York Times*, © 1981, The New York Times Company—Reprinted by permission; 1983—Editorial Board, in the *Miami Herald*, © 1982 by The Miami Herald, reprinted with permission; 1984—Albert Scardino, in the *Georgia Gazette*, reprinted by permission; 1985—Richard Aregood, in the *Philadelphia Daily News*, reprinted by permission; 1986—Jack Fuller, in the *Chicago Tribune*, © 1985, Chicago Tribune Company, all rights reserved, used with permission; 1987—Jonathan Freedman, in the *San Diego Tribune*, reprinted by permission; 1988—Jane Healy, in the *Orlando Sentinel*, © 1987, Sentinel Communications Co.; 1989—Lois Wille, in the *Chicago Tribune*, used with permission; 1990—Thomas J. Hylton, in the *Pottstown Mercury*, reprinted by permission; 1991—Ron Casey, Joey Kennedy, and Harold Jackson, in the *Birmingham News*, reprinted by permission; 1992—Maria Henson, in the *Lexington Herald-Leader*, reprinted by permission; 1994—R. Bruce Dold, in the *Chicago Tribune*, reprinted by permission; 1995—Jeffrey Good, in the *St. Petersburg Times*, reprinted by permission; 1996—Robert B. Semple, Jr., in the *New York Times*, © 2001 by the New York Times Co. Reprinted by permission; 1997—Michael Gartner, in the Ames, Iowa, *Daily Tribune*, reprinted by permission; 1998—Bernard L. Stein, in the *Riverdale (N.Y.) Press*, reprinted by permission; 1999—the Editorial Board of the *New York Daily News*, New York Daily News, L.P. reprinted with permission; 2000—John C. Bersia, in the *Orlando Sentinel*, reprinted by permission; 2001—David Moats, in the *Rutland (Vt.) Herald*, reprinted by permission; 2002—Alex Raksin and Bob Sipchen, in the *Los Angeles Times*, reprinted by permission; 2003—Cornelia Grumman, in the *Chicago Tribune*, © 2002, Chicago Tribune Company, all rights reserved, used with permission.

# Pulitzer Prize Editorials

AMERICA'S BEST WRITING
1917-2003

*Third Edition*

*1917*

# FRANK H. SIMONDS

for "The *Lusitania* Anniversary"

UNTIL the sinking of the ship *Lusitania* on May 7, 1915, Americans were widely split and many were truly neutral toward the contestants in World War I. But a turning point in public opinion came with the sinking. This was the opinion of many historians, including Frank Simonds, editor of the *New York Tribune*. In a multivolume history of World War I published in 1919, Simonds said that with the sinking Americans began to see the true, inhumane nature of Germany. Yet at the time of the *Lusitania* tragedy, fewer than half a dozen American newspapers asked for war. One of those that did was Simonds' *Tribune*. In a show of militant patriotism, it warned that "the nation which remembered the sailors of the *Maine* will not forget the civilians of the *Lusitania*." On the first anniversary of the sinking, Simonds wrote the editorial that won the first Pulitzer Prize. It was an attempt to characterize the European war as one between civilization and barbarism. Though today it may appear simplistic, it did mirror Simonds' true opinion and was not simply an artificial attempt to appeal to his readers' baser natures. In 1916 the editorial was effective propaganda considering the frame of mind of Americans.

# The *Lusitania* Anniversary

*New York Tribune* • May 7, 1916

On the anniversary of the sinking of the *Lusitania* it is natural and fitting that Americans should review all that has happened since a wanton murder first brought to this side of the Atlantic a nascent realization of the issue that was being decided on a world battlefield.

There will be no anger and no passion in American minds. We have never asked, never desired, that the slaughter should be avenged. No portion of the American people or of the American press has clamored for vengeance, no man or political party has demanded that there should be German lives taken because American lives had been ended.

It is not too difficult to reconstitute our own minds as we stood in the presence of that supreme atrocity. The horror that seized a whole nation in that moment has no counterpart in our history. We have known war, we have fought Great Britain twice, we have fought Spain and Mexico; within our own boundaries we have conducted the most desperate civil war in human history.

But it was not the emotion provoked by war or the acts of war which moved Americans. It was not even the emotion stirred by the sinking of the *Maine* nearly two decades ago. It was certainly something utterly remote from the feelings of our fathers and grandfathers on the morrow of the firing on Fort Sumter.

The *Lusitania* Massacre was not an act of war. The victims were not soldiers, only a portion of them were men. Essentially the thing was a new phenomenon to the American people. It was at first incomprehensible, unbelievable. Despite the solid and inescapable evidences of death, men's intelligence doubted what their senses told them.

So for days and weeks the American people stood doubtful and puzzled. They waited for that evidence they expected, they believed would come; that there had been an accident, a mistake, the blunder of a subordinate which would be repudiated by a government, the crime of a navy which would be disavowed by a people. But instead far borne across the seas they heard the songs of triumph of thousands of German men and women, who hailed the crime as a victory, the eternal disgrace as an everlasting honor.

Day by day, week by week, we Americans have since then been learning that we are not in the presence of a war between nations, a conflict between rival powers; that we are not the agonized witnesses of one more conflagration provoked by conflicting ambitions of hereditary enemies. We have been learning that what is going forward remorselessly, steadily, is a war between civilization and barbarism, between humanity and savagery; between the light of modern times and the darkness of the years that followed the collapse of Rome.

Time and again Americans have been murdered, time and

again our government, our people, have had recourse to the ordinary machinery and the ordinary conceptions of civilized life. But each time we have beheld the utter collapse of every appeal based upon reason, justice, common humanity. The Germans who slew our women and our children flung us back the challenge that they and not we possessed the true civilization, and that their civilization, their Kultur, was expressed in their works, which were altogether good and right.

Slowly, steadily, we have been learning. We still have much to learn, but the primary truth is coming home to many day by day. This German phenomenon which fills the world is a new thing and an old thing; it is new in our generation, it is new in recent centuries; but it is as old as that other barbarism which, descending upon the Roman civilization, beat upon it and spread destruction until it was conquered and tamed amidst the ruins and the desert it had created.

The French, who see things as they are, have beheld and appraised the German phenomenon justly. The British, like ourselves, have partially and temporarily failed to understand the nature of the German assault. We have insisted upon applying to the German mind our own standards and upon believing that the Germans thought as we thought, believed as we believed, but were temporarily and terribly betrayed by a military spirit and by dynastic madness

Nothing is less true, nothing more fatal to a just appreciation of the essential fact in the world in which we live. These things which we name crimes are neither accidents nor excesses; they are not regretted or condemned by a majority or even a minority of the German people. They are accepted by Kaiser and peasant; they are practiced by Crown Prince and private soldier; they are a portion of what Germany holds to be her right and her mission.

The *Lusitania* Massacre should have been a final illumination for us. Blazing up as it did, it should have revealed to us the ashes of Belgium and the ruins of Northern France. We should have seen in our slain women and children the sisters and fellows in misfortune of those who died more shamefully in Louvain and a score more of Belgian cities. We should have seen the German idea working here and revealing in each incident the same handiwork, the same detail. All these things were similar as the different impressions left by a single stamp.

We did not see. We have not yet as a nation, or as a people, perceived that the German phenomenon is an attack upon civilization by barbarism, a barbarism which combines the science of the laboratory with the savagery of the jungle, but a barbarism because it denies all those doctrines and principles which have been accepted after long years as the proof of human progress and the glory of mankind's advance.

In France the people will show you the atrocities of Germany commited not upon human beings, but upon the inanimate things, the destruction of the village church and the Rheims Cathedral, of the little thing of beauty quite as well as the larger and more famous thing, with far more emphasis than they will recount the horrors suffered by women and children. In the assault upon things beautiful because they are beautiful, an assault provoked neither by lust nor by passion, they recognize the revelation of that which is essential barbarism.

For us the *Lusitania* Massacre was a beginning. It was only a beginning, but it was not possible then, it is hardly possible now, for men and women, living in peace, under the protection of laws framed to protect human liberty and human rights, living in the full sunlight of this Twentieth Century, to believe that suddenly there has broken out from the depths the frightful and the all-destroying spirit of eras long forgotten.

We have been learning—we must continue to learn. The road of suffering and humiliation is still long. But the *Lusitania* was a landmark and it will endure in American history. Our children and our children's children recalling this anniversary will think of it as did the Romans over long generations, after the first inroads of the barbarians had reached their walls.

Today is not a day for anger or passion. It is not in anger or in passion that civilized men go forth to deal with wild animals, to abolish the peril which comes from the jungle or out of the darkness. We do not hate Germans and we shall not hate Germans because on this day a year ago American men, women and children were slain willfully, wantonly, to serve a German end, slain without regard to sex or condition, slain in the broad daylight by German naval officers and men whose countrymen hailed the killing as the supreme evidence of German courage, manhood, and Kultur.

But as we view the thing without passion we must see it without illusion. If the German idea prevails, all that we believe in government, in humanity, in the thing we call civilization, is doomed. If Germany succeeds in this war then it is not again time, as Pitt said after Austerlitz, 'To roll up the map of Europe,' but it is time to burn our ancient parchments and dismiss our hard won faith. All that there is in the German idea was expressed in the *Lusitania* Massacre, it was expressed in the killing of women and children, innocent of all offense, entitled to all protection as helpless, unoffending, as the children of a race not at war, at least entitled to immunity which hitherto was reckoned the right of women and children, neutral or belligerent.

The war that is being fought in Europe is a war for civilization. The battle of Great Britain, of France, of Russia, is our battle. If it is lost, we shall return to the standards and the faiths of other centuries. The truth of this is written in the wreck of the *Lusitania*, it is written in the wreck of Belgium and the desert of Northern France for those who may see. Where the German has gone he has carried physical death, but he has done more, he has carried spiritual death to all that is essential in our own democratic faith, which derives from that of Britain and France.

This war in Europe is going on until the German idea is crushed or conquers. The world cannot now exist half civilized and half German. Only one of two conceptions of life, of humanity, can subsist. One of the conceptions was written in the *Lusitania* Massacre, written clear beyond all mistaking. It is this writing that we should study on this anniversary; it is this fact that we should grasp today, not in anger, not in any spirit that clamors for vengeance, but as the citizens of a nation which has inherited noble ideals and gallant traditions, which has inherited liberty and light from those who died to serve them, and now stands face to face with that which seeks to extinguish both throughout the world.

# HENRY WATTERSON

for "Vae Victis!" and "War Has Its Compensations"

FROM the time World War I commenced in 1914, Henry Watterson, 74-year-old editor of the *Louisville* (Ky.) *Courier-Journal*, was the American press's leading exponent of American entry. In that year he had given a war cry to those Americans favoring the Allies: "To Hell with the Hapsburg and the Hohenzollern." When the United States entered the war in 1917, what Watterson had been urging for three years became reality. To celebrate the event, Watterson penned two editorials. Both were typical of his sonorous, flowery, marching style. When the Pulitzer committee met during a time of patriotic fervor to select the award for editorial writing, it gave Watterson's editorials a unanimous vote. The editorials, the judges declared, "were directed toward arousing the American people to their international duty and toward convincing a section of the country by tradition hostile to universal military service of the wisdom and necessity of its establishment." Now classic is the surprised and delighted "Marse Henry's" reply when informed of the award: "The gander-legged boys in the City Editor's room will find out that the old man is a promising journalist." He sent the $500 prize money to a war fund.

# Vae Victis!

*Louisville Courier-Journal* • April 7, 1917

"Rally round the flag, boys"—Uncle Sam's Battle song;
"Sound the bold anthem! War dogs are howling;
Proud bird of Liberty screams through the air!"
                    —The Hunters of Kentucky

It is with solemnity, and a touch of sadness, that we write the familiar words of the old refrain beneath the invocation to the starry banner, the breezy call of hero-breeding bombast quite gone out of them; the glad shout of battle; the clarion note of defiance; because to us, not as to Nick of the Woods, and his homely co-mates of the forest, but rather as to the men of '61, comes this present call to arms.

We may feel with the woman's heart of Rankin of Montana, yet repudiate with manly disdain the sentimental scruples of Kitchin of North Carolina.

There are times when feeling must be sent to the rear; when duty must toe the line; when the aversion brave men have for fighting must yield to the adjuration, "Give me liberty, or give me death!" That time is now upon us.

Unless Patrick Henry was wrong—unless Washington and the men of the Revolution were wrong, that time is upon us. It is a lie to pretend that the world is better than it was; that men are truer, wiser; that war is escapable; that peace may be had for the planning and the asking. The situation which without any act of ours rises before us is as exigent as that which rose before the Colonists in America when a mad English King, claiming to rule without accountability, asserted the right of Kings and sent an army to enforce it. A mad German Emperor, claiming partnership with God, again elevates the standard of right divine and bids the world to worship, or die.

From the beginning the issue was not less ours than of the countries first engaged. Each may have had ends of its own to serve. Nor were these ends precisely alike. At least France—to whom we owe all that we have of sovereignty and freedom—and Belgium, the little David of Nations—fought to resist invasion, wanton, cruel invasion; to avert slavery, savage, pitiless slavery. Yet, whatever the animating purpose—whatever the selfish interests of England and Russia and Italy—the Kaiser scheme of world conquest justified it.

In us it sanctifies it. Why should any American split hairs over the European rights and wrongs involved when he sees before him grim and ghastly the mailed figure of Absolutism with hand uplifted to strike Columbia where these three years she has stood pleading for justice, peace, and mercy? God of the free heart's hope and home forbid!

Each of these three years the German Kaiser was making

war upon us. He was making war secretly, through his emissaries in destruction of our industries, secretly through his diplomats plotting not merely foreign but civil war against us, and, as we now know, seeking to foment servile and racial insurrection; then openly upon the high seas levying murder upon our people and visiting all our rights and claims with scorn and insult—with scorn and insult unspeakable—at this moment pretending to flout us with ignominy and contempt. Where would the honest passivist draw the line?

Surely the time has arrived—many of us think it was long since overdue—for calling the braves to the colors. Nations must e'en take stock on occasion and manhood come to a showdown. It is but a truism to say so.

Fifty years the country has enjoyed surpassing prosperity. This has over-commercialized the character and habits of the people. Twenty-five years the gospel of passivism, with "business is business" for its text, has not only been preached—indiscriminately—oracularly without let or hindrance, but has been richly financed and potentially organized. It has established a party. It has made a cult, justifying itself in a fad it has called Humanity—in many ways a most spurious humanity—and has set this above and against patriotic inclination and duty.

Like a bolt out of the blue flashed the war signal from the very heart of Europe. Across the Atlantic its reverberations rolled to find us divided, neutral, and unprepared. For fifteen years a body of German reservists disguised as citizens have been marching and counter-marching. They grew at length bold enough to rally to the support of a pan-German scheme of conquest and a pro-German propaganda of "kultur," basing its effrontery in the German-American vote, which began its agitation by threatening us with civil war if we dared to go to war with Germany. There followed the assassin sea monsters and the airship campaign of murder.

All the while we looked on with either simpering idiocy or dazed apathy. Serbia? It was no affair of ours. Belgium? Why should we worry? Foodstuffs soaring—war stuffs roaring—everybody making money—the mercenary, the poor of heart, the mean of spirit, the bleak and barren of soul, could still plead the Hypocrisy of Uplift and chortle: "I did not raise my boy to be a soldier." Even the *Lusitania* did not awaken us to a sense of danger and arouse us from the stupefaction of ignorant and ignoble self-complacency.

First of all on bended knee we should Pray to God to forgive us. Then erect as men, Christian men, soldierly men, to the flag and the fray wherever they lead us—over the ocean—through France to Flanders—across the Low Countries to Koln, Bonn and Koblenz—tumbling the fortress of Ehrenbreitstein into the Rhine as we pass and damming the mouth of the Moselle with the debris of the ruin we make of it—then on, on to Berlin, the Black Horse Cavalry sweeping the Wilhelmstrasse like lava down the mountain side, the Junker and the saber rattler flying before us, the tunes being "Dixie" and "Yankee Doodle," the cry being "Hail the French Republic—Hail the Republic of Russia—welcome the Commonwealth of the Vaterland—no peace with the Kaiser—no parley with Autocracy, Absolutism and the divine right of Kings—to Hell with the Hapsburg and the Hohenzollern!"

# War Has Its Compensations

*Louisville Courier-Journal* • April 10, 1917

The man who is for peace at any price—who will fight on no provocation—for no cause—is apt to be either what men call "a poor creature," or an impostor set on by ulterior considerations. He may have an unworthy motive, or a selfish interest, or he may be a victim of the coward's fear of battle, or be obsessed by the doctrinaire's theory of universal brotherhood. But, craven or crank, or scheming rogue, he dishonors the noble heritage of manhood which, being common to us all, is only prized and extolled in conspicuous cases of sacrifice or prowess.

Pacifism, as it has shown itself in these times of emergency, has been compounded of each of these ingredients. But it would not have shown itself so strong if it had not been definitely organized, nor definitely organized if it had not been sufficiently financed. The Hague Arbitration movement, backed in this country by the Carnegie Foundation—actually started by the dethroned Czar of Russia—proposed a benefaction to humankind which few if any were disposed to question. It built itself upon a generally accepted truth. The gospel of "peace on earth, goodwill to men," was preached as never before. Professional warriors arrayed themselves in its behalf. Civilized nations flocked to the new religion and raised the benign standard. Many treaties embodying its aims were negotiated. One, and one alone, of the great Powers held out. That was Germany. Why, we now see clearly what we then did not see at all.

How much, if any, of the Carnegie Foundation money has been applied to the recent agitations against war with Germany, we know not. The activities of Mr. Bryan and of Dr. Jordan would lead to the conclusion that it has not been idle, or grudging, since neither of them works for nothing. But it is quite certain that it has been cunningly supplemented and enormously increased by money sent from Berlin to maintain a propaganda to divide our people and paralyze our Government. The prosecution of this now becomes treason and a pacifist who adheres to it is a traitor.

The conspirator who, claiming to be a pacifist, engaged in the nefarious business will be at no loss to save his skin. If he be a German emissary sent over for the purpose he has only to slip away. If he be a Kaiser reservist masquerading as an American citizen he can shift his foot and change his coat. If he be a selfish politician of the Stone-La Follette variety, with an eye on the Hyphenated Vote, he can wink his other eye, hoist the flag and sing "The Star-Spangled Banner" as lustily as the rest.

Those who are most in danger and only in danger are the honest simpletons who stick to it that war is crime; that we have no case against Germany, but, if we have, that it will keep; who go around mouthing socialistic and infidelistic platitudes about a paradisiac dreamland which exists nowhere outside their muddled brains. They cannot see that we have pursued peace to the limit and that peace longer pursued will prove more costly than war. Perverse and egotistical, prompted by the half truths of defective education, uninspired by ideals having any relation to the state of the country, or the spiritual needs of existence, they will not stop their vain chatter until, obstructing enlistments, or menacing public works, they land in jail.

It is grievous that this should be so. Yet it were not occasion for serious comment except that there is a middle class of non-descripts who are more numerous than an earnest and luminous patriotism would have them; men, who were born without enthusiasm and have lived to make money; men, with whom "business is business"; men who are indifferent to what happens so it does not happen to them; in short, men who recall the citation from "The Cricket on the Hearth," put into the mouth of Caleb Plummer:

> There was a jolly miller and he lived upon the Dee.
> He sang to himself, "I care for nobody and nobody cares for me."

"A most equivocal jollity," as Dickens does not fail to remark.

These people have sprung from the over-commercialism of fifty years of a kind of uncanny prosperity. Their example has affected injuriously the nation's reputation and has trenched perilously upon the character and habits of the people. It needs to be checked. They need a lesson. Nothing short of the dire exigencies which have come upon us would reach a mass so dense and stoic, so paltry and sordid, so unworthy of the blessings which the heroism of the fathers has secured them. That check and lesson they are about to receive. War is not wholly without its compensations.

The woman who is for peace at any price—whose imagination is filled with the horror of war—who, true to her nature, shrinks from bloodshed—is not as the man who skulks from the line and lowers alike the flag of his country and manhood. Ah, no! Peace is the glory of woman. Not upon the soul-stirring field of battle—rather in the dread field hospital after the battle—are her trophies to be found.

Well may she stand out against the strife of nations—yet equally with brave men she has her place in the orbit of duty and valor—and, when there is no peace, when war has come, the woman who whines "I did not raise my boy to be a soldier" forfeits her right and claim to be considered only a little lower than the angels, dishonors the genius of Womanhood and removes herself from the company and category of the heroic mothers of the world.

War, horrible as war is—"Hell," as a great warrior said it was—is not without its compensations. No man has more than one time to die. In bringing the realization of death nearer to us war throws a new light upon life. The soldier is a picked man. Whether he be a soldier in arms or a soldier of the cross, his courage, his loyalty, his love and faith challenge the confidence of men and the adoration of women. If he falls he has paid his mortal debt with honor. If he survives, though crippled, he is not disabled. His crutch tells its own story and carries its mute appeal, and there is an eloquence, though silent, resistless, in the empty sleeve.

Christendom stands face to face with the dispersion of some of its cherished ideals. There is much in its Bible that must needs be retranslated and readjusted. Although this will arouse the theologians, they will have to meet it.

Where this present cataclysm will leave us no man can foresee. Our world is, and will still remain, a world of sin, disease and death. This no man can deny. Science is minimizing disease. Death being certain, can creeds or statutes extirpate sin? Can they change the nature of man?

Before all else they must chasten it. For two thousand years theologic controversy has not only kept the world at war, but has driven its inhabitants further apart. It may be that this world war has come to cleanse the earth and to bring all tribes and races to a better understanding of what Christendom is, since there is no reason to doubt that the essential principles of Christianity will continue to dominate the universe.

'Tis a long way, we are told, to the Tipperary of Hibernia, but yet a longer [way] to the Millennial Tipperary of Scriptural mythology. The Christ-child must be born again in the heart of man. At this moment it is not the star of Bethlehem that shines. It is the luminary of the war god. The drums beat as for the men of old. "To your tents, O Israel," comes the word out of the deeps of the far away, and from highway and byway, as if in answer, the refrain "Tramp, tramp, tramp, the boys are marching."

Yet the Associated Press dispatches carry the following:

Washington, April 7.—Continuation of the pacifist fight on President Wilson's war programme was forecast to-day when the fifty Representatives who voted against the war resolution received the following identic telegram from Lelia Fay Secor, secretary of the Emergency Peace Federation:

"On behalf of the Emergency Peace Federation I thank you for your patriotic stand in opposition to war. May I request that you communicate at once with Representative Kitchin, to whom I have written a letter suggesting co-operation between ourselves and the pacifists in congress."

Mr. Kitchin is at his home in North Carolina and details of the scheme outlined in the letter to him could not be learned. He announced before leaving Washington that his opposition to the war programme would end with his vote against the resolution.

"Scissors!" shrieks Lelia Fay.

"Scissors!" cries good Mrs. Garrison Villard.

And away off yonder from the limb of a tree the Dickey Bird, impersonated by Claude Kitchin, responds, "Not on your life, ladies!"

*1920*

# HARVEY E. NEWBRANCH

for "Law and the Jungle"

IN September 1919 a black man was arrested for the rape of a white woman in Omaha, Nebraska. A mob gathered, broke the man from jail, and lynched him. Harvey Newbranch, editor of the *Evening World-Herald*, chronicled the episode and the rioting that followed. In a passionate editorial, he called on fellow citizens to respect the rule of law. It was the first of numerous editorials on the theme of law-and-order during racial crises to win the Pulitzer Prize. None of the later ones, however, surpassed the quality of Newbranch's work. While passion burned in the words, the editorial still exhibited a well-defined logic. Newbranch clearly stated the polarity between lawlessness and obedience to the law. A number of themes discussed are worth considering because they are common in later Pulitzer editorials—themes dealing, for example, with the necessity of obedience to law, the injustice of racial prejudice, the shame of rioters as cowards and animals, the blaming of authorities for their failure to uphold the law, and the appeal to civic pride in the good reputation of a town.

# Law and the Jungle

*Omaha Evening World-Herald* • September 30, 1919

There is the rule of the jungle in this world, and there is the rule of law.

Under jungle rule no man's life is safe, no man's wife, no man's mother, sister, children, home, liberty, rights, property. Under the rule of law protection is provided for all these, and provided in proportion as law is efficiently and honestly administered and its power and authority respected and obeyed.

Omaha Sunday was disgraced and humiliated by a monstrous object lesson of what jungle rule means. The lack of efficient government in Omaha, the lack of governmental foresight and sagacity and energy, made the exhibition possible. It was provided by a few hundred hoodlums, most of them mere boys, organized as the wolf-pack is organized, inflamed by the spirit of anarchy and license, of plunder and destruction. Ten thousand or more good citizens, without leadership, without organization, without public authority that had made an effort to organize them for the anticipated emergency, were obliged to stand as onlookers, shamed in their hearts, and witness the hideous orgy of lawlessness. Some of them, to their blighting shame be it said, respectable men with women and children in their homes, let themselves be swept away by the mob spirit. They encouraged if they did not aid the wolf-pack that was conspiring to put down the rule of law in Omaha—that rule which is the sole protection for every man's home and family.

It is over now, thank God!

Omaha henceforth will be as safe for its citizens, and as safe for the visitors within its gates, as any city in the land. Its respectable and law-abiding people, comprising 99 per cent of the population, will see to that. They have already taken the steps to see to it. The first step was taken when the rioting was at its height—taken belatedly, it is true, because they had placed reliance on the public authorities to safeguard the order and good name of Omaha. The blistering disgrace of the riot has aroused them. There will be no more faltering, no more fickleness, no more procrastination, no longer the lack of a firm hand. The military aid that has been called in is only temporary. It serves to insure public order and public safety for the day, for the week. But the strengthening of the police force of the city, its efficient organization under wise and competent leadership, is a policy that public sentiment has inaugurated and that it will sternly enforce. As to that there will be neither equivocation nor delay. Nor will there be any hesitancy or laxness in the organization, and rigid use if need be, of civic guards to keep the streets and homes and public places of Omaha secure.

The citizenship of Omaha will be anxious that the outside world should know what it was that happened and why it happened. Let there be no mistaking the plain facts. The trouble is over now. It was a flare-up that died as quickly as it was born.

Omaha is today the same safe and orderly city it has always been. It will be safer, indeed, hereafter, and more orderly, because of the lesson it has so dearly learned. And the flareup was the work—let this fact be emphasized—of a few hundred rioters, some of them incited by an outrageous deed, others of them skulkers in the anarchistic underbrush who urged them on for their own foul purposes of destroying property and paralyzing the arm of the law. If the miserable negro, Brown, had been removed from Omaha in time, as he should have been; if, failing to remove him, the public authorities had taken vigorous measures to prevent the congregation and inflaming of the mob, the riot would never have occurred. An organized and intelligently directed effort in advance would have preserved the good name of Omaha untarnished. It would have prevented the lynching. It would have saved our splendid new courthouse from being offered up in flames, its defense with the mob-victim in it, a costly sacrifice on the altar of law and order. There would have been no thought, even, of the amazing attempt to lynch the mayor of Omaha, bravely and honorably discharging his duty as chief magistrate in resisting the wolf-pack.

It would be impossible to speak too strongly in condemnation of the rioters or in the uncompromising demand for their stern and swift punishment, whoever they be, wherever they can be found. They not only foully murdered a negro they believed to be guilty. They brutally maltreated and attempted to murder other negroes whom they knew to be innocent. They tried to lynch the mayor. They wantonly pillaged stores and destroyed property. They burned the courthouse. In the sheer spirit of anarchy they pulled valuable records from their steel filing cases, saturated them in gasoline, and burned them. They burned police conveyances and cut the fire hose, inviting the destruction by fire of the entire city. Their actions were wholly vile, wholly evil, and malignantly dangerous. There is not a one of them who can be apprehended, and whose guilt can be proved, but should be sent for a long term to the state prison. And toward that end every effort of every good citizen, as well as every effort of the public authorities, from the humblest policeman to the presiding judge on the bench, must be directed. There can be no sentimentalizing, no fearful hesitancy, no condoning the offense of these redhanded criminals. The pitiful bluff they have put up against the majesty of the law, against the inviolability of American institutions, must be called and called fearlessly.

To the law-abiding negroes of Omaha, who, like the law-abiding whites, are the vast majority of their race, it is timely to speak a work of sympathy and support. Any effort on the part of any of them to take the law into their own hands would be as culpable and as certainly disastrous as was the effort of the mob. In the running down and maltreating of unoffending men of their color, merely because they were of that color, they have been done odious wrong. They naturally and properly resent having been confined to their homes, in trembling fear of their lives, while red riot ran the streets of the city. But their duty as good citizens is precisely the same as that of the rest of us, all of us, who have been outraged and shamed as citizens. It is to look to the law for their protection, for their vindication, and to give the law every possible support as it moves in its course. The law is their only shield, as it is the only shield of every white man, no matter how lowly or how great. And it is the duty of all, whites and blacks alike, to uphold especially the might of the law—to insist, if need be, on its full exercise—in protecting every colored citizen of Omaha in his lawful and constitutional rights.

For the first time in many years—and for the last time, let us hope, for many years to come—Omaha has had an experience with lawlessness. We have seen what it is. We have seen how it works. We have felt, however briefly, the fetid breath of anarchy on our cheeks. We have experienced the cold chill of fear which it arouses. We have seen, as in a nightmare, its awful possibilities. We have learned how frail is the barrier which divides civilization from the primal jungle—and we have been given to see clearly what that barrier is.

It is the Law! It is the Might of the Law, wisely and fearlessly administered! It is respect for and obedience to the Law on the part of the members of society!

When these fail us all things fail. When these are lost all will be lost. Should the day ever come when the rule that was in Omaha Sunday night become the dominant rule, the grasses of the jungle would overspread our civilization, its wild denizens, human and brute, would make their foul feast on the ruins, and the God who rules over us would turn His face in sorrow from a world given over to bestiality.

May the lesson of Sunday night sink deep! May we take home to our hearts, there to be cherished and never for a moment forgotten, the words of the revered Lincoln:

Let reverence of the law be breathed by every mother to the lisping babe that prattles on her lap; let it be taught in schools, seminaries and colleges; let it be written in primers, spelling books and almanacs; let it be preached from pulpits and proclaimed in legislative halls and enforced in courts of justice; let it become the political religion of the nation.

# FRANK M. O'BRIEN

for "The Unknown Soldier"

> ONE of the most popular winners of the Pulitzer Prize was Frank
> O'Brien's tribute on the occasion of the burial of America's "Un-
> known Soldier" November 11, 1921, in Arlington Cemetery. It
> was an opportune subject for journalism awards; Kirke Simpson's
> 1922 Pulitzer for reporting was given also for a story about the
> burial. The appeal of O'Brien's editorial derived from its noble-
> ness of ideas and the universality of O'Brien's descriptions. The
> editorial was more emotional and more "artistic" than most edito-
> rials of today, but despite the emotionalism of the subject the edi-
> torial really had a very simple, formal structure. Its lead
> sentence stated the three meanings of the burial, and the body
> simply explained each in order. The first two paragraphs were
> devoted to the burial as a "symbol," the next two to its "mystery,"
> and the final two long paragraphs and summary sentence to the
> "tribute." Tying all three together was a strong religious motif,
> unusual today but common among early winners of the Pulitzer.

# The Unknown Soldier

*New York Herald* • November 11, 1921

That which takes place today at the National Cemetery in
Arlington is a symbol, a mystery and a tribute. It is an entomb-
ment only in the physical sense. It is rather the enthronement of
Duty and Honor. This man who died for his country is the symbol
of these qualities; a far more perfect symbol than any man could
be whose name and deeds we knew. He represents more, really,
than the unidentified dead, for we cannot separate them spiritu-
ally from the war heroes whose names are written on their grave-
stones. He—this spirit whom we honor—stands for the unselfish-

ness of all.

This, of all monuments to the dead, is lasting and immutable. So long as men revere the finer things of life the tomb of the nameless hero will remain a shrine. Nor, with the shifts of time and mind, can there be a changing of values. No historian shall rise to modify the virtues or the faults of the Soldier. He has an immunity for which kings might pray. The years may bring erosion to the granite but not to the memory of the Unknown.

It is a common weakness of humanity to ask the questions that can never be answered in this life. Probably none to whom the drama of the Unknown Soldier has appealed has not wondered who, in the sunshine of earth, was the protagonist of today's ceremony. A logger from the Penobscot? An orchardist from the Pacific coast? A well driller from Texas? A machinist from Connecticut? A lad who left his hoe to rust among the Missouri corn? A longshoreman from Hell's Kitchen? Perhaps some youth from the tobacco fields, resting again in his own Virginia. All that the army tells of him is that he died in battle. All that the heart tells is that some woman loved him. More than that no man shall learn. In this mystery, as in the riddle of the universe, the wise wonder; but they would [sic] not know.

What were his dreams, his ambitions? Likely he shared those common to the millions: a life of peace and honest struggle, with such small success as comes to most who try; and at the end the place on the hillside among his fathers. Today to do honor at his last resting place come the greatest soldiers of the age, famous statesmen from other continents, the President, the high judges and the legislators of his own country, and many men who, like himself, fought for the flag. At his bier will gather the most remarkable group that America has seen. And the tomb which Fate reserved for him is, instead of the narrow cell on the village hillside, one as lasting as that of Rameses and as inspiring as Napoleon's.

It is a great religious ceremony, this burial today. The exaltation of the nameless bones would not be possible except for Belief. Where were Duty and Honor, the wellsprings of Victory, if mankind feared that death drew a black curtain behind which lay nothing but the dark? So all in whom the spark of hope has not died can well believe that we, to whom the Soldier is a mystery, are not a mystery to him. They can believe that the watchers at Arlington today are not merely a few thousands of the living but the countless battalions of the departed. "Though he were dead, yet shall he live"—there is the promise to which men hold when everything of this earth has slipped away.

All the impressive ritual of today would be a mockery if we did not believe that, out in an infinity which astronomers cannot chart or mathematicians bound, the Unknown Soldier and all the glorious dead whom we honor in his dust are looking down upon this little spinning ball, conscious of our reverence. And when noon strikes, signal for the moment of silent prayer, few of those who stand with bared head will lack conviction that the rites at Arlington are viewed by other than mortal eyes. Only in that spirit may we honor the Unknown Soldier and those who, like him, died for this Republic.

Unknown, but not unknowing!

# WILLIAM ALLEN WHITE

for "To an Anxious Friend"

WHEN railroad workers struck in 1922, the governor of Kansas attempted to use the full force of law and his office to suppress the strike. Placards that strikers asked merchants to display in support of the strike offended the governor, Henry Allen, and he ordered them down. William Allen White, a personal friend of the governor, told him the order was a violation of the First Amendment and that White was intending to display a placard himself. "If you do that," Governor Allen threatened, "I'll have to arrest you." White answered, "Come on and arrest me, and we'll test this matter in the courts." He posted in his newspaper-office window a placard similar to the type the governor had banned, and the confrontation between the two men became national news. Fred J. Atwood, a close friend of White, wrote the editor a warm and sincere letter to protest. White answered him, and then realized his answer to Atwood would be an answer to all people opposing White's stand. The answer echoed familiar reasoning on the importance of freedom of expression during times of stress. White's clear writing style, however, lent impact to the thought. "I worked over the phraseology of that editorial," White explained. "I cut out every adjective and used a verb instead, which greatly strengthens one's style. I shortened it, avoiding repetition, and finally ran it out." The editorial was picked up nationwide because, White surmised, "the moderation and strength of this boiled-down, concentrated, passionate reply to my opponents gave it wings." The strike soon ended, and the governor's suit against White was dropped.

# To an Anxious Friend

*Emporia* (Kan.) *Gazette* • July 27, 1922

You tell me that law is above freedom of utterance. And I reply that you can have no wise laws nor free enforcement of wise laws unless there is free expression of the wisdom of the people—and alas, their folly with it. But if there is freedom, folly will die of its own poison, and the wisdom will survive. That is the history of the race. It is the proof of man's kinship with God. You say that freedom of utterance is not for time of stress, and I reply with the sad truth that only in time of stress is freedom of utterance in danger. No one questions it in calm days, because it is not needed. And the reverse is true also; only when free utterance is suppressed is it needed, and when it is needed, it is most vital to justice.

Peace is good. But if you are interested in peace through force and without free discussion—that is to say, free utterance decently and in order—your interest in justice is slight. And peace without justice is tyranny, no matter how you may sugar coat it with expediency. This state today is in more danger from suppression than from violence, because in the end, suppression leads to violence. Violence, indeed, is the child of Suppression. Whoever pleads for justice helps to keep the peace; and whoever tramples upon the plea for justice, temperately made in the name of peace, only outrages peace and kills something fine in the heart of man which God put there when we got our manhood. When that is killed, brute meets brute on each side of the line.

So, dear friend, put fear out of your heart. This nation will survive, this state will prosper, the orderly business of life will go forward if only men can speak in whatever way given them to utter what their hearts hold—by voice, by posted card, by letter or by press. Reason never has failed men. Only force and repression have made the wrecks in the world.

# FRANK BUXTON

for "Who Made Coolidge?"

SHORTLY after Calvin Coolidge had become president on the death of Warren G. Harding, Frank Buxton of the *Boston Herald* wrote an editorial using a simple rhetorical device that answered the question "Who made Coolidge?" Repeatedly asking the question, the editorial each time gave a short answer. Although the editorial was distinctive for its structure, the announcement that it had won the 1924 Pulitzer Prize met with criticism. Critics said that its thought was superficial and its form simple. *Editor and Publisher* said of it: "The editorial prize winner seems to us a labored effort, freakish, without deep penetration and lacking qualities of spontaneity and purpose that one would expect in an editorial selected for distinguished merit from the year's production. The author might have carried his musical inquiry back to the biological source of human existence." In response to the criticism, it can be pointed out that the editorial was not typical of most editorial style or structure. Its mood was a pleasing combination of humor and adulation. Rather than being superficial, one could argue, its reasoning attempted to get at fundamental factors in Coolidge's rise to the presidency. This rise, the editorial implied, was the result of a combination of Coolidge's acquaintances, his character, and happenstance. It recognized the essentials of Coolidge's gaining national prominence: his honesty and frugality, his handling of the Boston police strike of 1919, the political astuteness of Frank Stearns and Senator W. Murray Crane, and the long line of accidents favoring his fortunes.

# Who Made Coolidge?

*Boston Herald* • September 14, 1923

"Who made Calvin Coolidge?"

Margaret Foley, of course. When Levis Grenwood was President of the Massachusetts Senate he opposed woman suffrage. She opposed his re-election in his district and prevailed. Senator Coolidge became President Coolidge on Beacon Hill and the signals were set clear for the road to the Governorship.

"Who made Calvin Coolidge?"

Edwin U. Curtis, of course. When he was a sick man in that old brick building at the dead-end of Pemberton Square, the heedless policemen went on strike to the refrain, "Hail, Hail, the Gang's All Here."

The sick man showed the strength of the stalwart, until finally Governor Coolidge sent a telegram to Samuel Gompers that tapped its way into national prominence, and is today a sort of Magna Charta of the people's rights.

"Who made Calvin Coolidge?"

James Lucey, the Northampton cobbler, of course. No explanation or argument is necessary here, but merely a reminder. The *Herald* published a facsimile a few days ago of President Coolidge's letter to him, which said: "If it were not for you, I should not be here."

"Who made Calvin Coolidge?"

Frank W. Stearns, of course. With as close an approximation to second sight as we may expect in these days, and with an ability to see around the corner years before Einstein told us how rays of light are bent, this substantial, self-made, self-respecting Boston merchant, with his quiet sense of obligation to the community, discerned qualities which hardly anyone else glimpsed. To go to the Republican Convention he left a Governor only to come back to pay his respects to a potential Vice President.

"Who made Calvin Coolidge?"

Senator Crane, of course. He made Coolidge by showing him, in precept and practice, the way of wisdom and by vouching for him in high places where his chance say-so was as good as his oath and bond. To the younger man he gave that mixture of personal attachment and respect of which he was none too prodigal, but always of mighty advantage to the few who won it.

"Who made Calvin Coolidge?"

The Republican Party of Massachusetts, of course, a canny organization, with some Bourbonism, some democracy, some vision, some solid traditions and no end of genuine appreciation of the merits of a trustworthy man. It always lined up behind him solidly even when he displayed that reticence which to the unknowing was some evidence of ingratitude, and to the knowing was merely Coolidgeism.

"Who made Calvin Coolidge?"

The people of Massachusetts, of course. They took him at more than his own modest valuation, whether he wanted to be a town officer or a Governor. They had that which thousands call a blind faith in him. More thousands called it a passionate intuition.

"Who made Calvin Coolidge?"

His mother, of course, who endowed him with her own attributes; a father that taught him prudential ways with all the quiet vigor of the old Greeks, who preached moderation in everything; his school and his college; his classmate, Dwight Morrow; and his guest of a day or two ago at the White House, William F. Whiting.

"Who made Calvin Coolidge?"

Calvin Coolidge, of course. From the reflective shoemaker and the furious Miss Foley to the complacent Frank W. Stearns and the watchful and discerning Senator from Dalton came some of the makings, but the man himself had the essentials of greatness. Give another man those same foes and friends and he might still be as far from the White House as most sons of Vermont.

*1925*

# ROBERT LATHAN

for "The Plight of the South"

> IN the 1920s the South was a neglected political region, offering
> no programs of national importance and receiving no acknowl-
> edgment in return. Its peculiar racial situation obscured its view
> and interest in other issues, and it had no strong political leaders
> capable of or interested in focusing its mind and strength on
> other areas. As a result, other sections ignored it politically and it
> suffered neglect in national programs. Much of the problem was
> created by the Southern mentality of peculiarity and isolation.
> Most newspapers did little to ameliorate the problem, looking at
> it from the same perspective as their readers and seeing little
> need for change. It was to stimulate awareness of this problem
> that Robert Lathan, editor of the *Charleston* (S.C.) *News &*
> *Courier*, wrote "The Plight of the South." Lathan emphasized
> particularly the void in national political programs and
> leadership coming out of the South. His editorial did not attempt
> to provide solutions to the problem—it simply presented and
> analyzed the situation, but with an obvious desire that answers
> be found.

# The Plight of the South

*Charleston* (S.C.) *News & Courier* • November 5, 1924

This article is being written on election day but before the
result of the voting can possibly be known. No matter. The suggestions it contains will still be pertinent whatever the story told by
the first page this morning. It makes very little difference what
any of us think about the outcome of yesterday's balloting. It
makes a considerable difference whether or not the people of the
South realize the precarious situation which this section has come

to occupy politically.

As yet we doubt if very many of them do realize this; and yet it is, we think, the outstanding political development of the time so far as we are concerned. Look at the facts. They are not pleasant to contemplate but they cannot be ignored longer. We are in a sad fix politically in this part of the country and if we are to find a remedy for our troubles we must first of all determine what they are. That will take considerable discussion and all we can hope to do now is to help start the ball of this discussion rolling. If that can be accomplished we may achieve the new program and the new leadership which we so much need.

For at the root of the South's present plight lies the fact that it has today virtually no national program and virtually no national leadership. Is it strange that it should be treated by the rest of the country as such a negligible factor? What is it contributing today in the way of political thought? What political leaders has it who possess weight or authority beyond their own States? What constructive policies are its people ready to fight for with the brains and zeal that made them a power in the old days?

The Plight of the South in these respects would be perilous at any time. In a period when politcal currents are deeper and swifter than ever before, with more violent whirlpools, more dangerous rocks and shoals, ours is truly a perilous position. Changes which used to be decades in the making now sweep over us almost before we know they are in contemplation. It is true everywhere. In all the countries of Europe the pendulum is swinging, now far to the left, now far to the right. Center parties have lost their power. They are in a very bad way. And the South has belonged to the school politically which sought as a rule the middle of the road, eschewing ultra-conservatism on the one hand and radicalism on the other. With Labor organized and militant, with radicalism organized and in deadly earnest, with conservatism organized and drawing the lines sharply, what is the South to do, what course shall she take, where do her interests lie, what is due to happen to her?

These are questions which already begin to press for answers. Who is to speak for the South? How many of her citizens are prepared to help formulate her replies?

*1926*

# EDWARD M. KINGSBURY

for "The House of a Hundred Sorrows"

THE *New York Times,* like many other newspapers, at one time
annually compiled a list of the neediest people in its city and
sponsored drives to help them during the Christmas season. The
problem for the editorial writer who must write such a yearly
piece is how to avoid cliché. For his editorial urging help with the
*Times'* "One Hundred Neediest," Edward M. Kingsbury won the
1926 Pulitzer Prize. Structured as if it were taking the reader on
a visit to a building filled with people in need, the editorial has a
distinctive approach. It also shows true sympathy and concern
for the needy. Edward P. Mitchell, editor of the *New York Sun,* of
which Kingsbury had been a staff member, said Kingsbury was
unique for his "exquisite humor, fine wit, broad literary appreciation and originality of idea and phrase." The executive secretary
of the Pulitzer Advisory Board said that, although the Pulitzer
Prize was awarded to Kingsbury on the basis of his "brilliant"
previous work, the award was made primarily because of this one
"beautiful" editorial.

# The House of a Hundred Sorrows

*New York Times* • December 14, 1925

The walls are grimy and discolored. The uneven floors creak
and yield under foot. Staircases and landings are rickety and
black. The door of every room is open. Walk along these corridors.
Walk into this room. Here is a sickly boy of 5, deserted by his
mother, underfed, solitary in the awful solitude of starved neglected childhood. "Seldom talks." Strange, isn't it? Some, many
children, never "prattle," like your darlings. They are already old.
They are full, perhaps, of long, hopeless thoughts. There are

plenty of other "kids" in this tenement. Here is one, only 3. Never saw his father. His mother spurned and abused him. He is weak and "backward." How wicked of him when he has been so encouraged and coddled! Do children play? Not his kind. They live to suffer.

In Room 24 is Rose, a housemother of 10. Father is in the hospital. Mother is crippled with rheumatism. Rose does all the work. You would love Rose if she came out of Dickens. Well, there she is, mothering her mother in Room 24. In Room 20 age has been toiling for youth. Grandmother has been taking care of three granddaughters who lost their mother. A brave old woman; but what with rheumatism and heart weakness, threescore-and-ten can't go out to work any more. What's going to happen to her and her charges? Thinking of that, she is ill on top of her physical illness. A very interesting house, isn't it, Sir? Decidedly "a rum sort of place," Madam? Come into Room 23. Simon, the dollmaker—but handmade dolls are "out"—lives, if you call it living, here. Eighty years old, his wife of about the same age. Their eyesight is mostly gone. Otherwise they would still be sewing on buttons and earning a scanty livelihood for themselves and two little girls, their grandchildren. The girls object to going to an orphan home. Some children are like that.

You must see those twin sisters of 65 in Room 47. True, they are doing better than usual on account of the coming holidays; making as much as $10 a month, whereas their average is but $6. Still, rents are a bit high; and the twins have been so long together that they would like to stay so. In Room—but you need no guide. Once in The House of a Hundred Sorrows you will visit every sad chamber in it. If your heart be made of penetrable stuff, you will do the most you can to bring hope and comfort to its inmates, to bring them Christmas and the Christ.

For I was ahungered, and ye gave me meat: I was thirsty, and ye gave me drink: I was a stranger, and ye took me in.

Naked, and ye clothed me: I was sick, and ye visited me: I was in prison, and ye came unto me.

*1927*

# F. LAURISTON BULLARD

for "We Submit"

IN 1921 the anarchists Nicola Sacco and Bartolomeo Vanzetti, accused of robbing and murdering a shoe factory paymaster, were convicted on what many people considered slender evidence. As execution was delayed six years by one appeal after another, Sacco and Vanzetti became the focus of worldwide attention and of debate over the fundamental nature of the American political system. Radicals and liberals argued that the two were found guilty not for an alleged crime but for their opinions. They cited as one piece of evidence the fact that trial judge Webster Thayer had expressed prejudice against the defendants. But an overwhelming majority of the public favored executing the two. Not only were they anarchists; but Italian immigrants, pacifists, and draft dodgers, too. It was not popular—especially in Massachusetts, where the murder occurred—to defend them. Despite such public opinion, the *Boston Herald* reversed its original position and began calling for a new trial. In a judicious editorial F. Lauriston Bullard argued the paper's point of view. A new trial was not granted, as the editorial urged; but the Massachusetts governor appointed a three-member commission, as Bullard suggested, to advise him. The commission, however, refused to propose executive clemency. Sacco and Vanzetti were executed August 22, 1927. Their deaths did not end the controversy; they added fire. The execution, as Bullard had implied in the editorial's final paragraph, gave radicals the argument they needed to persuade believers in justice to extreme positions and forced liberals to question the soundness of American institutions.

# We Submit

*Boston Herald* • October 26, 1926

In our opinion Nicola Sacco and Bartolomeo Vanzetti ought not to be executed on the warrant of the verdict returned by a jury on July 14, 1921. We do not know whether these men are guilty or not. We have no sympathy with the half-baked views which they profess. But as months have merged into years and the great debate over this case has continued, our doubts have solidified slowly into convictions, and reluctantly we have found ourselves compelled to reverse our original judgment. We hope the Supreme Judicial Court will grant a new trial on the basis of the new evidence not yet examined in open court. We hope the Governor will grant another reprieve to Celestino Madeiros so that his confession may be canvassed in open court. We hope, in case our supreme bench finds itself unable legally to authorize a new trial, that our Governor will call to his aid a commission of disinterested men of the highest intelligence and character to make an independent investigation in his behalf, and that the Governor himself at first-hand will participate in that examination if, as a last resort, it shall be undertaken.

We have read the full decision in which Judge Webster Thayer, who presided at the original trial, renders his decision against the application for a new trial, and we submit that it carries the tone of the advocate rather than the arbitrator. At the outset he refers to "the verdict of a jury approved by the Supreme Court of this Commonwealth," and later he repeats that sentence. We respectfully submit that the Supreme Court never approved that verdict. What the court did it stated in its own words thus: "We have examined carefully all the exceptions in so far as argued, and finding no error the verdicts are to stand." The Supreme Court did not vindicate the verdict. The court certified that, whether the verdict was right or wrong, the trial judge performed his duty under the law in a legal manner. The Supreme Court overruled a bill of exceptions, but expressed no judgment whatever as to the validity of the verdict or the guilt of the defendants. Judge Thayer knows this, yet allows himself to refer to the verdict as "approved by the Supreme Court."

We submit, also, that Judge Thayer's language contains many innuendos which surely are unfortunate in such a document. The petition for a new trial is based in part on the affidavits of two men, Letherman and Weyand, connected respectively with the United States Government for thirty-six years and eight years, and both now holding responsible positions out of the Federal service. Judge Thayer says that one of these men "seems for some reason to be willing to go the limit in his affidavits against the government of the United States," and he refers to "prejudiced affidavits, which appear to be quite easily obtained nowadays." The charges are rung on certain phrases also, as "fraudulent conspiracy between these two great governments," meaning the Governments of the United States and Massachusetts. The judge asserts a conspiracy charge which was not made by counsel for the defense; he asks "who pumped this curiosity into Madeiros"; he compliments the prosecution and refers slightingly to counsel for the defense.

We submit that evidence, if any, in the files of the Department of Justice having any bearing on this case ought to be examined in open court, or examined in private by the United States Attorney General and reported upon by him before this case shall finally be decided. We have no idea what the files may contain. Mr. Weyand said in his affidavit: "The conviction was the result of cooperation between the Boston agents of the Department of Justice and the District Attorney." We do not know that this is true, but we know there was cooperation; the department and the attorney joined in placing a spy in the cell next to Sacco's, and the prosecution admitted the fact in court.

Now as to Madeiros: A criminal with a bad record, true, and under sentence of death. But the Government relied in part on one of his confessions to convict him of a murder. His evidence was accepted against himself when his own life was at stake. His evidence now is offered in behalf of two other men whose lives also are at stake. We submit that Madeiros should be placed on the stand in open court, facing a jury and a judge, and subjected to examination and cross-examination. He may be lying, but the criterion here is not what a judge may think about it, but what a jury might think about it. The question is, Would the new evidence be a real factor with a jury in reaching a decision?

We submit that doubt is cast on the verdict of the jury by the important affidavit made after the trial by Captain C.H. Proctor of the State Police. On the stand, testifying as an expert, his evidence was understood by the jury and the judge to be that the fatal bullet issued from Sacco's pistol. Careful examination of the record discloses curious facts. Captain Proctor did not here reply to direct questions. His affidavit states what the record implies, that a device was fixed up in advance for dodging [a] direct answer to a direct question. His replies were understood to mean that he believed the bullet came from that weapon. He allowed that impression to go abroad. But his affidavit contradicts that testimony. Now, when the Supreme Court dealt with that point it expressed no opinion as to whether or not an "ambiguous answer" had been arranged to "obtain a conviction." The court ruled only that the trial judge had decided that no such pre-arrangement had been made, and that the Supreme Court could not "as a matter of law" set aside the ruling of the trial judge.

For these and other reasons we hope that the resources of our laws will prove adequate to obtain a new trial. Let it be remembered that the new trial is asked for on the basis of evidence never before the Supreme Court previously. The court has ruled on exceptions to the old trial, never on all evidence for a new one. If on a new trial the defendants shall again be found guilty we shall be infinitely better off than if we proceed to execution on the basis of the trial already held; the shadow of doubt which abides in the minds of large numbers of patient investigators of this whole case will have been removed. And if on second trial Sacco and Vanzetti should be declared guiltless everybody would rejoice that no monstrous injustice shall have been done. We submit these views with no reference whatever to the personality of the defendants, and without allusion now to that atmosphere of radicalism of which we heard so much in 1921.

# GROVER CLEVELAND HALL

for editorials against gangsterism and brutality

THE revival of the Ku Klux Klan became a major problem in the 1920s. In few other places was it as bad as in Alabama, where the Klan gained gruesome control of government at all levels. By 1927, a year in which both of the state's U.S. senators were Klan members, the organization had become daringly bold. The ministry and the press, whose ranks contained a number of KKK sympathizers, remained silent at the Klan's outrages. But the Klan had at least one opponent among Alabama's journalists, Grover C. Hall, editor of the *Montgomery Advertiser*. Born in Alabama in 1888, he joined the *Advertiser* in 1910 and was trained in its "tradition of tolerance." He was named editor in 1926. In July of the following year, his anger and indignation ignited by the flogging of a young black man at a rural church, Hall opened fire on the Klan. He followed with a four-month campaign to bring the Klansmen responsible to justice, to expose the Klan as brutish and cowardly, and to get legislation enacted that would limit its activities, including a law to prohibit the wearing of masks in public. State action did result. As a consequence of Hall's campaign, victims of floggings, too frightened before, talked to law officers and journalists; numerous Klansmen were convicted; and the number of floggings in Alabama declined dramatically. For his campaign, Hall was awarded the 1928 Pulitzer, the first year in which the award was given for no specific editorial but for a series. The editorial included here demonstrates the quality and power of Hall's writing. "Our Tom" is scathing ridicule of Senator Tom Heflin.

## Our Tom

*Montgomery* (Ala.) *Advertiser* • August 27, 1927

A bully by nature, a mountebank by instinct, a Senator by choice. Conceited and vain as the peacock is, but not proud as the nobleman is, for a choicer spirit would be too proud to assail the weak. He is bombastic and blustery, but is wanting in high courage; certainly he is wanting in that valor which scorns advantage, otherwise he would not select the class with the fewest votes in Alabama on which to heap contumely and indignities. The Roman Catholics cast less than two per cent of the total vote in Alabama. If they had political power in this state Tom would be afraid of them, for he is quite the biggest 'fraid cat in the United States senate, even as he is about the grossest demagogue there. Tom has spent a lifetime studying the art of dodging dangerous issues and otherwise playing safe.

Heflin hates and suspects the personal honor of all men who oppose his boundless ambition. In controversy he is intellectually without scruples, he is slanderous, cruel, cheap and absurd, and without a generous emotion. The monkeyshine is the only light he is capable of casting on any serious public question. Dressed like an Al Field tenor, Tom is gifted with the humor of mimicry, as Bert Swor is, but is entirely wanting in the higher quality of wit, for while the sight of an audience is to him the signal to release a deluge of words, an art long practiced by him, Tom never in his life fashioned an epigram. His diction is too sloppy even if his intelligence could provide the thought on which to hang the dainty language that adorns the epigram. He is a ham actor metamorphosed into a United States senator by a sorry trick of fate that invested Tom with lofty aspiration and immense gall. He is a clown on the platform and only as an entertainer is he interesting, for he is ill-informed, inaccurate in thought and unreliable in statement. But a hero to thousands nevertheless! Yet all of his daring has been spent in killing phantom dragons and doing battle with armored straw knights.

Good taste? Sense of propriety? Such terms merely amuse Tom. Fairness? Courtesy? Such qualities under the Heflin code are but signs of weakness in men and need not be respected by a gent with a mission and without a muzzle.

Thus this preposterous blob excites our pity if not our respect, and we leave him to his conscience in order that he may be entirely alone and meditate over the life of a charlatan whose personal interest and personal vanity are always of paramount concern to him.

*1929*

# LOUIS ISAAC JAFFE

for "An Unspeakable Act of Savagery"

IN the 1920s, when the revival of the Ku Klux Klan gave it a bigger heyday than it had enjoyed during Reconstruction, lynchings were considered local offenses. State prosecution had few supporters. A leader of the movement for state anti-lynching laws was Louis Isaac Jaffe, editor of the *Norfolk Virginian-Pilot*. In the mid-20s he outlined plans for a law in Virginia and finally convinced Governor Harry Flood Byrd to propose a law to the legislature. When the bill was adopted in 1928, Byrd said Jaffe's editorials "had more to do than any other single outside urging in convincing me that I should make one of my major recommendations the passage of a drastic anti-lynching law providing that lynching be a specific state offense." But Jaffe did not rest after enactment of the Virginia law. He urged a national law. Following a lynching in Houston, Texas, on the eve of the 1928 Democratic National Convention, he wrote "An Unspeakable Act of Savagery." Although Congress would delay in enacting anti-lynching legislation, Jaffe's editorial sparked national interest in such a law. For his campaign, Jaffe received the 1929 Pulitzer Prize, with the jury specifically mentioning the following editorial.

# An Unspeakable Act of Savagery

*Norfolk Virginian-Pilot* • June 22, 1928

As the Democratic hosts prepare to rededicate themselves anew to fairness and justice, the bustling Southern city in which they are to meet is disgraced by an unspeakable act of savagery. There is no other way to describe the performance of the eight armed white men who yanked Robert Powell, 24-year-old Negro, from a hospital cot on which he lay with a bullet in his stomach, and hanged him from a bridge just outside the city. Powell was under the charge of killing a detective in a shooting match from which he himself emerged with an apparently mortal wound. In the event of his recovery, he was headed for the courts. But to this Texas mob neither Death nor Justice was an acceptable arbiter. Nothing would satisfy them but a loathsome act of murder carried out against a human being while he lay in agony with a bullet in his entrails.

Houston, which is said not to have had a lynching in fifty years, is understandably stirred by this foul thing laid on its doorstep just when it was most anxious to show itself to the world at its cleanest. The City Council made an immediate appropriation of $10,000 for an investigation to be carried out by a committee representative of both races. A grand jury has been ordered to drop all other business to conduct an immediate inquiry. The Governor has offered a reward for the capture of each participant in the lynching and sent a special detail of Texas Rangers to assist the Houston police in the hunt. Apparently the spotlight that beats on Houston at this particular time has had something to do with the energy with which the authorities have acted. Ordinarily, Texas proceeds in these matters with considerably less dispatch and excitement. But this is no time to inquire too closely into motives. One of the proudest cities of Texas has been polluted by one of the foulest forms of mob murder, and it is a matter for general satisfaction that the authorities are moving so energetically to repair the damage to Texas' good name. If the perseverance of the authorities is in keeping with their initial burst of energy, one or more of the group that bravely did to death a crippled man lying on a hospital cot may see the inside of the Texas penitentiary.

The year that saw four months pass without a single lynching has now accumulated five of them. Five lynchings in six months represent a proportional reduction in savagery from last year's record of sixteen lynchings in twelve months, but the year is only half gone and no one may be too confident. We have come a long way from the dark days of 1892 when America celebrated the 400th anniversary of its discovery with 255 lynchings, but we have not yet arrived at that social abhorrence of this crime that must precede its practical extinction. When eight presumably decent and rational beings can gain the consent of their conscience to rob a hospital bed for the purpose of executing summary vengeance, and when, as was the case a few days ago in Louisiana, two Negroes are torn from their guards and lynched because they were brothers of another Negro who was accused of murder, it must be recognized that the rise and fall of the lynching curve is governed by racial passions that remain still to be brought under civilized control.

# CHARLES S. RYCKMAN

for "The Gentleman from Nebraska"

SATIRE is rare among Pulitzer Prize editorials. But while few satirical editorials gleam from the sea of analytical, reasoned ones, they also have been the most controversial. The most biting Pulitzer editorial may have been Charles Ryckman's 1931 winner. Even its title, "The Gentleman from Nebraska," was tongue in cheek. From a conservative Republican newspaper, the editorial was—depending on whose interpretation you accept—either an attack on Nebraska's progressive Republican Senator George W. Norris or a poke at the paradoxical political behavior of the state's provincial voters. It was an attempt to explain humorously why Nebraska voters continued to send Norris to Congress when he seemed more interested in other parts of the world than in Nebraska. While Norris undertook such crusades as attempting to have the federal government sell electricity from federally built hydroelectric plants directly to consumers rather than to private electric companies and to prevent federal subversion of civil rights, Ryckman charged that he did little more for Nebraska than make himself objectionable to federal officials. Liberals charged that the editorial was an underhanded, cruel, bad-tempered attack on Norris. Conservatives said it was a well-done explanation of the paradox of Nebraskans supporting the liberal Norris while their other political heroes were conservative. Nebraska's citizens thought it was an attempt to smear Norris and insult their intelligence.

# The Gentleman from Nebraska

*Fremont* (Neb.) *Tribune* • November 7, 1930

Senator George W. Norris, never lacking a mandate from the people of Nebraska in the course he has pursued as a member of the United States Senate, now returns to Washington doubly assured of the unquestioned approval of his state and its people.

The senatorial record of Mr. Norris, with all its ramifications, has been endorsed in as convincing a manner as anyone could wish. Many reasons have been advanced as to why such an endorsement should not be extended to him. The opposition to Norris has been conducted as ably and as thoroughly as any group of capable politicians could do the job. The candidacy of as fine a statesman as Nebraska ever produced has been presented to the state as an alternative to that of Mr. Norris, and has been rejected.

Acceptance of the situation is therefore a matter without choice. To continue the argument is to waste words. The opposition to Senator Norris has been so completely subdued and so thoroughly discredited that further jousting with the windmill is more quixotic than Quixote himself.

There is not even good reason for being disgruntled over the result. For the purpose of the Nebraska political situation, 70,000 people can't be wrong. The will of the state is seldom expressed in so tremendous a majority, and it must be taken not only as an endorsement of Mr. Norris but also as at least a temporary quietus upon his critics and opponents.

The state of Nebraska has elected Norris to the United States Senate this year, as it has many times in the past, mainly because he is not wanted there. If his return to Washington causes discomfiture in official circles, the people of Nebraska will regard their votes as not having been cast in vain. They do not want farm relief or any other legislative benefits a senator might bring them; all they want is a chance to sit back and gloat.

Nebraska nurses an ingrowing grouch against America in general and eastern America in particular. The state expects nothing from the national government, which it regards as largely under eastern control, and asks nothing. It has lost interest in constructive participation in federal affairs, and its people are in a vindictive frame of mind.

This grouch is cultural as much as political. Nebraska and its people have been the butt of eastern jokesters so long they are embittered. Every major federal project of the last half century has been disadvantageous to them. The building of the Panama canal imposed a discriminatory rate burden upon them. Various reclamation projects have increased agricultural competition.

Federal tariff policies increase the cost of living in Nebraska without material benefit to Nebraska producers.

Nebraska voters have long since ceased to look to Washington for relief, and they no longer select their congressional representatives with relief in view. Neither George Norris nor any of his Nebraska colleagues in congress have been able to combat this hopeless situation. If Norris were forced to rely upon what he has done in congress for Nebraska, he would approach an election day with fear in his heart.

But Senator Norris has found another way to serve Nebraska. By making himself objectionable to federal administrators without regard to political complexion and to eastern interests of every kind, he has afforded Nebraskans a chance to vent their wrath. He is, perhaps unwittingly, an instrument of revenge.

The people of Nebraska would not listen to George Norris long enough to let him tell them how to elect a dog catcher in the smallest village in the state, but they have been sending him to the senate so long it is a habit. If he lives long enough and does not get tired of the job, he will spend more years in the upper house of congress than any man before him. Death, ill health or personal disinclination—one of these may some day drive him out of the senate, but the people of Nebraska never will!

The state asks little of him in return. It gives him perfect freedom of movement and of opinion. It holds him to no party or platform. It requires no promises of him, no pledges. He need have no concern for his constituency, is under no obligation to people or to politicians. He can devote as much of his time as he likes to the Muscle Shoals power site, and none at all to western Nebraska irrigation projects. He can vote for the low tariff demanded by cane sugar producers of Cuba, while the beet sugar growers of Nebraska are starving to death. He can interest himself in political scandals in Pennsylvania, and be wholly unconcerned over the economic plight of the Nebraska farmer.

He can do all these things, and be as assured of election as the seashore is of the tide. He could spend a campaign year in Europe, and beat a George Washington in a Republican primary and an Abraham Lincoln in a general election.

And yet, George Norris is not a political power in Nebraska. The people of other states believe he is revered as an idol in his own state. As a matter of fact, he is probably held in lower esteem in Nebraska than in any other state in the union.

His endorsement of another candidate is of no real value. He could not throw a hatful of votes over any political fence in the state. He gave his tacit support to La Follette as a third party presidential candidate in 1924, and the Wisconsin senator could have carried all his Nebraska votes in his hip pocket without a bulge. He came into Nebraska in 1928 with a fanfare of democratic trumpets and of radio hook-ups, stumped the state for Governor Smith—and Nebraska gave Herbert Hoover the largest majority, on a basis of percentage, of all the states in the union.

As far as the people of Nebraska are concerned George Norris is as deep as the Atlantic ocean in Washington, and as shallow as the Platte river in his own state.

The explanation of this fascinating political paradox is to be found not in an analysis of Norris, but of Nebraska. As a senator, Norris has given Nebraska something the state never had before. He has put the "Gentleman from Nebraska" on every front page in America, and has kept him there. A resident of Nebraska can pick up the latest edition of a New York daily or of an Arizona weekly, and find "Norris of Nebraska" in at least three type faces.

But the publicity Norris gets for Nebraska is not the whole story. His real strength in Nebraska is measured by the antagonisms he stirs up beyond the borders of the state. His people take delight in setting him on the heels of the ruling powers, whether of government, of finance or of industry. The more he makes himself obnoxious to a political party, to a national administration or to Wall Street, the better they like him.

Nebraska is not interested in the smallest degree in what progress he makes, or what he accomplishes. It has been said of Norris that he has cast more negative votes against winning causes and more affirmative votes for lost causes than any other man in the senate. But every time he succeeds in pestering his prey until it turns around and snarls back at him, the chuckles can be heard all the way from Council Bluffs to Scottsbluff.

The summary of it all is that Nebraska derives a great deal of pleasure out of shoving George Norris down the great American throat. He has been an effective emetic in republican and democratic administrations alike, has worried every president from Taft to Hoover. His retirement from the senate, whether voluntary or forced, would be welcomed in more quarters than that of any of his colleagues.

The people of Nebraska know this, and enjoy it. Every time

Norris baits the power trust or lambastes the social lobby, Nebraska gets the same amusement out of his antics that a small boy gets out of siccing a dog on an alley cat. When he shies a brickbat at a president, Nebraska has as much fun as a kid pushing over an outhouse.

You have to know the isolation of the hinterland to understand why this is so. Nebraska has sent many men to the senate who were more capable than Norris, as his predecessors and as his contemporaries. It has had other senators who have done more for the state and for the nation than he has.

But it has never had another senator who let the whole world know there was a "Gentleman from Nebraska" in the manner he has succeeded in doing. Nebraska could send a succession of great men and good men to the senate, and the east and west and south would never know there was a state of Nebraska or that such a state was represented in the senate. But Norris lets them know there is a Nebraska, and Nebraska does not care how he does it.

There is an instinctive resentment in the hearts of these people of the states between the Mississippi and the mountains against the failure of the far east to understand and appreciate the middle west. It crops up in politics, in religion, even in sports.

Nebraska is one of the richest of all the agricultural states and yet the wealth of its industries exceeds that of its farms. It has given such names as Gutzon Borglum, Willa Cather, John J. Pershing, William G. Dawes, William Jennings Bryan and a hundred others of prominence to the nation. It has unsurpassed schools, progressive cities and towns, people of intelligence and culture.

And yet the rest of the nation persists in regarding Nebraska as provincial, its people as backward. If the east thinks of Nebraska at all, it is as a state still in a frontier period. The national conception of a Nebraskan is that of a big hayshaker, with a pitchfork in his hands, a straw in his mouth, a musical comedy goatee on his chin, a patch on the seat of his overalls and the muck of the barnyard on his boots.

Nebraska has resented these indignities, but has given up hope of avoiding them. Its only hope is to pay back in kind. In the days of the real frontier, it vented its wrath on the occasional luckless tenderfoot from the east. Now it sends George Norris to the senate.

Norris does not represent Nebraska politics. He is the personification of a Nebraska protest against the intellectual aloofness of the east. A vote for Norris is cast into the ballot box with all the venom of a snowball thrown at a silk hat. The spirit that puts him over is vindictive, retaliatory. Another senator might get federal projects, administrative favor, post offices and pork barrel plunder for Nebraska, but the state is contemptuous of these. For nearly two decades Norris has kept Nebraska beyond the pale of federal favor, but his people consider him worth the price.

George Norris is the burr Nebraska delights in putting under the eastern saddle. He is the reprisal for all the jokes of vaudevillists, the caricatures of cartoonists and the jibes of humorists that have come out of the east in the last quarter of a century.

*1933*

# HENRY J. HASKELL

for a series on national and international topics

THE *Kansas City Star* won the 1933 Pulitzer for nineteen editorials by its editor, Henry Haskell. The editorials composed three series: economic and political conditions in Europe, economic conditions in America, and the growth of government. The Pulitzer jury praised Haskell's work as "a compelling demonstration of editorial responsibility and leadership." Haskell, the jury said, "pointed out the need for national economy and cited specific cases where efficiency could be maintained in government at a lower cost to the taxpayer. ...[He] commented clearly and informatively on foreign developments without being sectionally selfish." The following editorial from the series on "Too Much Government" decried the growth of government bureaucracy, which Haskell argued was aimed solely at serving itself rather than the public. Although he saw the problem as grave, Haskell still was able to retain a sense of humor. He wondered, for example, how earlier American homemakers were able to make lemon pies without government instruction. In another editorial dated March 30 he pointed out that the growth of bureaucracy included the establishment of a federal bureau of efficiency. Writing from a conservative stance, however, Haskell faced the dilemma of deploring big government while accepting the fact that government must "aid and encourage" economic groups. Where to draw the line, therefore, between necessary and unnecessary government was a major point of focus for Haskell. Although our public debate faces the same quandary, Haskell's editorials of natural consequence now seem dated. In an editorial of April 1 he lamented the immensity of taxes and the national budget. The totality of the former for all levels of government was $13 billion annually in 1932; the latter was $4 billion. What would Haskell have hollered if he had known Roosevelt's New Deal was just around the corner?

# Too Much Government

*Kansas City* (Mo.) *Star* • March 25, 1932

The facts about the multiplying functions and agencies of the department of agriculture, laid before the house economy committee by Secretay Hyde, furnish another example of overproduction in government. The secretary has done well to recommend to congress that a number of these functions and agencies be abolished or turned over to the states.

The growth and expansion of the services supplied by this department are out of all proportion to the need or demand for them. They represent the aspirations of government rather than the needs of agriculture, which is true of all other departments. It is an evitable phenomenon of bureaucracy, which propagates itself, growing by what it feeds on.

The importance of the great agricultural industry of the United States cannot be overestimated; the propriety and necessity of the government to aid and encourage it never has been called in question. So well established is this principle, indeed, that it has become the convenient and unsuspected cloak behind which bureaucracy has chosen to operate. To aid agriculture, a market news service was established. That was proper and legitimate; but it is not proper and legitimate that this service should have been expanded until there are sixty-nine such market news service offices scattered throughout the country. The service itself is for agriculture; the operation of the service is in the interest of bureaucracy. It is proper and legitimate that the department should have field stations and laboratories for the benefit of agriculture; it is not proper nor legitimate that it should have 775 such stations, doing duplicate work. The expansion was not for agriculture, but for bureaucracy.

Agriculture, like all other business and industry, can best be served by a vigorous trimming of government. The country is being smothered by government services. It is being kissed to death. Many of these services are altogether unnecessary, others are a duplication of those furnished by the states and others, and, if they are proper at all, should be supplied wholly by the states. Some of them, indeed, should not be furnished by either the federal government or by the states, but by the homes, if they are required at all. In that class of services may be lumped all those by which government now seeks to instruct the American housewife in how to make lemon pies and rompers. How those problems were met by the wives and mothers of America before the department of agriculture was established, a little more than sixty years ago, nobody now knows, but in some way the Civil War was carried on and the western wilderness and deserts subdued without the bureau of home economics.

In reducing government to a size where it can be put into the clothes provided for it by the Constitution, congress should observe the simple rule that government is the servant of the people of the United States and not their master. Its function is to serve the people and not itself. When it gets out of bounds, as it now is, and assumes to build itself up for its own benefit at the cost of the people whose welfare it is supposed to promote, it should be put back in its place and with no gentle hand.

*1934*

# EDWIN P. CHASE

for "Where Is Our Money?"

LIKE at least two earlier winners, Edwin P. Chase's prize-winning
editorial was greeted with criticism. Written during the Great
Depression when great numbers of people were out of work and
banks were idle, the editorial attempted to explain the causes of
the troubles. Marked by a conservatism typical of newspapers of
the day, it was essentially an attack on Franklin Roosevelt's approach of remedying the problems through government programs.
Although its sentiments were out of touch with the desires of the
majority of the public, the editorial was picked up by a number of
the nation's leading newspapers, whose editors believed it accurately dissected the cause of America's economic problems. Criticism of the editorial's selection for the Pulitzer Prize came mainly
from liberals, who chided Chase's piece for shallow, faulty reasoning and poor writing. In defense of the editorial, it might be said
that it was a good attempt at providing an understandable analysis of an abstract, complicated problem. Stylistically, though the
editorial is punctuated with rather crude phrasing, its satire and
its strength of feeling are occasionally effective.

# Where Is Our Money?

*Atlantic* (Iowa) *News-Telegraph* • December 2, 1933

It is announced that at 10 o'clock tonight, Iowa time, William
Randolph Hearst, well known publisher, will broadcast an address
on the subject which appears at the caption of this article.

The subject is a broad one and permits of many ramifications. Likewise the query is a live one and has been for several
years with many people who formerly were in comparative afflu-
ence and have found themselves suddenly in a position where

money is a scarce article. The whereabouts of the money of the individual is perhaps beside the point in this comment, if we stick to
the text, as doubtless Mr. Hearst's broadcast will deal with the
whereabouts of the funds of the nation as a whole, rather than the
financial plight of the individual citizen; but the subject intrigues
one and suggests a line of thought relative to the part the individual has played in rendering himself particularly susceptible to the
injuries inflicted by the period of economic stress.

Where is our money? Here in Iowa, if competent statistics
are to be believed, during the ultra-prosperous years of the world
war period when money flowed like water into the coffers of the
farmer and the business man and everyone else, some 200 million
dollars of good Iowa money went for stocks, shares in half-mythical
concerns which were worth exactly their value as a piece of printed
paper. During that period and shortly thereafter a good many
hundreds of millions from the middle-west went into the first and
second mortgage bonds of apartment hotels and the like, security
issued on appraisals inflated to the nth degree. The most of these
bonds are now worth just what the stocks we referred to are
worth—the value of the paper and the printing contained therein.
There is no way of estimating how many hundreds of millions of
money the country over went up in smoke and vanished in thin air
when it suddenly dawned on us that even the most productive land
in a section like ours is not worth $300 or $400 an acre. It took
only the simplest mathematics to arrive at that conclusion, for
even at the prices brought by farm products at their peak, the return on the land in this section would not pay interest on an in-
vestment of $300 or $400 an acre. It can easily be recalled that
during that hectic period it was considered a mark of provincialism
not to buy a new automobile every year. A lot of fur coats and a lot
of diamonds and a lot of expensive clothes for both men and
women were indulged in by all classes. The wage earner suddenly
awoke to the fact that by buying on the installment plan he could
keep up with the Joneses and he not only spent every cent he could
get his hands on in many instances, but he pledged the major
portion of his wages or salary months ahead to pay for automobiles
and other articles which were worn out by the time he had
completed the payments.

These are but a few instances, cases in point. One might go
on indefinitely telling of the wild orgy of spending and of contracting obligations without thought of the pay day and with little or no

thought of the economic soundness of such spending. Then came deflation. We got down to cases. We danced and are still paying the fiddler. Like children we have sought someone to blame for our plight and also like children we now seek some magic way to cure our ills and expect the government to provide the cure. The man who contracted debts does not want to pay them just now, because in some instances, he cannot pay them. In every way we have met the crisis which was thrust upon us as though we had nothing to do with producing it. As a matter of fact, we had all to do with producing it. In the proportion that the individual citizen went haywire with extravagance and reckless spending governmental units went on the same kind of an orgy and whooped our taxes 100 per cent in ten years. Bond issues were pyramided by communities with the same disregard of the coming of the pay day which characterized the individual. We built great cathedrals of education, with motion pictures and swimming pools and all sorts of gewgaws and frills. We erected public buildings in many cases entirely beyond possible needs of communities for a hundred years. Just as private enterprise overbuilt in every direction, governmental building activities got out of bounds. The people have to pay the bill. The saturnalia of expenditure created fixed taxes, and taxes have a habit of certainty in good times and bad times alike. With our incomes and our business revenues depleted our tax bill in the main has remained the same. All an echo of the period of extravagance and wild-eyed inflation which brought about our troubles. We were talking about "two cars in every garage and a chicken in every pot," and we made much about the so-called American standard of living, whatever that meant. We insisted that all the various elements of our population should attain that standard, and we instilled into the minds of many people who could not afford it a desire for the things had by others more fortunate in life. Oodles of people who had no more business with an automobile than a wagon has with five wheels bought cars. Oodles of people learned to live beyond their means. It began to look as if it would not be long until there would be no one to do the work of the country, as all were seeking the same mythical standard to which we referred. And we still have the automobiles.

The bottom went out of things. Or it might be more appropriate to say that the top was blown off. Then the people of the United States commenced to take stock. Seeking someone to blame they listened to the fulminations of the politicians who represented the "outs" and who told that the way to cure their ills was to convert the outs into the "ins" and the ins into the outs. This they did, with their usual disregard of essentials and fundamentals. It became a pleasing fiction to attribute our plight to the tariff, and later to our money standard. The people were told that all that was necesary was to reduce the tariff which protects American manufacture and agriculture, and all would be jake. Now they are being told that the way to put money into the hands of those who are penniless, and make it possible for the debtor to pay his obligations and start things moving on a normal basis is to cheapen our money. A lot of other experimental schemes are being worked out by an administration of which the people demand action. We are spending huge sums of money, borrowed for the purpose, in an endeavor to squander ourselves back to prosperity. In the face of the fact that debt is one of the basic causes of our troubles, we are following the theory that incurring more debt would cure us. And in the face of the fact that excessive taxation is another of the causes of our trouble we are laying the groundwork for more of the same, under the delusion that the application of all of these methods will relieve us of the trouble which we brought on ourselves, aided and abetted by worldwide economic upheaval.

We are a queer lot, we Americans. We expect whichever party happens to be in charge of the government to so manipulate the handling of public affairs as to afford us a cure for the results of our own folly. We seem to assume that it is possible for us to get well economically by the waving of some magic wand. We think we can force prosperity, and to the majority of the people of the country prosperity means a return to the hectic days preceding the stock market crash of 1929. This theory disregards the fact that those hectic days were created by false and inflated values which in turn were created by a false and inflated philosophy. In the creating of this inflation we disregard all natural laws of economics, so it is but natural for us to expect to cure the trouble by the same process. But it cannot be done.

The only way back to solid ground and to a degree of prosperity and well-being commensurate with common sense and economic soundness will be by the application of thrift and hard work and the balancing of the budget of every individual. The old haywire days are gone forever. But a large percentage of our population still believes in Santa Claus and good fairies. The cause of the present economic condition of the country in large measure can be ascertained by every citizen by looking in the mirror. Each one of us contributed his share. There is nothing new about all of this. It has been the history of things in the world since the earliest dawn of civilization. Particularly has it characterized every postwar period. Humanity never learns. We have not progressed so far in our thinking, after all.

Where is our money? The answer is not difficult. It can be told in one short sentence. We spent it.

*1936*

# FELIX MORLEY

for distinguished editorial writing

FELIX MORLEY submitted 34 editorials for his Pulitzer entry in 1936. That bundle of writings covered almost any subject imaginable, from Christmas to the trial of Bruno Hauptman for kidnaping the Lindbergh baby to the Supreme Court to taxes to politics to world affairs. Most of the editorials on the last subject dealt with the League of Nations and the growing threat of Adolph Hitler and Benito Mussolini. With the editorial entitled "Bankrupt," Morley criticized what he called the "bankruptcy of European statesmanship" and what he saw as the hypocrisy of League members in condemning Hitler's tactics. Apparent in the editorial was the opposition of conservative American politicians to the League. While their rejection of the United States' participation in the League undermined the organization from the beginning, they had no compunction about criticizing its failure. Morley conveniently and, it might seem, blindly ignored this fact. Senator William Borah was in such agreement with the editorial that he had it placed in the *Congressional Record*. On the positive side, it can be said that the editorial did attempt to give an analytical overview of why League actions were unsuccessful.

# Bankrupt

*Washington Post* • April 18, 1935

In a sanctimonious resolution, which carries little hope for any fundamental improvement in the European situation, the Council of the League of Nations has formally rebuked Germany for her recent denunciation of the disarmament sections of the Treaty of Versailles.

The wording of the resolution, which declares that "Germany

has failed in the duty which lies upon all members of the international community to respect undertakings which they have contracted," will make it virtually impossible for the German government to resume its membership in the League. But the action taken at Geneva yesterday does more than block that desirable step. It also calls for the development of a policy of economic and financial sanctions "which might be applied should, in the future, a state, whether a member of the League of Nations or not, endanger peace by unilateral repudiation of its international obligations."

This, in effect, means the development of a definite anti-German alliance under the leadership of the victors in the last war. It is a tragic confirmation of the criticism of those who have maintained that the chief function of the League has always been to enforce the terms of the Versailles Treaty. It is a step toward surrounding Germany with a ring of steel which may, because of German economic weakness, for the present preserve an uneasy absence of actual hostilities. But it is the direct opposite of that policy of constructive statesmanship which would have sought to build real peace on a freely admitted equality of national rights.

Of course, the brutal, headstrong character of the Nazi government has invited this resolution at Geneva. But few of the nations which have so piously condemned the German action of March 16 are in a position to throw stones effectively. Six countries which have defaulted on their war-debt agreements with the United States solemnly approved the resolution's statement that "it is an essential principle of the law of nations that no power can liberate itself from the engagements of a treaty nor modify the stipulations thereof unless with the consent of the other contracting parties."

One of the council members denouncing Germany in this lofty language was Russia, which has always maintained that obligations of the Czarist regime are not binding on its present government. Another condemnatory vote came from Poland, which less than a year ago unilaterally repudiated her obligations to the League in respect to minorities in her territory. Yet another rebuke to German came from Turkey, which shortly after the war pointed the way to Germany by forceful overthrow of the Treaty of Sevres. Italy, so scrupulous with respect to the treaty rights of Abyssinia—a fellow member of the League—is also prominent in the parade of Geneva Pharisees. In fact, only Denmark, with a clean record on treaty observances, dissociated herself from the denunciation of the German kettle by other European pots.

The refusal of the victorious powers to regard Germany as an equal was primarily responsible for driving that country into the hands of the fanatics who now control her destiny. Confronted with a situation for which they must share the responsibility before history, the only concession of the war victors is to gild their mailed fist with a veneer of self-conscious rectitude. Nor is it to be overlooked that this portentous resolution makes no distinction between the violation of negotiated and dictated treaties.

The bankruptcy of European statesmanship was never more apparent than in the approval given this sorry declaration by the Council of the League of Nations.

# GEORGE B. PARKER

for distinguished editorial writing

GEORGE B. PARKER shared the 1936 Pulitzer with Felix Morley. This was the first of two times that two recipients shared the editorial writing award. Like Morley, Parker apparently covered a wide range of topics, although he had a particular interest in freedom of the press. Precisely what editorials his entry contained is uncertain, since neither the official Pulitzer Collection at Columbia University nor the archives of Scripps-Howard contains the material. His most frequently cited editorial was the following, which in the past has been available in incomplete fragments only. It showed Parker's concern not only for freedom of the press but for how European events in the pre-World War II period affected the press. Parker especially attempted to explain to readers how censorship imposed by European governments could affect the reliability of newspaper reports and how readers should react to war news.

# Censorship, You—and Us

Scripps-Howard Newspapers • October 11, 1935

With war and sanctions now well under way and with hostile alignments crystallizing throughout the world, we want to talk frankly with you about censorship and how it may affect the war news you read in your paper.

"We were fooled once, aplenty," one reader writes. "Early in the World War, for example, England shut off the cables to Germany and from then on all we got was through Allied channels. What about it now? What reason have we to believe what we are reading today from abroad?"

The answer is that you are right to be suspicious. By no

means should you put complete confidence in foreign dispatches. Use salt whenever you feel it is needed. We will do the best we can to spot the lies, and so will our correspondents abroad, but we can't guarantee accuracy when censorship is in the saddle. So we want to ask your help in a problem that must necessarily be yours as well as ours.

All we can guarantee is plenty of diligence, over there and here—diligence reinforced by considerable experience with the tricks of censorship learned from the World War. We are more sophisticated now then we were then. War was a new and fresh thing to us in those days and we were pretty green. A good deal of credulity was squeezed out in that affair. So we hope to guard against many of the things we fell for once. But don't expect too much. Be ready to make your own discounts and your own deductions.

Censorship and war go together just as censorship and dictatorships do. A correspondent working in a zone of censorship is not like a correspondent working in a free country. He is under wraps, and can't defy the government, including the military forces, of the country where he is stationed. He just has to make the best he can of a bad journalistic situation. By exercising wisdom born from training, by checking his sources, by being on watch for propaganda "plants," by writing objectively, he can minimize the danger of being "used." But what he writes must be filed through the censor.

Propaganda is as much a part of war as are machine guns and airplanes. In many respects it is the most important part. By it, nations in conflict seek to build up sentiment at home and support around the world. The Belgian baby story was more of an asset to the Allies than a score of regiments. "All is fair in war," and as someone has said, the first casualty in every war is truth.

So you may expect propaganda from many sources. Even on this side, in a neutral country trying its best to "keep out of it," there will be carefully hidden propaganda agencies, working for this side and that, putting forth stories plausible enough on the surface, but loaded with the dynamite just the same, designed to dislodge your neutrality and to deliver you over into one camp or another.

Accordingly, the best we can do is to ask you to join us in being wary, and to assure you that you can depend upon us to be just as cautious as it is possible for us to be.

This is no time for artlessness either on the part of newspapers or newspaper readers. We wish we were all-seeing, but we must agree with Mr. Dooley, who said:

"Newspapers are not perfect, and neither is the human race."

*1937*

# JOHN W. OWENS

for distinguished editorial writing

ALTHOUGH a number of editorials were submitted as John W. Owens' Pulitzer entry, members of the Pulitzer committee let it be known that the editorial "The Opposition" had particularly influenced them in awarding him the 1937 prize. Written shortly after the Republicans' disastrous loss in the 1936 presidential election, the editorial analyzed why the GOP's fortunes had sunk so low. Within the structure of a political history of the party, the editorial argued that the GOP was suffering from "intellectual poverty" and an absence of any well-designed proposal to solve society's problems or provide political direction. Owens concluded that in 1936 the intellect of the Republican party had dived to its lowest level ever. In addition to his writing as editor of the *Baltimore Sun*, Owens authored a number of articles on politics for various magazines and journals and was considered an astute observer of the political scene. It might be pointed out as a matter of coincidence that the Nicholas Murray Butler mentioned in the latter part of this editorial was the president of Columbia University, through which winners of the Pulitzer Prize are selected. Many of the political figures mentioned in this editorial may be unfamiliar to today's reader. Among the most important ones were the following: Dean Acheson, Under Secretary of the Treasury under Franklin Roosevelt; William Allison, Republican senator from Iowa and 1888 presidential hopeful; William E. Borah, Republican senator from Idaho and 1936 presidential hopeful; John W. Davis, 1924 Democratic presidential candidate; Jonathan Dolliver, Republican senator from Iowa in the late 1800s and early 1900s; Lewis Douglas, Franklin Roosevelt's Director of the Budget; Carter Glass, Democratic senator from Virginia and Secretary of the Treasury under Woodrow Wilson; Mark Hanna, Republican senator from Ohio and a leading national political figure in the late 1800s; Charles Evans Hughes, 1916 Republican presidential candidate; Hiram Johnson, California governor and Progressive candidate for vice president in 1912; Robert LaFollette, Republican senator from Wisconsin and leader of the Progressives; Alf Landon, 1936 Republican presidential candidate; George W. Norris, Republican senator from Nebraska and 1928 presidential hopeful (he was the subject of Charles Ryckman's 1931 Pulitzer Prize winning editorial); Elihu Root, Secretary of State under Theodore Roosevelt; John Sherman, Republican senator from Ohio and 1880 presidential hopeful; Thomas J. Spellacy, Democratic National Committeeman from Connecticut; and James Warburg, Franklin Roosevelt's treasury advisor.

# The Opposition

*Baltimore Sun* • November 6, 1936

The careful reader may have observed in the recent campaign one important fact which was not mentioned in public discussions. It is the fact that no spokesman of the Republican party made the front page in the regular run of things save Mr. Landon himself. Democratic leaders made the front page—Davis and Griffith and others. But there were no Republican successors to the Roots and the Hugheses of other Presidential years. Not a single sledge-hammer speech, of the sort that Hughes and Borah made in the campaign of 1928, appeared on the Republican side in the entire campaign of 1936. Not a single Republican speech deserved the front page. And this, we think, is a fact that needs the attention of those who are trying to understand the present and prepare for the future.

In part, this intellectual poverty of the Republican party may be described as a quirk of fate. For, in part, it is due to the rise of the descendants of the immigrant groups in New England and New York. It is nearly twenty years now since Al Smith became a major figure and his appearance signaled a political revolution. It signaled the increasing power in the Democratic party in the Northeast of leaders who spring from the loins of the party's rank and file. Mr. Roosevelt's patrician leadership in the last four years does not alter the essential fact. And, simultaneously, Smith's appearance as a major figure signaled the increasing supremacy of the Democratic party over the Republican party in the Northeast. Not only in New York but in Massachusetts, in Connecticut, in Rhode Island, even in Maine a new order was at work which brought to the seats of power the Watshies, the Parleys, the Laucygans, the Spellacys. Their individual fortunes varied, but their collective power was established.

Quite suddenly, as history goes, the breeding grounds of Republican intellect failed. The sons of the immigrants were defeating the sons of the Puritans, and the latter were turning from politics. Compare the intellectual quality of the Republican representation in the Senate from the Northeast when Hoover yielded to Roosevelt with that when Taft yielded to Wilson. Other forces were at work. Probably the materialism which always had been the teammate of the austere idealism of the Puritan had acquired excessive weight. But, in any event, there was the plain fact that scions of Puritan wealth and Puritan education were being defeated by the sons of immigrants, and New York and New England were failing as the breeding ground of Republican intellect. Anyone who saw the party leaders who met Mr. Landon at Buffalo on his first trip into the East could measure the collapse with his own eyes.

At the same time, logic was doing a similar work in the Middle West and the West. Those areas had provided more Presidents for the Republican party, but less intellect. They had, however, produced their Shermans and their Hannas and their Allisons and, in later years, their Dollivers and La Follettes and Borahs and Norrises. And these Republicans of the Middle West and the West, representing to a very large extent yeoman constituencies, were insisting with ever-increasing vehemence upon the extension to their constituencies of the paternalistic government to which their party was committed.

Borah and Norris and Hiram Johnson might now and again inveigh against the special privileges accorded powerful interests by their party, and might even vote against them. But their real interest has been in extending paternalism to the little fellow in their constituencies. Their passion was reserved for fights to give him the benefit of the Government's resources. They were not so much against the Hamiltonian idea as they were in favor of means to augment the trickling down from top to bottom of largess bestowed by the Federal Government. Most of them would fight ten times for "benefits" for their own people to the one time they fought against the whole system of special favors.

And along came Mr. Roosevelt in 1933 and gave them in the White House a benediction they never had been able to get from their own party. He, no more than they and no more than Mr. Hoover and the Old Guard, made a frontal attack upon the whole system of special privileges. The structure of monopoly was never safer than in the plans and projects of the New Deal. But, whereas Mr. Hoover and his Republican predecessors insisted upon rugged individualism for the little fellow, though they could stomach a veritable mountain of special favors indirectly given to the big fellow, Mr. Roosevelt sought to make the scheme universal. Everybody was to get some sort of bounty.

The result was that he appropriated what was left of the intellectual vitality of the Republican party. At the very moment that the collapse of the Northeast as the great breeding ground of Republican intellect was complete, Mr. Roosevelt met the demands of the secondary breeding ground of Republican intellect and thereby absorbed it. Norris, Borah, Hiram Johnson, La Follette, Abuzens and the other Republicans of force in the Middle West and the West supported him generally in the New Deal and in the 1936 campaign backed him openly or passively.

The news editors who thrust Republican speeches other than Mr. Landon's into the inside pages were simply giving mute testimony to a great historical fact. There was left in the country scarcely a Republican who had anything to say (and was willing to say it) which deserved a place on the front page of any important newspaper. And how did Mr. Landon meet the situation? In the worst possible way.

He had been given a party platform that was a creaking, lopsided omnibus of vote-buying dodges, often mutually contradictory. Immediately after the Cleveland convention it was bruited that Mr. Landon was cognizant of the weakness of his platform and intended in his acceptance speech and in a few speeches that would follow to give coherence and order and an enlightened direction to his party's policy. His acceptance speech failed to carry forward this purpose, but the first few of his speeches on tour seemed to lay the foundation for a structure of genuine political liberalism. The parochial counselors overcame him. When he got down to specific issues, he was offering special favors to this group of States and that group of citizens.

The man who had spoken strongly and intelligently at Portland for liberalism committed himself at Des Moines, at Minneapolis and at Indianapolis to the sorriest schemes of reckless and extravagant paternalism, of sectionalism, of nationalism and of isolationism. By the time he was through, his own position was a hodge-podge of Old Guardism and New Dealism. His personal position was a reflection of the ramshackle platform given him at Cleveland.

Intellectual opposition to Mr. Roosevelt from the Republican party had simply ceased to exist. There was no semblance of any central idea of government in the Republican campaign. The campaign consisted in stimulation of ultra-conservative and reactionary fervors, on the one hand, and extension of New Deal bounties on the other. It closed as an amalgam of the worst features of Hooverism and of Rooseveltism.

Three brilliant and able young men had resigned from the Roosevelt Administration on issues which involved principle. They were Douglas, Acheson and Warburg. They wished to fight Mr. Roosevelt on questions of principle. Moreover, the circumstances attending their departure had been such that, as human beings, they craved the opportunity to fight. But when Mr. Landon had passed from the general to the particular in those speeches at Des Moines, Minneapolis and Indianapolis, those three men divided very much as the millions of the voters in the country divided. Warburg and Acheson made their way back into the Democratic camp. They found Mr. Landon accepting and even extending much that was worst in the Roosevelt regime and opposing that which they believed to be good. Douglas went through a mental struggle of weeks before he could decide that the balance still lay against Mr. Roosevelt.

In the small group that was left of the old intellectuals among the Republicans of the Northeast, there was almost unanimous silence. Perhaps it may be said that Mr. Root's great age barred him from participation in the campaign. But there is his spiritual son, Henry L. Stimson, the last Republican Secretary of State. He was not in the Republican campaign. And there is Nicholas Murray Butler, whose traditional Republican conservatism has given place in these days of violent nationalism to consistent preaching of the essentials of historic liberalism. He was not in the Republican campaign. For that matter, John Davis, the Democratic bolter who had the clearest understanding of Mr. Roosevelt's departure from Democratic liberalism, contented himself with an indictment of the President and avoided endorsement of the Republican candidate.

It is this intellectual collapse of the Republican party that, to those who have some understanding of the need of a two-party system in democratic government, is the worst feature of the recent campaign. Those who look superficially at the figures in the election totals may conclude that the opposition to Mr. Roosevelt has been reduced numerically to negligible proportions. Actually, the change of one voter in ten would lift the opposition to a very dangerous level. There would be no serious difficulty in building a formidable opposition to Mr. Roosevelt, and in thus preserving the two-party system in effectual form, if there were intelligence in the leadership of the Republican party. But the bald and unvarnished fact is that the intellect of the Republican party is at the lowest ebb in its entire history.

It follows, of course, that whatever opposition Mr. Roosevelt may invite as his policies are disclosed must come from the Democratic party, as was the case in 1933. And, if evoked, this opposition will have influence in 1937 as it had in 1933. But obviously the opposition of a Carter Glass must fall of its full force if the natural political opposition to Mr. Roosevelt can do no more than wallow in a sea of confused expediencies. If the Republican opposition is so stupid that it cannot understand why Carter Glass's opposition to New Dealism does not mean Carter Glass's support of Old Guardism, then Carter Glass may expect to fight a lonely fight. If the Republican opposition is so stupid that it cannot understand a fight on principle against Mr. Roosevelt's paternalism, if it is so stupid that it can only conceive a fight against wholesale paternalism in terms of a fight for paternalism in the interest of a few, then, indeed, is the outlook poor.

Which means that the responsibility of the historic liberal, the historic Democrat, is all the greater if and when Mr. Roosevelt shows the whites of his eyes in specific issues, as he did not do at any time in the campaign that gave him 523 electoral votes out of 581.

*1938*

# WILLIAM WESLEY WAYMACK

for distinguished editorial writing

ALTHOUGH the Pulitzer Prize administration does not have a file of the work for which William Wesley Waymack received the 1938 award, it is believed his editorials dealt primarily with growing farm tenancy in the United States in the 1930s. L.W. McGuire, former promotion manager for the *Des Moines Register,* said he thought "Waymack came to the attention of the Pulitzer judges with a series of articles on farm tenancy written late in 1936 and entered in 1937. Apparently the judges were waiting for the entry the next year and gave him the prize." Waymack's entry, McGuire added, probably covered a "wide range of subjects," including, in addition to farm problems, political issues, civil liberties, international affairs, and industrial relations. The *Register*'s Pulitzer Prize file contains articles on farm tenancy written by Waymack in 1936. These, assumed Don Benson, later director of public events for the paper, "were among those submitted on Waymack's behalf for the Pulitzer Prize." In the editorial below, Waymack argued that tenancy was not simply a regional or farm problem but that it was national. Showing an understanding of the implications tenancy had for the future of the country, he called for national awareness and action to eliminate it.

# Tenancy Problem Is National

*Des Moines Register* • November 27, 1936

It is announced that regional hearings will be held between the first and the middle of next month by the president's committee on farm tenancy—two meetings in the south, two in the middle west and one on the west coast. The one on the west coast is in a sense supplementary.

68

These regional hearings, which are intended to bring out every possible point of view or proposal that thoughtful individuals or groups may be nursing, tend to emphasize the regional phase of the tenancy problem.

And there are regional differences, sharp and significant ones.

There is by no means an adequate understanding as yet between the several sections most vitally affected. Not even among our more well-informed people. We in the cornbelt know too little about the special aspects and urgencies of the problem in the cotton south, and they of the cotton south are deficient in acquaintance with cornbelt conditions.

Yet the big thing to get in mind, as we begin for the first time to face the problems of conserving our soil and creating or conserving a high type of rural population, is that the problem is basically national, not sectional.

In its long run effects, if we are to remain a united country with freedom of movement for both goods and people between the sections, the broad problem of land tenancy is indivisible.

It is true that conditions in the deep south are infinitely worse than they have become in our part of the country.

There, thanks to the Civil War, the race question, a vicious system of one-crop, cash-crop production, and other factors, we have a population of millions of low grade farm tenants.

They have a high birth rate. They include vast numbers of Negroes, but a larger number of whites. Many of them are thoroughly incompetent, though they may come from the purest American stock. They exist far below the level of European peasants, who at least have homes, a reasonable degree of security, and a wholesome way of life.

Some millions of these southern tenants are in reality not tenants at all. They have no capital. They own no stock or equipment. They are wage slaves on the farm, working year after year to catch up with current debts to merchants and others and never catching up. Their houses are often shanties, lacking windows or cook-stoves. They know nothing of modern sanitation. They have practically no educational opportunity. By various devices they are often disenfranchised—by cumulative poll taxes, for instance.

Of course the soil has suffered, soil not so good as ours in any case.

Of course the existence of such conditions has begun to produce bitterness and radicalism.

That, drawn starkly, is the ugliness of the situation in parts of the south.

Now, does any sane man think that conditions of that sort can go on forever without somehow affecting us?

The future population of our cities is going to be drawn largely from these southern low-castes. Our citizenry of tomorrow is in their seed.

The squeezing out of both Negroes and whites, who move north to compete not only with our industrial workers but also with our farm renters, tends inevitably to lower standards both in our cities and on our farms. Already in southern Iowa there has been some influx of renters from the south. This accentuates the yearly shifting of tenants. It accentuates the mining of soil. It accentuates the lowering of human values. Father Ligutti of the Granger Homestead enterprise has pointedly referred to one phase of it as the "importation of illiteracy."

Moreover, there are other very specific economic ways in which south and north are inseparable.

Merely as one illustration, let us consider the matter of foreign markets for the south's cash crops. If our national tariff or other policies should result in permanent loss of any large part of our European and Japanese cotton markets, millions of acres of cotton land would inevitably go into other production in competition with the cornbelt, including the crops of which we already tend to have annual surpluses for export.

There are great regional differences with respect to the farm tenancy problem, as we said in the beginning.

In the south there is the enormous social task of somehow reversing the degenerative tendencies of generations, of starting to build the lower levels of the population up to the point at which a sound rural civilization is even possible. That—we may as well face it—is probably going to call for some species of governmental paternalism that we should prefer not to engage in.

In the cornbelt we have more fertile land and more competent people. We have the handicaps of a speculative tradition that are extremely difficult to counteract. And we have leasing practices that no longer fit our type of agriculture and that run contrary to the public interest.

We have an "agricultural ladder" that used to enable people to climb from farm laborer to farm renter to farm owner, but which in recent years has worked in reverse—it has given us farm owners descending to tenants, farm tenants descending to lower levels of tenancy, and the lower levels descending to farm labor.

But the main thing is that the problem as a whole is a distinctly national problem.

The degree of emphasis on different phases of such solutions as the country may adopt will vary in different sections.

But it is vital to each affected section that solutions be found in all sections.

We are members one of another. There is no escaping that.

*1939*

# RONALD G. CALLVERT

for distinguished editorial writing

As the world became slowly entangled in the tragedies that led to World War II, the American press—as it had done during the era of the first global war—again took on a cloak of patriotism. The war theme dominated the Pulitzer Prize for editorial writing. A presage of things to come was Ronald Callvert's editorial "My Country 'Tis of Thee . . . ," a patriotic song of America. Like few other editorials, it was blatantly lyrical, an effect gained by its repetition of the phrase "in this land of ours, this America." As luck would have it, Callvert wrote the editorial because another writer was unavailable. When he thought of the idea, Callvert said, "It occurred to me as a good editorial for Ben Hur Lampman to write." Lampman was noted for his lightness of touch as an *Oregonian* editorialist. The editorial quickly drew the attention of readers and of churches, schools, and patriotic organizations. To meet the demand for reprints, the *Oregonian* issued the editorial in leaflet form and distributed more than 14,000 copies. It received journalism's highest honor when judges selected Callvert for the 1939 Pulitzer Prize and pointed out "My Country 'Tis of Thee . . . " as exemplary of his work.

# My Country 'Tis of Thee . . .

*Portland Oregonian* • October 2, 1938

In this land of ours, this America, the man we choose as leader dons at no time uniform or insignia to denote his constitutional position as Commander in Chief of armed forces. No member of his Cabinet, no civil subordinate, ever attires himself in garments significant of military power.

In this land of ours, this America, the average citizen sees so little of the army that he has not learned to distinguish between a major and a lieutenant from his shoulder straps. When the Chief Executive addresses his fellow-countrymen they gather about him within handclasp distance. Goose-stepping regiments are not paraded before him. When he speaks to the civilian population it is not over rank upon rank of helmeted heads.

In this land of ours, this America, there is no tramp of military boots to entertain the visiting statesman. There is no effort to affright him with display of mobile cannon or of facility for mass production of aerial bombers.

In this land of ours, this America, there is no fortification along the several thousand miles of the northern border. In the great fresh water seas that partly separate it from another dominion no naval craft plies the waters. Along its southern border there are no forts, no show of martial strength.

In this land of ours, this America, no youth is conscripted to labor on device of defense; military training he may take or leave at option. There is no armed force consistent with a policy of aggression. The navy is built against no menace from the Western Hemisphere, but wholly for defense against that which may threaten from Europe or Asia.

In this land of ours, this America, one-third of the population is foreign born or native born of foreign or mixed parentage. Our numerous "minorities" come from fourteen nations. The native born, whatever his descent, has all political and other rights possessed by him who traces his ancestry to the founding fathers. The foreign born of races that are assimilable are admitted to all these privileges if they want them. We have "minorities" but no minority problem.

In this land of ours, this America, the common citizen may criticize without restraint the policies of his government or the aims of the Chief Executive. He may vote as his judgment or his conscience advises and not as a ruler dictates.

In this land of ours, this America, our songs are dedicated to love and romance, the blue of the night, sails in the sunset, and not to might or to a martyrdom to political cause. Our national anthem has martial words, difficult air. But if you want to hear the organ roll give the people its companion—"America . . . of thee I sing." In lighter patriotism we are nationally cosmopolitan. Unitedly we sing of Dixie or of Ioway, where the tall corn grows, of Springtime in the Rockies, or of California, here I come.

In this land of ours, this America, there is not a bomb-proof shelter, and a gas mask is a curiosity. It is not needed that we teach our children where to run when deathhawks darken the sky.

In this land of ours, this America, our troubles present or prospective come from within—come from our own mistakes, and injure us alone. Our pledges of peace toward our neighbors are stronger than ruler's promise or written treaty. We guarantee them by devoting our resources, greater than the resources of any other nation, to upbuilding the industries of peace. We strut no armed might that could be ours. We cause no nation in our half of the world to fear us. None does fear us, nor arm against us.

In this land of ours, this America, we have illuminated the true road to permanent peace. But that is not the sole moral sought herein to be drawn. Rather it is that the blessings of liberty and equality and peace that have been herein recounted are possessed nowhere in the same measure in Europe or Asia and wane or disappear as one nears or enters a land of dictatorship of whatever brand. This liberty, this equality, this peace, are imbedded in the American form of government. We shall ever retain them if foreign isms that would dig them out and destroy them are barred from our shores. If you cherish this liberty, this equality, this peace that is peace material and peace spiritual—then defend with all your might the American ideal of government.

*1940*

# BART HOWARD

for distinguished editorial writing

> BART HOWARD was known for his skill at capturing a situation
> with a phrase and for the sparkle of his writing. He was espe-
> cially fond of graphic description and alliteration. These charac-
> teristics are apparent in many of the editorials included in his
> entry for the 1940 Pulitzer Prize. More than for his talent, how-
> ever, Howard surpassed other editorial writers because, said a
> fellow staffer on the *St. Louis Post-Dispatch*, of his sincerity, his
> "deep and abiding convictions," and a "great faith in the dignity
> of the individual and in the validity of democracy." The following
> editorial—analyzing Adolph Hitler's conquests—was typical of
> his work. It makes apparent his use of language and was
> prophetic in its vision of the destruction that Hitler would bring
> to Europe.

# Europe's Emperor

*St. Louis Post-Dispatch* • March 17, 1939

The massive memory of Bismarck shrivels in the blazing sun
of Adolf Hitler's conquests. The former won by "blood and iron" uti-
lizing intrigue as a preface. The latter wins by strategy of conference, fortified by force, to be sure, and punctuated by the threat of
marching armies.

Schuschnigg is summoned to Berchtesgaden for an afternoon
in the torture chamber, and Austria is expunged from the map
while Vienna becomes Berlin's scrubwoman.

How many a plotting hour ticked secretly across the clock as
Hitler suggested and Henlein [Konrad Henlein, leader of the Sudeten German Party] acquiesced may only be surmised. But at last
the Sudeten Germans, under superb coaching, were letter-perfect

in their parts, and the Reich was ready to rescue their brothers from the tyranny of "ruthless Czecho-Slovakia." What would the neighbors say—the great Powers pledged to safeguard that one green isle of democracy in stormy Central Europe? France was explicitly committed; Russia conditionally; England impliedly. Chamberlain made his pilgrimage to the Fuehrer's mountain retreat, and later, with Daladier, consented to the pillage of the little Republic at Munich's midnight.

With Austria and the Sudetenland securely possessed and the plunder respectably approved, Herr Hitler's hunger was satisfied, rapacity was foresworn, there would be no more raids in Europe. "The Sudetenland," said Hitler at the Berlin Sportspalast on September 26, 1938, "is the last territorial demand I have to make in Europe." And in an earlier September speech at Nuremberg, he said he had given the guaranty to Chamberlain: "We do not want any Czechs any more."

England believed, officially. So did France. Russia refused to be deceived, distrusting Hitler's vow and subsequently impugning the motives of both Chamberlain and Daladier. Russia's suspicions have been frightfully vindicated, and today London and Paris join with Moscow in pronouncing worthless the word of Hitler. And Mussolini's Rome, at the other end of the paper axis, sees in the once barred doors of the Brenner Pass an open gateway for a Colossus in growing pains.

In Dr. Tiso of Slovakia [Josef Tiso, prime minister of Slovakia and head of Slovakia's delegation to the Munich Conference], Hitler seems to have found a craftier confederate than Henlein of the shriekingly managed Sudeten affair. Or perhaps Der Fuehrer has acquired a more polished technique. Surely the consummate skill of this latest coup, that caught the world flat-footed, may not be denied. Machiavelli could write it. Hitler does it. The revolt of Slovakia, inspired, promoted and directed in Berlin, is a masterpiece of statecraft. Moralists may deplore. Lights may burn late in sleepless chancelleries. The thing is done. A *fait accompli*, in the language of diplomacy, and the architect of the German Empire awakes in the historic castle of centuries-old Prague to breakfast contentedly and to count his gains.

He counts his gains realistically. Slovakia's independence lived but a day. Tiso, the politician, may now turn back to the priestly beads he seemingly had forsaken. The swastika is his country's flag.

What a vulturous Ides of March for the ravished, murdered homeland which Masaryk's genius had guided into the stature of a fine nation! The swastika flies over Bohemia and Moravia, and Hungary comes up from the south to seize Carpatho-Ukraine, with Poland ghoulishly hurrying to the feast of death.

The German Empire, territorially, is mighty today, and Hitler has inventoried the spoils with barbaric gusto.

The continental balance of power, deftly maintained, with grave lapses, of course, by Britain's ministerial jugglery, trembles under the tread of Europe's Emperor.

# REUBEN MAURY

for distinguished editorial writing

WHILE many of the Pulitzer Prize editorials, and perhaps most of the recent ones, are thoughtfully reasoned but routinely written, a few are shallow in thinking but facile in wording. Reuben Maury's editorials in the *New York Daily News* are examples of the latter. Maury received the 1941 award for six editorials:

• "Chemistry—The New Frontier" (January 3, 1940), a review of technical advances during the preceding decade and a speculation of things to come;
• A three-part editorial (January 27) endorsing a drive to save the Metropolitan Opera, discussing the presidential election, and urging continuation of work relief;
• "Satellite Nations" (March 24), an expression of doubt that small nations could continue to exist independent of a large, aggressive neighbor;
• "Moses' Crosstown Highway Plan" (May 26), an approval of a plan to erect three elevated highways across Manhattan;
• "Anti-Semitism in This Country" (September 24), an argument against the belief that Jews were pushing the United States into World War II;
• "Toward Totalitarianism," reprinted below.

The editorials generally were marked by a superficiality of thought and written in an interesting, simple manner aimed at a huge mass audience, reminiscent of the techniques of Arthur Brisbane, former editorialist for the Hearst newspapers. Critics greeted the announcement of Maury's award with charges that he was a "self-confessed hireling" who wrote for two publications of differing political views and that his editorials were irresponsible. In the editorial reprinted here, Maury argued that Roosevelt's New Deal policies, especially those regulating business, were moving America "toward totalitarianism."

# Toward Totalitarianism

*New York Daily News* • February 11, 1940

We often get the feeling in these wartime days that a strong current in human affairs is running somewhere, but that we can only guess from chips on the surface whither the current is going.

We think the best guess is that it is setting toward totalitarianism all over the world—meaning toward state control of the individual and of business.

Russia and Germany have arrived at complete totalitarianism; Italy has the forms of it; General Franco's Government in Spain is heading toward a "vertical syndicalist" state which reads like totalitarianism to us.

Even more significant to a person trying to dope out world trends, Great Britain has gone a long way toward totalitarianism since the war began last September. When the government begins to tell people to douse their lights, send their children to the country, and how much meat they can eat, that is state control of the individual where he lives. Now that this control has been clamped on Englishmen, we doubt that it ever will be fully relaxed.

As soon as the war broke out, France put civil liberties on the shelf for the duration—outlawed the Communist Party, began arresting people for saying so much as a kind word for Hitler, and so on.

The United States is on the road toward totalitarianism, though whether we'll eventually go the whole route is another question.

Time was in this country when business, any business, was practically a free agent.

Those big, expansive, devil-take-the-hindmost days began coming to an end in 1887, when Congress set up the Interstate Commerce Commission to curb some of the predatory habits of some of the railroads. Social control after social control has been fastened on business and the individual in this country since then—income, inheritance and gift taxes, soft coal commissions and workmen's compensation boards and Indian Welfare bureaus, labor relations acts and the Wage-Hour Law, etc., etc., etc., and a few more etc.'s.

Under the impetus of the New Deal, we've gone a longer way toward totalitarianism in seven years than we went in the previous 20 years. By the same token, the European war is taking Britain and France toward totalitarianism much faster than they would have gone had the horrors of peace continued to afflict them. Wars hurry economic changes along, every time.

We think the history of Europe since 1914 adds support to our theory that the world is headed toward totalitarianism.

The World War tossed into the ash can the thrones of three great empires—Germany, Austria-Hungary, Russia—along with the idea that some people are born to lord it over a lot of people who are born to be lorded over.

This war is rapidly taking away money and property from those who have a lot of those things—conscription of securities in England, confiscation of the Thyssen fortune in Germany, savage income taxes everywhere.

Life under totalitarianism is apparently not as pleasant for most people as life in a democracy. But neither, we should think, is it unbearable.

For one thing, the New Deal's government controls had to happen if there wasn't to be an attempt at revolution in this country against concentration of too much wealth in too few hands. It was evolution that brought those things to us, not a malevolent Mr. Roosevelt determined to smash up the Hooverian paradise of 1929-33.

For another thing, everybody who has a job is more or less caged anyway; there's no such thing as perfect freedom.

We do hope, though, that if the United States goes in for totalitarianism some way can be found to preserve the freedom of the mind. We mean freedom of speech and press, liberty to say what you think, whether your thoughts are worth a hoot or not. A system under which we had not only to live and do business as the Government ordered but also had—as in Russia and Germany—to think as the Government thought, would be unendurable, we believe, to most Americans.

*1942*

# GEOFFREY PARSONS

for distinguished editorial writing

As events leading to World War II burned hotter in Europe in 1941, Americans still faced domestic disagreements. In a series of 17 editorials, Geoffrey Parsons issued a "plea for unity" in the *New York Herald Tribune.* Coming from a Republican paper, the editorials called for Republicans to put aside partisanship and for Republicans and Democrats to unite for the common good. In nominating Parsons for the Pulitzer award, the jury for the editorial writing prize pointed out the integrity of Parsons' stance. "This series by the chief editorial writer of a leading Republican newspaper," the jury stated, "urges national unity behind the national leader whom this editorial writer and his paper had vigorously opposed for re-election and whose domestic policies Mr. Parsons still asserts leave much to be desired. These editorials seem outstanding examples of cooperation in a crisis by an opposition newspaper, are carefully reasoned, contain scholarly background, and are vigorously expressed in excellent and calmly persuasive prose." In announcing the award of the Pulitzer to Parsons, the Columbia University trustees added this citation: "The selection of these editorials over others of great distinction and to the same patriotic purpose was chiefly influenced by a wish to recognize an outstanding instance where political affiliation was completely subordinated to the national welfare and a newspaper firmly led its party to higher grounds." The first editorial from Parsons' series follows.

# The Urgent Need of Unity

*New York Herald Tribune* • January 15, 1941

That the nation is face to face with the gravest crisis since the Civil War hardly admits of dispute. Within the next few months—perhaps within two months, perhaps within six—there seems certain to be decided the tremendous issue, whether this country will face Germany and the future with allies or without them. If the latter, then our children and our children's children are all too likely to live in a world at war, perpetually arming for military combat, in economics endlessly struggling against totalitarian controls. To say that our national standard of living may be put back fifty years by such a world-wide warfare is certainly not to exaggerate.

Before such a crisis the need of national unity grows hourly. We do not mean a unity artificially imposed by law or threat or social pressure. We mean a unity achieved through frank debate, respect for disagreement and a realization that personalities and partisanship have no place in such an hour.

It is a matter for sincere regret that the President still refuses to take the lead in bringing about such a spirit of union. That he should have consulted the opposition in Congress before the submission of the lease-lend bill is now generally conceded. That that bill contains no provision for keeping both sides of the Houses informed as to steps taken under the tremendous grants of power contained in it, is equally a matter for regret. Passage of the bill could have been expedited and sources of friction and disunity avoided had Mr. Roosevelt approached the problem from a broader outlook, with partisanship forgot.

But the opposition will only make an unfortunate situation worse if it responds in kind. Now, if ever, Republican statesmanship has a chance to demonstrate its capacity by placing the patriotic needs of the time above personal irritations or factional disputes. We ask Republicans to be generous toward one another in this period of stress and that all who debate the issues, of whatever party, hold the national purpose clearly before them in all they say and do.

This is not to suggest that debate be slighted or hurried decisions reached. We trust that ample discussion will be insisted upon and that the excesses of the bill will be relentlessly lopped off. Similarly, in the more general debate in the nation at large there must be the fullest opportunity for every side to be heard— those who oppose any aid to Britain as well as those who believe that full aid to Britain is essential to American defense.

But it is possible to conduct such a debate without personal recriminations and with the hope and resolve to seek out the common wisdom of the American people. The time calls, above all else, for open minds, clear thinking and fair, generous discussion. There should be no petty questioning of motives, no substitution of epithet for reason.

For one important thing, let us be sure of our facts. For this reason we think Mr. [Wendell] Wilkie is rendering an important public service by undertaking the risks of a first-hand study of the English problem. For another, let us as far as possible, abandon catch phrases and formulae that no longer apply. For another, let us summon all our national gifts of imagination that we may see the issues not only for the immediate present but for the long future.

This newspaper believes firmly that aid to Britain is the only possible means to avoid war. It also believes that the issue of peace and war does not and has not for a considerable time been within our power to control or decide. The leader of Germany will or will not make war upon us as the coldest of military calculations determine; and if he decides upon war he will fix the moment by the same relentless logic. And, whether he decides to war upon us in a military sense or not, a long and vastly more destructive economic warfare is inevitable unless we should yield and become, like France and the small democracies, in an economic sense, a slave nation.

But we welcome the contrary views of our readers, and we shall, as always, be glad to give them full voice in our columns. We ask only that debate be about realities and that, in view of the gravity and urgency of the crisis, the discussion be kept upon a high plane of good will and patriotic endeavor. The goal is "Unity"; only in such a spirit and by such ideals can it be achieved in time.

*1943*

# FORREST W. SEYMOUR

for editorials published during 1942

> FORREST SEYMOUR became the fifth winner of the Pulitzer for edi
> torials inspired by World War II. His entry was composed of 23
> editorials covering generally three themes: the home front, bring
> ing about an intelligent peace, and making democracy work.
> Most of the editorials dealt specifically with aspects of the war,
> but they also covered such topics as politics, the national
> economy, and the poll tax. The editorial receiving most attention,
> "Statesmanship in the Legion," applauded the American Legion's
> adoption of a resolution favoring an anti-isolationist role for the
> United States when World War II should end and the Legion's
> recognition that the United States must assume a role of leader
> ship to assure world order. The editorial also received the Ameri
> can Legion Editorial Appreciation Award for 1943.

# Statesmanship in the Legion

*Des Moines Register* • May 3, 1942

In the *Register*'s opinion, the statement about America's role
in the world ahead that was adopted by the national executive
committee of the American Legion Friday is one of the notable contributions of our time to statesmanlike public leadership.

The Legion does exercise an important leadership. Though
occasionally during its quarter century of life we have disagreed
with one or another of its policies, its influence on the whole has
been excellent. We have frequently said this. Especially during the
last ten years, after the disasters that international suspicion and
disunity were breeding had become apparent, the voices of national Legion leaders began to be heard more and more frequently
on the side of intelligent recognition of this nation's world respon-

sibilities. More than one of these leaders, incidentally, were Iowans.

Since the Legion is quite representative of the whole American people, it has naturally gone through the same period of debate in this epoch that all of us have. But because it has been essentially progressive and attuned by its very character to popular sentiment, it has been "out ahead" of many comparable forces in its recognition of the political realities and its shift to practical and courageous policies.

Now, through its national executive committee, it has "gone to bat" for the principle upon which all of our long-run hopes for a decent future world hinge. That part of the committee's statement which sums up this principle is worth repeating. Here it is:

> It was considered that what the last war proved and what this war emphasizes is:
>
> That, whether we like it or not, we are a part of the entire world; that as a nation we cannot escape repercussions from mighty social, economic and political upheavals in any quarter of the world; that isolationism is dead; that now is the time to condition the public mind for full acceptance of this inexorable fact.
>
> That, however complete the military victory may be, we cannot win the peace, we cannot provide assurances to our people against periodic repetition of our involvement in world catastrophes, unless we as a major nation recognize and assume our responsibilities and take our position of leadership in organizing the world to establish and maintain order; that there can be no assurance of permanent national security except through world security.

That says it all, and says it magnificently.

We would call attention to two or three other things with respect to this.

First, the Legion took this stand by approving the report of its coordinating committee, which had been consulting with spokesmen for a half dozen other national groups exerting a similar wide influence among their respective memberships. They were the National Grange, the American Federation of Labor, the National Association of Manufacturers, the Elks, the Knights of Columbus, B'nai B'rith, and the Masonic lodge of New York.

This sort of consultation among large national associations exercising a broad influence and leadership is certainly nothing to be sneezed at. We do not know how it got started. But it is a grand thing. We assume that it will continue to develop.

Second, this statement of principle was hinged, naturally and properly, on an acknowledgement that winning the war has to come first.

That goes without saying.

The wisdom that is being displayed in America, by committing ourselves to intelligent participation in the postwar organization of the world, does not need to detract a whit from the energy with which we fight for the essential military victory. On the contrary, the prospect of wise and informed leadership after the war will give point to our sacrifices, and permit more zealous concentration on the job at hand.

More than that, the faith and valiance of all the harassed and suppressed peoples of the world—both our existing and potential allies—depend in large measure on our clear understanding of what they are struggling for and of our own urgent place in the world's future.

The Legion by its nature is a symbol of the best of military experience and valor, combined with the best of civilian leadership and statesmanship.

It is no small matter, as we see it, that this organization's strength and influence are plainly going to be exerted in the years ahead on the side of intelligent world order.

*1944*

# HENRY J. HASKELL

for editorials written during 1943

> HENRY HASKELL is the only person who has received the Pulitzer
> award for editorials twice. For his second prize, he submitted as
> his entry seven complete editorial pages from the *Kansas City*
> (Mo.) *Star*, of which he was editor. While the editorials covered a
> wide range of topics such as education, politics, and Social Secu-
> rity, the predominant subject was World War II and related in-
> ternational problems. Reprinted here are two editorials from the
> February 28, 1943, editorial page. "How Germany Fooled the
> World" recited a history lesson to support Haskell's analysis of
> why the Treaty of Versailles ending World War I was unsuccess-
> ful. It urged that similar "mistakes" be avoided when World War
> II should end and that strong measures be imposed on post-war
> Germany. "That Valley Falls Latin Teacher" criticized attempts
> by the National Education Association to use the war as an ex-
> cuse for eliminating cultural studies from high schools.

# How Germany Fooled the World

*Kansas City* (Mo.) *Star* • February 28, 1943

The Commission to Study the Organization of Peace has just
made its third report. Other committees and groups are busy with
the same studies. We are constantly and properly reminded that
unless we are both intelligent and vigilant we may win the war
only to lose the peace. Whether any generally accepted plan is
worked out or not, all this discussion is to the good. The problems
of the post-war world are as formidable as those of the war itself.

It was the American Patrick Henry who said: "I know of no
way of judging the future but by the past." At this time it is important to survey what happened after the first World War in order to

avoid the mistakes made in that fateful period.

Some of the discussion of the new world order has a familiar ring to those whose memories go back to the other war—the kaiser's war, just as this is supposed to be Hitler's war.

We keep hearing that whatever is done about Germany, the German war criminals must be punished; the officers, that is, who ordered the shooting of hostages, who were responsible for the vast and ghastly atrocities against Poles and Jews, who ordered the bombing of Rotterdam and the machine-gunning of refugees on the roads of France, who planned the destruction of Lidice.

After the war, it is agreed, Germany must be disarmed and an army of occupation maintained on German soil. Then some sort of a world authority must be set up; something comparable to the League of Nations, but with more power to keep the peace. In all these plans we are cautioned to bear in mind that the German people were not responsible for Hitler and the war. At the last free election for the Reichstag Hitler's party received only a minority of the vote. The Germans are like every other civilized people. All they really desire is to live comfortably at home in peace. They were dragged into an unwanted war by a paranoiac dictator who had established his rule by intimidation and the Gestapo, so the argument runs.

The idea of punishing the war criminals is not new, but probably few Americans recall that such punishment was included in the Treaty of Versailles. The kaiser was to have been punished, but he was out of reach in Holland. Evidence, however, had been collected in the cases of 900 lesser men, and under the treaty Germany agreed to hand them over to an Inter-Allied tribunal for trial and punishment.

But unexpected difficulties developed. A cry of protest to the civilized world went up from Germany. Such procedure would be an intolerable insult to a great nation. The new German democratic government appealed to the Allies not to burden it with the odium that would attach to any government that attempted to carry out this provision of the treaty. The French were obdurate, but liberals elsewhere turned a sympathetic ear to the plea. After all why humiliate a proud people needlessly? The Weimar republic offered to have the criminals publicly tried by the German supreme court at Leipzig. The British government yielded and the

French could not hold out against it. The preliminary proceedings took a year. Finally twelve of the 900 were tried, and six convicted. The British solicitor general asserted in the House of Commons that the trials were "a new milestone in the course of international justice." The official English observer at the trials, Sir Ernest Pollock, declared that while they might not have fulfilled the expectation of the public "they were of real importance and value. They had made history." And that was that.

Naturally the victims of German aggression were determined after the last war that Germany should be completely disarmed, just as they are today. The army was to be reduced to 100,000 men and there was to be no general staff. An Inter-Allied Control commission was set up under a French general with an English general as second in command. It was at work for several years. There were disagreements as to the size of the army. The English general took the position that the private armies with which Germany abounded were to be considered as part of the Reichswehr. When Hitler came to power it was estimated that the army included 250,000 highly trained troops instead of the 100,000 permitted by the treaty. A general staff was set up under another name. The republic's minister of defense confided to his friends that he would establish the general staff as the Institute of Textile Studies, if necessary.

There was complaint that word was always received two days in advance of the visits of the commission and that machine tools and supplies mysteriously disappeared, German airplane factories were set up on friendly Russian soil and a submarine plant established on the Spanish coast, so that experimental work could be carried on.

When Germany was admitted to the League of Nations in 1926 it was necessary that the control commission issue a final report that the disarmament provisions had been complied with. The report was made and suppressed by the democracies anxious to get Germany into the League. Later General John H. Morgan, adjutant general of the commission, wrote: "Germany has never disarmed, has never had the intention of disarming, and for seven years has done everything in her power to hinder, deceive, and countercontrol the commission appointed to control her disarmament."

At Versailles the French had contended that disarmament was not enough. Foch [Ferdinand Foch, French military chief of staff during World War I and representative at the Paris Peace Conference] had insisted on the Rhine as a natural defense and he had urged the setting up of an autonomous Rhineland as a buffer state. He was overruled, but all the Allies agreed that Allied forces should occupy at least part of the Rhineland until 1935. In the conference Clemenceau [Georges Clemenceau, premier of France] said: "In fifteen years I shall be no more. In fifteen years, if you do me the honor of visiting my grave you will be able to say, I am sure, 'We are watching on the Rhine and we shall remain there.' "

But in 1929 as a gesture of appeasement and good will Briand [Aristide Briand, French foreign minister] consented to the withdrawal of all Allied troops, with the Rhineland itself remaining a demilitarized zone. Seven years later the Reichswehr marched in and France again was under the guns. The British government, and liberals everywhere said this was only natural. Any nation of course would insist on the right to do what it chose within its own territory, and Hitler's move was no threat to world peace.

When Germany entered the League of Nations in 1926 there was universal rejoicing and a general feeling that the millennium was at hand. But within a few years national dissensions paralyzed the League and it proved helpless to stop aggression anywhere. Even when Germany withdrew and openly threw off the mask of disarmament, nothing was done.

In retrospect it is evident that all the policies adopted to make Germany a peaceful, good neighbor were vitiated by one fundamental mistake. That mistake was the assumption that a peace-loving German nation had been forced into war against its will by a wicked government. Germany did not change with the flight of the kaiser. The ideals of a militaristic Germany able to dominate by force persisted under the republic as they had under the empire. What Mirabeau [a French Revolutionary orator] said more than a century ago was still true. Germany was "not a country with an army, but an army with a country."

The mistakes of the post-war years are obvious. How to avoid similar mistakes in the future involves problems of immense difficulty. But certainly we must build on a foundation free from the fundamental error that followed the last war. At Versailles under the idealistic leadership of President Wilson the assumption prevailed that the German people were misrepresented by their government; that once the government was changed, they could be trusted. In the light of the evidence we must assume that Hitler is right in saying that he speaks for the mass of the German people. An entire nation must be deprived of its power to do harm until it is re-educated in the essentials of civilization. Our post-war measures must be framed with this fact steadily in mind.

# That Valley Falls Latin Teacher

*Kansas City* (Mo.) *Star* • February 28, 1943

The campaign of the National Education Association to take advantage of the war to drive out cultural studies from high schools has evoked wide protest. One of the replies to the association's pamphlet on the subject comes from Justice William S. Smith of the Kansas Supreme court. The association took the ground that the teaching of ancient languages and literatures should be confined to "the very few" who might be expected to use them "in their scholarly pursuits," or whose cultural life might be enriched by them.

Justice Smith inquires how a high school teacher is to determine which students would achieve sufficient cultural value from Latin and Greek to warrant their studying these languages. The justice adds: "I was fortunate enough to come under the tutelage of a dear little old maid who loved to teach Latin in the Valley Falls high school. Under her influence I studied Caesar and Cicero and read the Aeneid twice. At that time my experience in Valley Falls constituted my entire cultural life. I have thanked the memory of that schoolteacher many, many times."

The advocates of the purely practical education would turn out a generation of trained cooks and machinists—which is all very well, for our civilization needs them. But they would smother the cultural life, which is destructive of civilization itself.

It would be a drab world if the National Education Association succeeded in banishing from American high schools the Valley

Falls teachers who love the classics and in keeping from the Bill Smiths of the future that contact with the past that helps to an understanding of the present.

# GEORGE W. POTTER

for editorials, especially on freedom of the press

GEORGE POTTER'S winning entry consisted of a number of editorials dealing with various aspects of World War II, but the Pulitzer jury especially noted his editorials on freedom of the press, covering such subjects as wartime censorship. These, the jury said, "expressed accurately and pertinently the American view of freedom of the press." It called special attention to one editorial, "Relations of Freedoms," dealing with the importance of a sound economic base for the press. The system of income through advertising, Potter argued, is what guarantees press freedom. Without this or some such system independent of the government, he said, the press cannot be free of influence by the government or corrupt private interests since it would have to rely on one or the other for its financial support. While this theme was constructed in the first half of the editorial, Potter in the latter part switched emphasis to the importance of private property. Thus the editorial, economically conservative, was as much a defense of private property as of press freedom.

# Relations of Freedoms

*Providence* (R.I.) *Journal-Bulletin* • Date uncertain

In the proper spirit of nonpartisanship, both Republicans and Democrats in Congress, using spadework material gathered by the State Department, are uniting on a resolution to guarantee world freedom of news. The aim is to incorporate in the peace treaties guarantees underwritten by the signatory nations affording the right to gather news anywhere and to permit the unhindered receipt into their countries of news gathered elsewhere.

The premise of this resolution is so obvious that it does not require laboring. It is that war, or the threat of war, is minimized and that better relations prevail among the nations of the world when there is free access to honest and unbiased news and information, objectively presented. We know from bitter experience that the first thing that totalitarian [governments] and dictatorships do when they come into power is to seize the press and make of it an instrument of totalitarian design to poison the minds of their people, color their thinking and stir up hatred and rancor against other nations. Through their control of the press, the totalitarian authorities effectively blanketed their people from information of or contact with the outside world.

But it is merely a counsel of perfection to suppose that there can be genuine world freedom of news without a genuine free press. A genuine free press is one that is economically free, that is, one that can support itself by its own revenues and stand on its own two feet independent of subsidy or subvention from government or self-seeking or selfish private interests. In France before the war, freedom of the press was guaranteed as a right, but in fact the French press was venal and corrupt because it was not economically free and depended upon subsidies and bribes for its bread and butter, often from foreign powers, with results that were calamitous to France. Pertinax, the most profound student of journalism in France, put his finger exactly upon the solution of how to get a genuine free press in that country: "The French people," he said, "will have to develop the advertising habit or be prepared to pay much more for their papers." In other words, the French press must be able to pay its own way in order to have real freedom, and that truth applies in any country that wants a free press.

Some people in this country do not understand or deliberately misinterpret what freedom of the press actually is. They father the idea that it is a right belonging to newspapers solely, giving them the privilege of doing as they please. As a matter of fact, freedom of the press is a specific grant of a right by the Constitution not to the newspapers solely but to all the people for their protection. We have the freest press in the whole world, thanks not alone to a jealously guarded popular right but also because the American press is economically independent, stands on its own two feet without subsidy or subvention and can pay its own way, depending upon its own competency for survival. Through our cooperative system of newsgathering, which serves newspapers of all shades of opinion, the American people are assured of objective news.

Thus we see in the instance of the American press a definite and inextricable relationship between a flourishing human freedom and the sound fruits of a healthy economic freedom. One depends upon the other, and both will prevail so long as conditions are maintained which permit this economic freedom.

Does the individual in America see clearly that his human freedoms are tied in with economic freedom?

There is a well-known generalization that human rights come before property rights. It is used by demagogues, because of its surface appeal, to play upon the emotions of the unthinking. Like all glib generalizations it should be subject to critical examination. We would not say that property rights come before human rights or that human rights come before property rights. Unqualified absolutes like these do not contain the truth as tested by human experience. What we do say is that human rights and property rights are related to one another, are intertwined with one another, work with and play upon one another for the general good, depend upon one another.

Pope Pius, in a recent statement of most far-reaching significance for the reconstruction of the world, said this much better than we can hope to say it, said it out of [a] background of deep human experience for the guidance of the men who will help build the new world. He related private property, a "natural fruit of labor," to man's determination "to create for himself and his own an existence of just freedom, not only economic but also political, cultural and religious."

He condemned a capitalism that "arrogates unlimited right to property without any subordination to the common good," and he condemned a system that, depriving men of any direct or indirect security in their lives, leaves them slaves of any political party that promises them bread and security. "By defending private property," said the Pope, "the Church . . . also pursues a lofty ethical-social aim. . . . The aim of the Church is to render the institution of private ownership such as it should be in accordance with the plans of Divine wisdom and the dictates of Nature: one of the elements of the social order, a necessary premise of human initiative, an impulse of labor for the advantage of the temporary and transcendental aims of the goal, the prize and dignity of man, who was created in the image of God. . . . Future social and economic-policy organizing activity of the State, of local bodies, of professional organizations will not be able to achieve their lofty aims in continuing the fruitfulness of the social life and normal returns of a national economy unless they respect and protect the vital function of private property in its personal and total value."

In other words, the Pope says that human rights and property rights, human freedom and economic freedom, are not antagonistic or divided into separate categories. They go hand in hand in a proper and related balance for the welfare of all. An understanding of this fundamental relationship will make for a better and more prosperous condition for us all.

*1946*

# HODDING CARTER

for a series on racial, religious, and economic tolerance

AFTER serving in World War II on the *Stars and Stripes,* Hodding
Carter returned to his newspaper in Greenville, Mississippi, and
immediately began attracting nationwide attention. In numerous
editorials he concentrated on building respect between races. For
such writing he was awarded the 1946 Pulitzer Prize. "I had been
protesting editorially against racial and religious injustices for a
long time before our editorials won a Pulitzer Prize," he said.
"But . . . the Pulitzer Prize induced more people at home to con-
cede that there might be some merit in what we were saying."
The most popular editorial of his prize-winning series was "Go
For Broke," written shortly after V-J Day. Although it was out-
wardly a challenge to white Americans to treat Japanese-Americans as equals, there is little doubt that Carter intended it to call
for racial tolerance for blacks also. "Go For Broke" was widely
reprinted and is one of the most frequently quoted Pulitzer Prize
editorials in the history of the award. After winning the award,
Carter was known to have proposed tongue-in-cheek a new slogan for his small chicken enterprise: "All our pullets are prizes."

# Go For Broke

*Delta Democrat-Times* (Greenville, Miss.) • August 27, 1945

Company D of the 168th Regiment which is stationed in
Leghorn, Italy, is composed altogether of white troops, some from
the East, some from the South, some from the Midwest and West
Coast.

Company D made an unusual promise earlier this month.
The promise was in the form of a communication to their fellow
Americans of the 442d Infantry Regiment and the 100th Infantry

Battalion, whose motto is "Go For Broke," and it was subscribed to unanimously by the officers and men of Company D.

In brief, the communication pledged the help of Company D in convincing "the folks back home that you are fully deserving of all the privileges with which we ourselves are bestowed."

The soldiers to whom that promise was made are Japanese-Americans. In all of the United States Army, no troops have chalked up a better combat record. Their record is so good that these Nisei were selected by General Francis H. Oxx, commander of the military area in which they are stationed, to lead the final victory parade. So they marched, 3,000 strong, at the head of thousands of other Americans, their battle flag with three Presidential unit citationed streamers floating above them, their commander, a Wisconsin white colonel, leading them.

Some of those Nisei must have been thinking of the soul-shaking days of last October, when they spearheaded the attacks that opened the Vosges Mountain doorway to Strasbourg. Some of them were probably remembering how they, on another bloody day, had snatched the Thirty-Six Division's lost battalion of Texans from the encircling Germans. And many of them were bearing scars from those two engagements which alone had cost the Nisei boys from Hawaii and the West Coast 2,300 casualties.

Perhaps these yellow-skinned Americans, to whose Japanese kinsmen we have administered a terrific and long overdue defeat, were holding their heads a little higher because of the pledge of their white fellow-soldiers and fellow-Americans of Company D. Perhaps, when they gazed at their combat flag, the motto "Go For Broke" emblazoned thereon took on a different meaning. "Go For Broke" is the Hawaiian-Japanese slang expression for shooting the works in a dice game.

The loyal Nisei have shot the works. From the beginning of the war, they have been on trial, in and out of uniform, in army camps and relocation centers, as combat troops in Europe and as frontline interrogators, propagandists, and combat intelligence personnel in the Pacific where their capture meant prolonged and hideous torture. And even yet they have not satisfied their critics.

It is so easy for a dominant race to explain good or evil, patriotism or treachery, courage or cowardice in terms of skin color. So easy and so tragically wrong. Too many have committed that wrong against the loyal Nisei, who by the thousands have proved themselves good Americans, even while others of us, by our actions against them, have shown ourselves to be bad Americans. Nor is the end of this misconception in sight. Those Japanese-American soldiers who paraded at Leghorn in commemoration of the defeat of the nation from which their fathers came, will meet other enemies, other obstacles as forbidding as those of war. A lot of people will begin saying, as soon as these boys take off their uniforms, that "a Jap is a Jap," and the Nisei deserve no consideration. A majority won't say or believe this, but an active minority can have its way against an apathetic majority.

It seems to us that the Nisei slogan of "Go For Broke" could be adopted by all Americans of good will in the days ahead. We've got to shoot the works in a fight for tolerance. Those boys of Company D point the way. Japan's surrender will be signed aboard the *Missouri* and General MacArthur's part will be a symbolic "Show Me."

*1947*

# WILLIAM H. GRIMES

for distinguished editorial writing

OCCASIONAL Pulitzer-winning editorials seem to have struck a popular chord and gained wider currency than the columns of the parent newspaper. One such editorial was William H. Grimes' "Apathetic and Pathetic," one of 15 writings submitted as his 1947 Pulitzer entry. Most of his editorials dealt with economics, business, or labor. "Apathetic and Pathetic" included references to these subjects, but it was more concerned with what Grimes saw as America's abandonment of its traditional values. Grimes, the *Journal's* editor, criticized economic and political trends in the United States and the apparent contradiction between what Americans said they believed and how they acted. The editorial was reprinted in a number of newspapers, and the *Journal* received more than 30,000 requests for reprints.

# Apathetic and Pathetic

*Wall Street Journal* • March 7, 1946

Concerning Premier Stalin's Russia and its international conduct, there are a great many puzzling aspects. To us the most puzzling is not rooted in Russia. It grows in America. It can be expressed in the form of a question: Why should anybody expect Stalin to do anything different than he is doing? If any surprise is due, it is in the fact that Stalin, being what he is and having the opportunity that he has, should be even as moderate as he has been.

The opportunity is that a ruthless man believing in the law of force has no opposition. And he has none because the only nation in the world around which could rally "a decent respect to the opinions of mankind" is losing its faith. It is becoming ashamed of its traditions. The light of freedom for the individual which has heartened men for a century and a half flickers and burns low in a fetid atmosphere from which the sustaining oxygen has been drained.

Try this if you will. Go into any group—the more prosperous and fashionable the better the test—and speak of the "self-evident truth" that "all men are endowed by their Creator with certain unalienable rights, that among these are life, liberty and the pursuit of happiness." Say to this group that "to secure these rights governments are instituted among men."

We venture that you will be startled by the number of people, particularly younger people, who do no know that you are quoting the Declaration of Independence. And of those who know, a large number will not agree with the philosophy expressed. And of those who agree—and this is the most tragic thing—many will not have the courage to say so.

Perhaps the dominant attitude was summed up by a young man who would probably think of himself as an "intellectual." He said:

"Only a few people in the Bible Belt believe those things now."

Or listen to the young minister of the gospel who came to this office sneering at those who "operate in a vacuum of idealism."

We gave our government encouragement—it did not need much—to connive with Stalin. In the criminal decision of Yalta an American President accepted secret agreements which bartered thousands of human beings and which, if carried out, will send thousands more to exile and death.

We did that and a chorus of writers and commentators defaulted their obligation to ask questions and said that Yalta was good. They said Stalin was a man of his word. He would not grab territory. He would not suppress the churches. He would cease to send his agitators into every corner of the world. He would not use his military power to force on other peoples his own social and political system. Each of those things he has done. Some illusionists, who said he would not, now have the decency to acknowledge disillusion. They suggest that we shake an admonitory finger at Stalin.

This is a ludicrous suggestion. Does anyone imagine that Stalin is such a fool that he thinks we can or will oppose his armed might with ours? And if we are not ready to do that, what other means of opposition have we? We have none, for we have besmirched our own moral precepts. We have dropped our faith and stand grotesquely naked.

Yet we tell other peoples of the world how they must act. We have abandoned the tradition that peoples have the right to work out their own destiny.

We denounce a Colonel Peron of Argentina as a dictator and a bad man suspected of aggression and therefore he must not rule that unhappy republic. He certainly is those things. But who is the United States to denounce the man that the people of his country apparently have chosen in a free election and to condemn any other government for cooperating with dictators? The fact is that Colonel Peron helped himself to power by borrowing more than one page from the book of the New Deal.

But Colonel Peron and General Franco, another unsavory character ruling Spain, are, we say, corrupt. Furthermore, they suppress the rights of the people. They poison the wells of free information. They certainly do those things.

Let us see what government it is that hurls these accusations of corruption and extralegal sanctions.

It is a government where the family and friends of a President could use their prestige to enrich themselves and those who publicly protested are denounced. It is a government against which, for the first time in American history, Americans fear to speak. It is a government which is spending the people's money on a bureaucracy with which men abhor contact because resistance means reprisals. The system has the expected results. Many businesses feel that they must have a friend at court and so some who have official access are paid as "advisers." There was a time when we called such men lobbyists and investigated them. Now they are appointed to high office.

Looking at our record of connivance with dictators and looking at our domestic scene, is it any wonder that the people of Argentina decided that Colonel Peron might be the lesser of two evils?

And while we condemn the dictators for suppressing and distorting the free flow of information, our own State Department proposes a plan to blanket the world with propaganda.

Why should Stalin take us and our pious protestations seriously? Why should he give us any attention at all? He knows what is happening and he knows that we are treading the path to his philosophy and his orbit. He thinks he has only to wait—and he may be right.

We have told the world about four freedoms but the number of men who live under the heel of dictatorship is greater, not less. We have not stood for freedom. We are in the thick of the game of power politics. We are in it in Europe and in Asia and we have imported it to the American continent. It is Stalin's game and of course we do it badly.

There are men not afraid to speak out. One is John Foster Dulles who dares speak and knows whereof he speaks. We quote:

> I am afraid we've got very few friends in the world today. There was a time when we had more friends than any other people of the world. Today we have influence because of our production capacity, because people are trying to get the physical things we produce. I don't detect any real friendship on the part of other peoples. This leaves us in a dangerous and vulnerable position; one which we should do our utmost to correct.

A man's standing in his community is a projection of his own character. A nation's standing in the world is a projection of its domestic life.

What we see at home is a condition where public trust is openly accepted as an avenue to private gain; where a government is so steeped in propaganda lies that it must give the wrong reasons for its policies; where in the name of freedom the citizen is being handcuffed to rules of a troupe of brilliant pygmies who write the prescription for a fuller life on an adding machine; where debt is prosperity and thrift a social crime; where it can be asserted that there exists a "moral right" to steal and bribe; where men shout free enterprise and then seek better and bigger government subsidies; where women leaving black markets stop to sign petitions for continuation of price control; where groups demanding "When do we get ours?" no longer whisper but shout and where officials no longer consider it necessary to conceal that they are the creatures of these groups.

Is it any wonder that in our international relations we cannot combat the assertion that black is white and that the goal of human freedom is the slave state?

Is it any wonder that Mr. Dulles laments the lack of those policies, "expressive of the righteous faith of the best in America?"

We are apathetic: We are rapidly growing pathetic.

*1948*

# VIRGINIUS DABNEY

for distinguished editorial writing

VIRGINIUS DABNEY, former editor of the *Richmond* (Va.) *Times-Dispatch*, was one of those few writers who received the Pulitzer Prize without submitting an entry. The Pulitzer committee, Dabney later said, "decided to make the award to me on the basis of my work 'during the year' and with nothing before them." As a result, there is no file of Dabney's work for which he received the 1948 prize. Unsuccessful at selecting an editorial appropriate for inclusion in this anthology, Dabney explained to the compilers that he was "unable to recall any 1947 editorial that is exceptional in any way." It is generally believed, however, that Dabney was awarded the Pulitzer for his stands on racial issues in the South. During the 1940s he was a staunch opponent of the poll tax and the one-party political system while favoring increased opportunities for black Americans and equal though segregated facilities. His attitude toward editorial policy has been that writers must take stands on important local issues and not waste space on trite or irrelevant subjects. To improve the editorial page, Dabney wrote in a 1945 magazine article, the page "must be dedicated to the welfare of all the people, not merely to the interest of one exclusive and fortunate class. . . . More money will have to be spent on it, and more talent allotted to it. Then readers will turn to it in the expectation of being informed, stimulated, or amused, not in the confident knowledge that they will find there the same old sloppily written pontifications, the same dreary and bumbling half-truths, the same pachydermatous attempts at humor, where there is any humor. The effective editorial page . . . should be put together with some consideration for style, it must be vigorous, independent and free, and its judgments must have perspective, while permeating the whole there must be a passionate concern for the truth." Included here is the editorial for which Dabney won the 1948 Sigma Delta Chi (now Society of Professional Journalists) award for editorial writing. A defense of freedom of the press, it made evident the *Times-Dispatch*'s determination to oppose the Virginia legislature's intention of investigating the newspaper. One of its primary persuasive appeals was its equating the state house of delegates with historic despots, while its apparent reasonableness on the issue of libel law moderated a stand that some readers might have considered nothing more than self-serving.

# We Will Not Be Intimidated

*Richmond* (Va.) *Times-Dispatch* • March 15, 1948

The Virginia House of Delegates has passed a resolution instructing the State Corporation Commission to investigate Richmond Newspapers, Inc. This absurd action was taken in retaliation for criticisms leveled at members of the General Assembly, and more particularly members of the House, during the session just ended.

The *Times-Dispatch* does not intend to be silenced by any such political skulduggery. This newspaper has spoken its mind freely during the recent session of the State Legislature, and it will continue to speak its mind. No threats from any section of the State, or from any branch of the General Assembly, nor yet from the Democratic machine, will influence its course.

The issue here is far bigger than the question [of] whether a Richmond newspaper should criticize the Virginia Legislature. One of the bulwarks of free peoples is involved.

George Mason's immortal Bill of Rights, which is a part of the Virginia Constitution and has been virtually copied in the Constitution of the United States, as well as in the constitutions of the other 47 States, says (Article 1, Section 12, Virginia Constitution): "That the freedom of the press is one of the great bulwarks of liberty and can never be restrained but by despotic governments."

The laws of libel, both criminal and civil, are always available, of course, to any citizen who is aggrieved by improper newspaper criticism.

There are all kinds of newspapers, just as there are all kinds of people, but once the freedom of newspapers or individuals to criticize public figures is hampered or curtailed, the first step toward dictatorship has been taken.

In country after country where the liberties of the people

have been quenched, under Fascist, Nazi or Communist rule, one of the first steps has always been the smashing of the independent press.

The Second World Congress of the Communist International had this to say:

> Only when the proletarian dictatorship has deprived the bourgeoisie of such powerful weapons as the press, the school, parliament, church, the government apparatus, etc., only when the final overthrow of the capitalist order will have become an evident fact—only then will all or almost all the workers enter the ranks of the Communist Party.

Adolf Hitler said in *Mein Kampf*:

> It [the State] must not let itself be misled by the boast of a so-called "freedom of the press" and must not be persuaded to fail in its duty and to put before the nation the food that it needs and that is good for it; it must assure itself with ruthless determination of this means for educating the people.

Here in America there have been examples of interference with liberty of newspaper expression by officials or legislatures. One of the earliest occurred at the end of the eighteenth century, when the *Richmond Examiner*, a Jeffersonian organ, was attacked under the notorious Sedition Act for its political editorials. The effort to stifle the *Examiner* was unsuccessful.

The late Huey P. Long, as Governor of Louisiana, had his servile legislature impose a ruinous tax on all the Louisiana newspapers of large circulation because they had criticized his administration and exposed its rottenness. The tax was pronounced unconstitutional by the Supreme Court.

Frank Hague, the Jersey City boss, struck at the *Jersey Journal* by firing any county or city employee seen reading the paper, and by bringing about the withdrawal of certain advertising.

Similar techniques have been employed both in this and other countries. Those who employ them violate one of the principles on which American liberty has been founded, a principle for which oceans of blood have been spilled.

The resolution of the House of Delegates is a threatening gesture designed to arouse public prejudice. It is not motivated by ethical intent to correct economic injustice; its purpose is to gag the press.

So long as this newspaper is in the hands of its present ownership and management, it will not be gagged.

It will fight fiercely the concentration of governmental functions in a few hands, and the making of governmental policies by a small group of insiders.

It will not be muzzled, by the House of Delegates, or any other agency.

The *Times-Dispatch* will not be intimidated.

# JOHN H. CRIDER

for distinguished editorial writing

IN 1949, for the second time, the Pulitzer Prize for editorial writing was shared by two journalists. One of the winners, John Crider, editor of the *Boston Herald*, concentrated primarily on the 1948 presidential election in the editorials submitted as his Pulitzer entry. All the editorials were datelined outside Boston, although it is uncertain whether they were actually written in those places or in Boston. The *Herald*'s publisher, Robert Choate, in his cover letter with the entry, expressed his enthusiasm for datelined editorials. "The exhibit," he wrote, "is limited to [Crider's] out-of-town editorial writing because I believe it represents a novel and constructive departure from the conventional editorial style. ... It does impress the reader with the editor's proximity to the news." Typical of the style and Crider's anti-Harry Truman sentiment was the editorial below.

# Imagine, One Billion!

*Boston Herald* • October 1, 1948

ABOARD PRESIDENT TRUMAN'S TRAIN, in Illinois, Sept. 30— President Truman said a most significant thing yesterday before his audience in the stadium at Tulsa. He said that for the first time in the history of Oklahoma its farm crop topped one billion dollars in value. There were some cheers and quite a bit of applause. "Imagine," he added, "one billion dollars."

Of course, this was just another attempt by the Democratic candidate to appeal to the native pride of the very proud Oklahomans. As a matter of fact, the $1,000,000,000 he mentioned would be around $600,000,000 or less if spoken in terms of 1939 purchasing power of the dollar.

But the funny part of it was that the President never mentioned "inflation," one of his favorite themes. In that Tulsa speech, it was mighty flattering to tell the Oklahomans they had produced such a crop.

He soon spoiled it, however, by adding that this huge production record was due in very large part to the farm policies of the late President Roosevelt which he had carried forward. He wouldn't let the people of Oklahoma rest in the belief that they had done something great themselves.

But worse, he didn't explain that the reason the produce income was so large was at least partly due to the inflated value of the dollar. Nor did he say that Oklahomans had to pay almost as much more than the value of their ordinary crops for what they bought from the East. Nor did he talk about what the President has tried to do to let union leaders run hog wild, as they say in this part of the country, with wage rates and monopoly control by deeply rooted union leaders.

That one billion dollar brag was the strange case of the loud-spoken anti-inflation President boasting about inflation. It is one of the strangest brags on record.

# HERBERT ELLISTON

for distinguished editorial writing

As his entry for the Pulitzer Prize, Herbert Elliston submitted 23 editorials covering a wide range of topics from politics to religion. Elliston was formerly on the staff of the *Christian Science Monitor*, and a number of his editorials reflected a particular interest in religion. "Church Unity" was typical of his approach. A commendation of the intent of the World Council of Churches to become a permanent organization, the editorial provided the opportunity for Elliston to express his hope that the action would help "restore vitality to religion." The editorial appeared to reflect Elliston's personalized view of Christianity, but it is not clear exactly what his view was since the editorial tended to jump quickly from one sub-theme to another. The primary problem with the editorial's style comes from Elliston's attempt to cover too many aspects of the major theme in such a short space. As a result, the editorial is disjointed and a number of ideas are presented without being adequately defined in the context of the editorial. We get a mention of Communism, an interchurch schism, religious form and content, philosophy, particularism, and a number of other topics without ever being shown their particular relevance. Then we are left with the "hope that [the Council decision] will not degenerate into words signifying nothing" without being given any reason to suspect why such an unhappy result might occur.

## Church Unity

*Washington Post* • August 29, 1948

Arnold Toynbee in his recent volume *Civilization on Trial* says that Western civilization has been "living on spiritual capital. Practice, unsupported by belief, is a wasting asset, as we have suddenly discovered, to our dismay, in this generation." This is a passage that John Foster Dulles quoted in his address to the World Council of Churches meeting at Amsterdam. Out of the conference came a decision which represents a great and worldwide effort to put enough belief into practice to restore vitality to religion. After ten years as a provisional body, the World Council, with 450 delegates representing 150 churches in 40 countries, has formally declared itself a permanent organization. There are big gaps even in this formidable nucleus of churches. The Roman Catholic Church, whose fold embraces the greatest number of Christians of any church, was not present, nor were the Russian Orthodox Church and the Southern Baptist Convention of the United States. But, if the new body falls a long way short of a reunion of Christendom, a historic event occurred, nevertheless, at Amsterdam. It "will go on working daily," as Mr. Dulles said, "to mobilize Christian power to break down the walls of division."

Clearly the fact that a pseudo-religion is on the march is the major event that has awakened the churches. Communism has flourished in a soil compounded of many elements. But one of them is undoubtedly the undermining of religious faith by the deepening and extension of schism and the deadening influence of mere ritual without works. This has diverted men to the worship of such false gods as nationalism, communism and fascism. It may be argued that extreme sectarianism has developed as a result of a series of rebellions against the elevation of form above content. If unity in diversity could have been maintained, the total effect would have been beneficial, but with splinteration has gone a dissension and a pride in theological dogma which fly in the face of Holy Writ. If the fatherhood of God is the fundamental belief of most of mankind, surely the corollary—the brotherhood of man—cannot be denied. The great gulf fixed between the two conceptions in the hearts and minds of most of the God-worshipping world is an abomination in the sight of God.

In this respect philosophy, which, according to Bertrand Russell, is something intermediate between theology and science, is coming to the support of religious belief, though organized religion fails to take advantage of it. The part is being rejected for the whole, and the only reality is the reality of relations—in the arts and sciences no less than in life itself. In other words, particularism of any kind has ceased to be acceptable on philosophical, let alone on religious, grounds. The time is thus overdue, in terms of the modern enlightenment no less than in those of the great challenge, when the whole armor of the church should be put to the task of restoring God in our daily life, lest Satan take possession of the vacuum. We hail the Amsterdam decision, and hope that it in turn will not degenerate into words signifying nothing.

# CARL M. SAUNDERS

for distinguished editorial writing

WITH world tensions increasing in 1948, Carl M. Saunders of the *Jackson* (Mich.) *Citizen Patriot* and his clergyman asked one day over dinner what could be done. Strain between the United States and the Soviet Union was deepening, and the Cold War was starting to heat up. Saunders came up with the question and an answer: "Why don't we—all of us in America—pray for peace? We've tried rattling our tanks and planes; we've tried calling names; we've tried the United Nations. Let's put first things first—let's have a day of prayer for peace." He wrote an editorial pointing out that since Memorial Day is commemorated in honor of those who have died in war, no observance could be more appropriate than prayer that there be no more war. His idea caught on. Two of Michigan's congressmen introduced a joint resolution, and it received unanimous congressional approval. President Harry Truman issued a proclamation calling the nation to prayer. Saunders then wrote what he considered an appropriate "Prayer for Peace" and printed it. It was read in most Jackson churches and at the Tomb of the Unknown Soldier on Memorial Day, with radio carrying the program nationwide. Again in 1949 Congress and Truman approved the request for designating Memorial Day as a day of prayer, and in 1950 Congress asked the president to proclaim observation of each Memorial Day by prayer. For his 1949 work, Saunders received the Pulitzer Prize. After the award of the 1950 Pulitzer Prize, the *Citizen Patriot* received so many requests for copies of the editorial and prayer that it printed them in a pamphlet to meet the demand. Included here are both the editorial and the "Prayer for Peace."

# First Things First

*Jackson* (Mich.) *Citizen Patriot* • February 20, 1949

A year ago the *Citizen Patriot* proposed that a period during Memorial day be set aside to pray for peace.

Our suggestion was approved by the Congress of the United States in the form of a resolution sponsored by Senator Homer Ferguson and Representative Earl C. Michener. The resolution called upon President Truman to proclaim a period of Memorial day for prayers for peace.

The White House issued the proclamation. From Arlington Cemetery the chief of chaplains of the United States Army delivered the Prayer for Peace, the phrasing of which we proposed.

America, commemorating the memories of the men who have fallen on far scattered battlefields that this nation and its way of life might endure, prayed that further sacrifices of war be avoided.

What's more logical than that Memorial day be marked by such a Prayer for Peace?

We recite these circumstances only for the purpose of urging that again this year the President proclaim a period of Memorial day as the proper occasion for nation-wide supplication for peace.

Last year the original suggestion was made only two weeks before Memorial day. This year we make the suggestion early enough to permit normal, routine procedure in Congress and again we remind our readers that this is inspired only with realization that armaments and men alone cannot mold the shape of things to come in this world. First things should come first, and a nation which believes in God should not depend upon the materialism of earth to save it from the great tragedy of war.

We repeat in part the editorial of last May:

"The United States is generally classified as a 'Christian nation.'

"If this means anything at all, it means that the vast majority of our people accept the basic tenets of the Christian faith. Beyond that there is a large minority of Americans who worship in the Hebrew faith. Both Christian and Hebrew believe in God as the maker of Heaven and earth.

"Yet as a nation we seem utterly unaware of God or His place in the making of history."

As individuals many Americans worship. Many pray to God daily or more often.

Why then should not America pray as a nation in a time when as a nation we are in dire need of help and guidance?

We do have one day in the year supposedly dedicated to Thanksgiving when we as a people are expected to offer thanks to the Supreme Being for the blessings showered upon us.

But we have no day or hour or minute when as a people we turn to prayer.

If we are a Christian nation, isn't a national moment of prayer a logical, natural course?

Differences in creeds or systems of worship or dogma need not enter into this discussion if as a people we believe that there is a God who shapes the course of our lives.

It should be possible for Protestants, Catholics, Jews and others to join in a common appeal to a common God.

The world is troubled today. America is deeply troubled. The threat of war hangs over all of us. Yet we want peace. We are not a warlike people. We cherish the lives of those young people who become sacrifices in war. We are ready to be tolerant of all nations which do not menace us regardless of divergent ideologies.

So far as this newspaper is concerned, it believes that the preparation for defense of our country is wise and is not in contravention of basic religious beliefs. We appreciate, of course, that some good people disagree with us. They do not believe a fire department is needed to protect us from war's flames even though conflagration threatens.

But first things should come first.

And the first defense against disaster should be prayer. The first appeal for peace should be to the Omnipotent Master of the universe.

PRAYER FOR PEACE

O Lord, Father of All Men, We come to Thee in humble supplication.

Thou knowest we have strayed much from Thy laws.

Yet, O God, Thou hast blessed us abundantly, and our children.

Thankful for these blessings and hopeful in the promise of Thy forgiveness, we now beseech Thy special guidance and care.

Again in this world of mortal men wars and threats of wars beset us.

Jealousies and rivalries of nations plague us.

Fears are all about us.

We turn to Thee, O God, to ask that in Thy good time peace may be restored to all nations of men.

We ask that men may live together in understanding and respect.

We ask that governments may rule in Thy wisdom.

We ask that intolerance, bigotry, and greed as between nations, and men, and races, may be overcome by the force of Thy will.

We ask that this United States and its people may be guided by Thee and that its mothers may be spared the sorrows and its sons the sacrifices of further wars.

Bless our leaders with wisdom.

Show us the way to better understanding one with another among our own people.

To that end we seek Thy benediction and light, ready always in faith that Thy will be done and confident that in the end Thy good purpose will triumph.

Amen.

# WILLIAM H. FITZPATRICK

for a series on "Government by Treaty"

WITH the United Nations' adoption of the Universal Declaration of Human Rights in 1948, it began construction of a "Covenant on Human Rights." Supporters termed it an international bill of civil rights, guaranteeing the basic rights fundamental to the Western system of justice. Some Americans, though, feared the proposed Covenant as a danger to their traditional rights. The Covenant with its conditional guarantees of freedom, they felt, would allow unacceptable restrictions to be placed on the exercise of these rights. In two series of articles in December of 1950, William H. Fitzpatrick, editor of the *New Orleans States*, set forth what he considered to be the dangers the Covenant posed to the United States Constitution. The four editorials in a series entitled "The Covenant on Human Rights" discussed the dangers to constitutional rights. A second series, "Government by Treaty," analyzed how a treaty adopting the Covenant would supersede constitutional law. Three years later, in 1953, reacting to sentiment against adoption of the Covenant and to a movement to amend the Constitution to limit the authority of treaties, the Eisenhower administration announced it would not submit any human rights agreements to the Senate for ratification. This ended any chance the Covenant might have had for U.S. approval. Included here is the final editorial in Fitzpatrick's three-part series on "Government by Treaty."

# Government by Treaty: What We Can Do About It

*New Orleans States* • December 18, 1950

This newspaper is opposed to government by treaty. This newspaper is opposed to ratification of the Genocide Convention and the Covenant on Human Rights, because it believes them to be dangerous to our liberties and freedoms.

Members of the American Bar Association's Committee on Peace and Law through the United Nations ask:

"Can we sacrifice fundamental principles of freedom on the altar of necessity for a compromise?

"For which standard of free speech and a free press will we be fighting under the banner of the United Nations—the standard of the Covenant or the standard of the Constitution of the United States?"

Proponents of these treaties say that we must ratify them to assume the leadership expected of this nation in the conflict of ideologies and the battle for men's minds.

But is it leadership to endanger the rights of our citizens to meet upon the common ground of agreement with other countries whose nationals do not possess nor understand nor, in some cases, desire the rights we as Americans hold dear?

If the government's policy is to set an example, then we recommend the example set by the representatives of the United States, Great Britain and Canada in refusing to approve the proposed Treaty on Public Information because it included the same sort of general restrictions of public safety and public security that the Covenant includes.

But if the policy of our government is to agree to these lower standards on the premise that forsaking our own historic ideals is necessary in the interest of world peace and understanding, then there is a way to implement that policy of compromise and still maintain our own traditional rights and freedoms.

This can be done by amending the Constitution to:

*Forbid the invasion of domestic law by treaty unless specifically authorized by Act of Congress;*

*Forbid the Congress to make treaties effective by laws not otherwise authorized by the Constitution; and*

*Forbid any fundamental change in our form of government as now constituted by the device of treaty ratification.*

The American Bar Association has authorized a committee to study this suggestion of amending the Constitution to protect our Bill of Rights. But until these three steps—or some equally acceptable safeguards—are adopted to prevent destruction of the United

States Constitution through government by treaty, the Senate should reject summarily any and all treaties which are judged to contain unacceptable restrictions on and derogations of our rights as free Americans.

*1952*

# LOUIS LaCOSS

for "The Low Estate of Public Morals"

"THE Low Estate of Public Morals" may have evoked more public response than any other Pulitzer Prize editorial. Numerous letters and telegrams to the *St. Louis Globe-Democrat* applauded its stand, and the paper received around 50,000 requests for reprints. The editorial was inspired by a cheating scandal at the United States Military Academy, West Point, but writer Louis LaCoss tied the scandal into the climate of dishonesty and low morals throughout America. "The editorial," LaCoss surmised, "said nothing particularly new—I had written many times previously on the general subject—but, as reader response indicated, it packaged the thinking of many Americans." Following publication of the editorial in 1951, the *Globe-Democrat* received a volume of suggestions from readers that resulted in a series of articles by leading Americans on solutions to the problem of public immorality. Now, four decades later, in an era that has been marked by scandal in government and in public life—an era in which we perhaps have come to accept cheating among our officials, our students, our college sports programs—it may be difficult to comprehend how Louis LaCoss' editorial could have elicited so strong a public response. A change in moral climate was evident, for example, when in 1994 a cheating scandal shook the U.S. Naval Academy and some of the Academy's top administration—rather than vigorously pursuing the culprits—were accused of covering up the scandal and showing favoritism in meting out punishments.

# The Low Estate of Public Morals

*St. Louis Globe-Democrat* • August 6, 1951

The discharge of 90 West Point cadets for cheating at examinations is only one facet of the many-sided problem of moral disintegration nationally that is causing many persons to wonder whether America is going down the path of decay that caused the Roman empire to fall. It is a sobering thought. But the facts must be faced.

The West Pointers were dishonest. They cheated. Some did so because they couldn't play football and keep up with their studies. Others who were not athletes cheated because that was the easy way to make passing grades.

The excuse of the athletes accents the abnormality of thinking in many institutions of higher education as to the part sports should play in college life. The necessity of having a good team to assure big revenue to build a bigger stadium to make more money, has led many of our colleges into the evil devices of buying players, of competing in the open market for a star half back. Some colleges have recognized the error and have de-emphasized sports, as should be done.

At West Point the incentive was a bit different because Uncle Sam foots the bills there, but there was the incentive for the individual to "make" the team that was tops or near it in the nation. So, if practice on the field interfered, cheat a little and make the necessary grades.

But fundamentally what happened at West Point reflects a present distorted attitude toward old-fashioned honesty and integrity that obtains not only in our schools but in America's social and political life.

It is seen in the high places in government, which after World War II practiced plain deception on the people. We were told no secret agreements had been made with anybody. Later, we discovered pacts were signed at Tehran, Yalta and Potsdam that made the Korean war inevitable.

In the New Deal era was born the idea that an administration can perpetuate itself in power by buying the voters with handout money. Remember how Harry Hopkins tapped the WPA till to win an election in Kentucky? During that era was born the fiction that cities and states as well as individuals need not look to their own resources or ingenuity to survive—let Washington do it. Out of the mating of depression and political trickery came the insidious thinking by millions of Americans that hard work is positively silly; that if one does work, do the least possible, draw the biggest pay possible—and strike for more.

The youths, such as the West Pointers, with whom we are concerned today, were babies then. They have grown into manhood in an environment of take-it-where-I-find-it entirely alien to the American tradition. They are the unpretty fruit of the mistakes of the past two decades.

What do we see in Washington today? Corruption and scandals. The close link between the underworld and politics was revealed by the Kefauver committee. The Fulbright committee turned the spotlight on the RFC [Reconstruction Finance Corporation] and the influence peddlers, some within the shadow of the White House, who sold their contacts for a price.

We hear of doubtful goings-on in the government department that collects our income taxes.

We hear of patronage bought and sold like so much goods over the counter.

An Army General sees no wrong in accepting gifts from those with whom he does government business, nor in diverting government materials to private use.

The chairman of the Democratic National Committee yells "smear" when it is discovered that he is on the payroll of a St. Louis company for the ostensible reason that he has influence on RFC loans.

The close personal friend of the President, a Major General, has a desk in the White House where he conveniently hands out receipts for deep freezers presented him gratis and which he distributes where they will do good politically.

Campaigns for the Senate in Ohio and Maryland last year were conducted along lines that set a new political low.

So, when 90 West Point cadets stray from paths of honesty, when nauseous revelations are made of the bribing of college basketball teams, when youths charged with robbery stand up in court, as they did in New York, and brazenly admit their guilt, but excuse it by saying that "everybody's doing it," when teenagers become delinquent via the narcotics road, when too many youths of both sexes flout the laws of chastity and decency—when these derelictions of the youths of our land are totted up, there comes a time for sober questioning among the adults.

Where does the fault lie? In the home? Perhaps. In the schools? In part. In the churches? In part. But in the main the fault lies in that nebulous field of public morals and spirituality which was so highly cultivated by the founding fathers and which of late has been so scantily tilled. Among too many of us the accepted premise is that anything is fair unless we are caught; that each of us is entitled to something for nothing; that the world owes us a living; that an honest day's work for an honest day's pay is almost unethical; that gypping the other fellow before he gyps you is the only policy that pays off.

The level of public morals is low. Unfortunately, the good example is not set in Washington. The President is victimized by his friends, but a false sense of loyalty prevents him from moving forthright against them. His reluctance condones wrong-doing. Leadership in both parties is weak, because it is consistently attuned to the next election, not to what is best for the public welfare. In fact, public morals are low because politics at all levels is played at an historic low. The one is the coadjutor of the other.

Yet, we strut the earth telling everybody else to look at us and see democracy in fairest flower—and please copy; we'll foot the bill. We wonder, for instance, what Pravda will have to say about the 90 West Point cadets.

The time is here for moral regeneration. West Point is just one item in the sad chronology. The Roman empire fell, not because it was overwhelmed from without, but because it decayed from within. If this is an appeal for a return to the day-by-day practice of old time religion, and respect for God's moral law, so be it. When the moral fabric of a nation begins to unravel, it is time to do some patching before the entire garment is gone. The cause and effect of this deterioration nationally will be issues in next year's presidential campaign.

## 1953

# VERMONT C. ROYSTER

for distinguished editorial writing

"THE Quality of Morality" reminds one of Louis LaCoss' 1952 editorial winner on public morals. Vermont Connecticut Royster's Pulitzer entry consisted of 13 editorials covering topics from politics to Christianity and from prizefighting to public morality. The Pulitzer Advisory Board cited Royster for his "ability to decide the underlying and moral issue, illuminated by a deep faith and confidence in people of our country ... [and his] warmth, simplicity and understanding of the basic outlooks of American people." It mentioned the editorial included here as typical of his work. Written shortly after the 1952 presidential election, the editorial attempted to analyze Dwight Eisenhower's defeat of Adlai Stevenson as a difference between their stands on moral issues. While the editorial is commendable for its effort at perceiving underlying principles, there is a question of whether Royster adequately defined "morality" in equating it with such issues as inflation. His definition also included a strong correspondence of morality to Republicanism, and the question immediately arises of whether Democrats would have argued that their social policies showed more concern for humanity than Republican policies did and, thus, deeper morality.

# The Quality of Morality

*Wall Street Journal* • November 12, 1952

One of the puzzlements of the politicians and political commentators over the election seems to be that the people voted overwhelmingly against the Administration during a period when the country is supposed to be prosperous.

Well, the first question raised by the election is whether the people thought themselves as "prosperous" as they were told they were. What was exploded as a myth may have been all this talk about good times for everybody.

It is true enough that an inflation seems to make a lot of people better off than otherwise. But a lot of other people are obviously worse off. And still more people who at first think they are better off soon find that they are not, even though they may be told over and over that they are.

The simple fact is that inflation does not make good times. It makes bad times. Long continued, it makes the worst of times. The election figures suggest that a great many people have discovered that fact.

And to us the election figures suggest one other fact—or at least one other quality in the American people deeply imbedded in their history. That is the quality which when the crucial moment comes makes a moral issue ascendant above all others.

In 1862 someone asked Lincoln where he differed with Mr. Douglas, since both would preserve the union, both opposed the extension of slavery, both would leave it alone where it was. Mr. Lincoln said only on a moral issue: he believed slavery was wrong, Mr. Douglas believed it was all right, and that in the end the moral answer would override all else. A century's veneration is tribute to Lincoln's understanding of his fellow citizens.

In 1952 the electorate was presented with a moral issue. Often on specific programs it was difficult to tell Mr. [Dwight] Eisenhower from Mr. [Adlai] Stevenson; Republican policies from Democratic ones. But there was a great difference in the answer to one simple question.

Was the sort of government we were getting right or wrong?

Mr. Stevenson perforce said it was right. Mr. Stevenson agreed that corruption and betrayal and inflation and all the rest were bad. But perforce he argued extenuating circumstances. He could not be morally indignant about our government without disowning his own party and its erstwhile leader.

Mr. Eisenhower said the kind of government we have been getting was wrong. He said inflation was wrong not only because it was bad economics but because it robbed people. He said the present Korean situation was wrong because there was in sight no end to the slaughter. He said big and omnipotent government was wrong not merely because it was unmanageable but because it deprived people of their liberties.

Mr. Eisenhower won the people, we think, because he said corruption, Communism, inflation, war waste and all the rest were morally wrong. He appealed not to cupidity but to the sense of right and wrong.

In an adjacent column Mr. Chamberlin reminds us of great nations that fell because the people could be debauched to the point where they were no longer capable of moral indignation.

We do not think Americans are immune to human frailties. Other things being equal they can be grateful for bread and circuses and express their gratitude at the polls. But present them a moral issue and nothing else is equal.

Once convince the people of a moral issue, be it at city hall or Capitol Hill, and they will set aside even cupidity. Long is the list—and now longer—of the would-be buyers of the electorate who have had their power snatched from them by the people's moral indignation.

# DON MURRAY

for a series on the "new look" in national defense

DON MURRAY'S entry of more than 100 editorials was the largest ever submitted for the Pulitzer Prize. Yet all the editorials were part of a series on a proposed "new look" in national defense. To gather information for the series, Murray interviewed experts in Congress and the military, made field studies, and examined numerous documents. His goal in the series was to analyze changes in U.S. military policy and examine means of improving America's defense capabilities. The editorials were critical but constructive and were credible enough to be cited in congressional debates. Reprinted below is the first article of the series. From it, Murray's outlook and approach should be clear. He strongly favored military power but did not agree blindly with military practice in developing a defense program. Instead, he analytically examined the question of why American defense was muddled and called for a well-defined policy arrived at free of military bureaucracy. Murray, at age 29, was the youngest editorial writer ever to receive the Pulitzer.

# Still Wanted: A New Look—1

*Boston Herald* • December 2, 1953

It is eight years since the United States stood victor in two wars—one in the Pacific and one in Europe.

It is four years since Russia exploded our monopoly of atomic weapons. It is three-and-a-half years since Communist forces invaded South Korea.

Yet we still do not have a long range military policy, with well defined goals and priorities, which would make steady, efficient military growth possible.

Unprepared for every war in our history, we run a great danger of being unprepared for another. For while we have spent huge sums for defense there is evidence we have not spent it all effectively. We have allocated our dollars in wasteful fits and starts, instead of by orderly plan.

The absence of a military policy motivates this series of editorials. We will show:

(1) Why we don't have a long term military policy.
(2) Why one is essential now.

We will suggest:

(1) What our military policy should include.
(2) How it can be created.

This is why we don't have a military policy today.

The new Joint Chiefs of Staff sat down in chains to formulate a fresh military policy.

The Secretary of Defense had indicated their budget was not to exceed $35,000,000,000, a sharp cut from the interim budget adopted earlier in the year.

The administration was not prepared to eliminate any of the commitments made under larger budgets. We were still to keep troops in Europe and Korea, navies on both oceans, air bases on four continents—all as we probably should.

But our foreign commitments and our fiscal restrictions closed off two main avenues to a new look. In a meeting at Quantico the President indicated he would not tolerate any dissension within the Joint Chiefs of Staff. They turned to themselves. Admiral Radford announced they would meet alone—without advisers—and he brought the Marines in as an equal member whenever possible.

With understandable but dangerous dedication, each head of his service fought for his men. Blinded by years of service devotion, apparently unable to accept the deep meanings of new weapons and new ways to carry them to battle, the Joint Chiefs of Staff ran to an unhappy compromise.

They adopted the interim budget drafted in haste by the new administration last spring. It had, of necessity, been made without thorough investigation or profound military consideration.

But the JCS turned to it, for it maintained the Army and Navy at their present high levels. The Air Force, unable to appeal, accepted their previously established cut, even though it, alone of all the services, is in the middle of a building program. The Air Force may have had little choice. The other services had the votes.

This budget was passed by the Defense Department to the National Security Council. There it was turned down and sent back to the military.

Why? Because the Secretary of the Treasury said it cost too much and because other members of the Council recognized that it was no new look. And the people had been promised a new look.

At the moment a special committee of junior officers, according to *Fortune* magazine, are trying to come up with a new look. We'd like to bet that it's more of a barroom brawl than a profound re-evaluation of our military situation. The men on this committee may justifiably believe that their career depends on what they get for their service, not what they accomplish for the country.

In future editorials we will show how important it is we correct this situation and how we may go about it.

*1955*

# ROYCE HOWES

for "An Instance of Costly Cause and Effect
Which Detroiters Should Weigh Soberly"

THE editorial for which Royce Howes won the 1955 Pulitzer was
as much a reporting job as an editorial one. In a work of about
2,000 words, Howes attempted to explain why laborers at a
Dodge automotive plant in Detroit went on strike. He was aided
by two *Detroit Free Press* reporters who helped gather information. Although the editorial was successful as a news report,
Howes also attempted to make a point, that the city and its residents could not afford strikes based on "insignificant" causes. The
editorial attempted to place the blame for such a strike on both
management and labor. Indeed, the Pulitzer jury lauded it for
"impartially ... analyzing the responsibility" of the two groups.
But a hint of management favoritism was apparent. Howes, formerly a public relations employee for a Detroit steel company, did
not adequately emphasize the significance of the "little holes"
that were the point of the strike. It was not the holes themselves
(to which Howes gave exaggerated emphasis) but the amount of
work expected of laborers that was the crux of the trouble. When
this is recognized, Howes' contention that the strike was for a
frivolous reason becomes questionable. Thus the central theme of
the editorial is opened to challenge.

# An Instance of Costly Cause and Effect
# Which Detroiters Should Weigh Soberly

*Detroit Free Press* • July 16, 1954

In auto shops the strip which frames the insides of your car's
windows is called garnish molding. Screws hold it in place, and of
course, there must be holes for the screws.

How many of those holes can reasonably be drilled in eight hours by Dodge assembly line men was the seed of the disagreement which last week made almost 45,000 Chrysler Corporation workers idle and payless.

The insignificance of the little hole in contrast to the immensity of loss to all whom the strike touched reminds of nothing so much as the old nursery rhyme that tells how what began with the loss of a horseshoe nail ended with the loss of a kingdom.

The question we want to examine here is whether Detroit can afford that kind of cause-and-effect sequence.

We are not thinking of just the pay which the strike cost Chrysler workers who participated or whose jobs stopped temporarily because of the strike. Nor are we considering primarily the cost to the corporation in production and dislocation. And while we are not forgetting all the merchants of goods and services whose cash registers rang up less money because so many were out of work, that isn't the cause of our primary concern, either.

What troubles us most gravely is the long-term damage to Detroit as a place to prosper, whether you are a production worker, management man or merchant. Accumulatively, affairs such as last week's strike hurt Detroit's reputation. And when its reputation goes, hope of an ever-building prosperity goes with it.

Industries do not like to locate, or even continue, in a place where the trivial can cost so much. Workmen don't like to establish where instability is so great that a triviality can cost them a week's pay—or more.

We would not attempt to allocate the degrees of responsibility for the Chrysler Corporation stoppage last week.

Nor do we contend that either union or management should have shrugged off everything as trivial that occurred between the disagreement over drilling little holes and the idling of nearly 45,000.

After all, between loss of the horseshoe nail and loss of the kingdom events became increasingly less trivial. So with the progress of the dispute at Dodge.

What happened was this, and here we relate the company's story and then the Dodge local's version:

Until June 28, there were 26 men installing garnish moldings. Each accomplished the entire process. The molding was adjusted, clamped in place, holes drilled, screws driven and clamp removed by the individual man.

On that day, following an efficiency study, engineers changed the operation. A man did just one thing in the installation process. Those who fitted didn't clamp, those who clamped didn't drill, and so on.

One thing this did was to enable a man to work more or less in place as the car passed him. Formerly he rode down the line in the car and walked as much as 100 feet back to resume his station. In time, it was anticipated, the new way would reduce the garnish molding crew to 18 men and permit transfer of the other eight to new work.

The system, according to the engineers, has been used for some time in almost all—and perhaps all—other auto plants. They say it involves no speed-up, but a greater production proficiency.

Under this plan at Dodge, four men were assigned the drilling job. July 12, one of them was warned he was not keeping pace and causing other drillers to lose position. The next day he was sent home, and the three other drillers were warned that they were not keeping up to standard. At the same time, extra drillers were assigned.

July 14, the drillers again lost position, extra ones were added and supervisors demonstrated how the job could be done without losing position. But the next day the other three original drillers lost position so rapidly that they fell 15 cars behind.

They were sent home and warned that they would be discharged if their work wasn't satisfactory when they came back. This brought a resentment among other workers, the line became jammed, it had to be shut down and 5,000 men were sent home.

The next day two of the drillers returned, failed to turn in the work required of them and were fired. That was a Friday. Nearly 100 men didn't return from lunch, the line had to be stopped once more and the next Monday the strike was called—so improperly, it now turns out, that it had no legality in the eyes of not only management but of the UAW.

Officials of the Dodge local say that with the change of procedure in the matter of garnish molding there was no chance for a "rest break" possible formerly because a man could get his immediate job done by working fast and finishing it in less than the required time. Now, the local says the next job is constantly waiting and a 10-minute relief can be had only when the foreman grants it.

No time study, says the union, has been made, though in early July a grievance was filed and such a study requested. The management asked that the study be postponed 30 days to give men opportunity to accustom themselves to the new system. That would be necessary, it was explained, to determine actually what the method should call for in work output.

What has happened, says the local, is that production line man-power is set up to handle an even flow of 75 cars an hour, but frequently must handle 85 cars an hour. This occurs, it is explained, because unavoidable stoppages of the line (breakdowns, absence of materials, etc.) are compensated for by increasing speed so that the day's output averages 75 cars an hour.

The local's version of the discharge of the two men, which touched off the strike, parallels that of the company—except that the company says the firing was "for deliberate refusal to put out a fair day's work and refusing to do what they were told."

First the matter of how and by whom the holes, five in each molding, were to be drilled. Then two men fired. After that close to 45,000 idled.

We don't think very many people will see any necessity for the drastic consequence of so little. Nor do we think when the cause is analyzed it can do anything but bring harm to the whole city.

We remarked that we would not attempt to assess degrees of responsibility—not exact degrees.

But it seems apparent that the Dodge local was anything but free of fault. In fact that much was ruled Friday when the parent UAW ordered the strike called off and said that the vote under which it was called was improper.

Under UAW rules a strike vote must be taken on a specific grievance, and any subsequent strike actually called can only relate to that grievance. The vote taken several months ago under which the Dodge local's leadership acted concerned a matter having nothing to do with how a garnish molding shall be installed.

Perhaps management let dissatisfaction run too far and get out of hand. It seems to us there could have, for instance, been a tentative time study. Its results need not have been final, but at least some guidance might be had from it and the workers who thought there should be one somewhat mollified.

The UAW, at the international level, might have been better advised had it stepped in sooner instead of giving the Dodge local so much time to work its way out of an untenable position.

The weakness and danger in the union position, as we see it, is that it endeavors to assume management prerogatives in trying to say how a plant shall run; what production methods shall be employed; how much patience must be shown employes who cannot or will not do the same job which has been demonstrated as reasonable elsewhere.

Names need not be named, but anyone casually acquainted with Detroit's latter day industrial picture knows that just such relinquishments of management function have had a prominent part in the departure from this region of certain industries, and the abolishment of thousands of jobs forever.

It is the condition which drives industry from a place. It is prominent among the reasons why some industries have not been able to meet the challenge of competition.

What labor shall receive in wages, what hours it will work, what benefits it will receive are properly matters for the union in collective bargaining. So are working conditions free from avoidable hazard to safety. Other items proper to union bargaining can be named.

But assumption of the right to manage is not one of them, and assumption of that right is inevitably destructive. It can only lead to fewer jobs.

Firm retention by management of the right to manage, on the other hand, makes more jobs. The plants where work is steady and employment high are those where management—even at the cost of riding out strikes—has kept a firm grip on its right to say how things shall be done and what standards those who ask employment will be expected to meet.

We believe that realization of this fact of life is extremely essential to meet.

Ours is a tremendous industrial city, its might and prosperity rest on the payrolls of industry in very great part. There is every reason to believe that unless unnecessary discouragements to industrial growth are presented it will attract more industrial wealth, offer more jobs and increased security.

But what is reflected in the strike and compelled shutdown

which put almost 45,000 men and women on the street is a definite and emphatic discouragement. Such exhibitions can turn enterprise from Detroit despite a great many factors here which normally would attract it—as they have attracted it in the past.

Our purpose in discussing the incident of the Dodge strike is not to castigate any individuals or groups as such. But we do believe it represents something which Detroit can ill afford. And our interest in this city's welfare requires that we cite to *Free Press* readers the implications and the portents involved.

What they point to is something neither Detroit nor any other community can afford if its people and its institutions want to maintain a competitive position—and we are thinking of men and women who must compete for jobs just as much as we are of industries which compete for markets.

*1956*

# LAUREN K. SOTH

for "If the Russians Want More Meat ..."

RARE are the editorials that have an effect on a major public event. Lauren K. Soth's "If the Russians Want More Meat ..." was one of those rare editorials. During the midst of the Cold War, he suggested that the Soviet Union send a delegation to Iowa to study agricultural methods. The invitation was made casually, and Soth did not believe it had a chance of being accepted. To his surprise, it was, and it opened up a program of exchanges between the Soviet Union and the United States, helping to thaw the chill that had developed between the two nations. A Russian delegation visited Iowa farms and later introduced Iowa methods to their country's agriculture. In return, an American delegation was invited to Russia. Soth, who toured with the group, wrote that the Soviet Union remained secretive but that "the freedom we had was a far cry from the way foreigners have been treated in Russia during most of the last ten years."

# If the Russians Want More Meat ...

*Des Moines Register* • February 10, 1955

Nikita Khrushchev, who seems to be the real boss of the Soviet Union now, signaled his emergence to power by a well-publicized speech before the Central Committee last month, lambasting the performance of the Soviet economic managers. In this speech Khrushchev especially attacked the management of agriculture. And in doing so, he took the rare line of praising the United States.

Khrushchev advocated the development of feed-livestock agriculture as in the United States. "Americans have succeeded in achieving a high level of animal husbandry," he said. He urged Soviet collective and state farms to plant hybrid corn to provide more feed for livestock. And he demanded an eightfold increase in corn production by 1960.

Speaking as an Iowan, living in the heart of the greatest feed-livestock area of the world, we wish to say that, for once, the Soviet leader is talking sense. That's just what the Russian economy needs—more and better livestock so the Russian people can eat better.

We have no diplomatic authority of any kind, but we hereby extend an invitation to any delegation Khrushchev wants to select to come to Iowa to get the lowdown on raising high quality cattle, hogs, sheep, and chickens. We promise to hide none of our "secrets." We will take the visiting delegation to Iowa's great agricultural experiment station at Ames, to some of the leading farmers of Iowa, to our livestock breeders, soil conservation experts, and seed companies. Let the Russians see how we do it.

Furthermore, we would be glad to go to Russia with a delegation of Iowa farmers, agronomists, livestock specialists, and other technical authorities. Everything we Iowans know about corn, other feed grains, forage crops, meat animals, and the dairy and poultry industries will be available to the Russians for the asking.

We ask nothing in return. We figure that more knowledge about the means to a good life in Russia can only benefit the world and us. It might even shake the Soviet leaders in their conviction that the United States wants war; it might even persuade them that there is a happier future in developing a high level of living than in this paralyzing race for more and more armaments.

Of course the Russians wouldn't do it. And we doubt even that our own government would dare to permit an adventure in human understanding of this sort. But it *would* make sense.

# BUFORD BOONE

for editorials on a segregation issue

AUTHERINE LUCY was the first black person to enroll at the University of Alabama. There was harsh opposition from the beginning. Admission was granted under order of the U.S. Supreme Court, but even then university officials refused to give Miss Lucy a room or cafeteria privileges. On the nights after her first two days of class—Friday, February 3, 1956, and Saturday, February 4—crowds gathered on campus. Students made up a large portion of the crowds, but their numbers were swelled by townspeople, high school students, and non-local members of extreme pro-segregation groups. By noon Monday, a crowd of some 1,000 students and outsiders had grown unruly, even threatening to lynch the young woman. Finally, she escaped from campus lying on the floor of a highway patrol car that drove through the crowd. That night, the university's board of trustees voted to expel her temporarily "lest greater violence should follow." She subsequently charged that school authorities had conspired to create mob action. In early March the trustees permanently expelled her for her "baseless accusations." Throughout these events, Buford Boone, editor of the local *Tuscaloosa* (Ala.) *News*, stood up for Miss Lucy's right to be admitted to the university and rebuked his fellow townspeople for their actions, despite the probability of endangering his paper's circulation and advertising. Eventually, his courage, moderation, and perseverance were credited with giving leadership to his troubled community and allaying some of its opposition to integration. "What a Price for Peace" appeared the day after the trustees' night session barring Miss Lucy.

# What a Price for Peace

*Tuscaloosa* (Ala.) *News* • February 7, 1956

When mobs start imposing their frenzied will on universities, we have a bad situation.

But that is what has happened at the University of Alabama. And it is a development over which the University of Alabama, the people of this state, and the community of Tuscaloosa should be deeply ashamed—and more than a little afraid.

Our government's authority springs from the will of the people. But their wishes, if we are to be guided by democratic processes, must be expressed by ballot at the polls, by action in the legislative halls, and finally by interpretation from the bench. No intelligent expression ever has come from a crazed mob, and it never will.

And make no mistake. There was a mob, in the worst sense, at the University of Alabama yesterday.

Every person who witnessed the events there with comparative detachment speaks of the tragic nearness with which our great university came to being associated with murder—yes, we said murder.

"If they could have gotten their hands on her, they would have killed her."

That was the considered judgment, often expressed, of the many who watched the action without participating in it.

The target was Autherine Lucy. Her "crimes"? She was born black, and she was moving against Southern custom and tradition—but with the law, right on up to the United States Supreme Court, on her side.

What does it mean today at the University of Alabama, and here in Tuscaloosa, to have the law on your side?

The answer has to be: Nothing—that is, if a mob disagrees with you and the courts.

As matters now stand, the university administration and trustees have knuckled under to the pressures and desires of the mob. What is to keep the same mob, if uncontrolled again, from taking over in any other field where it decides to impose its wishes? Apparently, nothing.

What is the answer to a mob? We think that is clear. It lies in firm, decisive action. It lies in the use of whatever force is necessary to restrain and subdue anyone who is violating the law.

Not a single university student has been arrested on the campus and that is no indictment against the men in uniform, but against higher levels which failed to give them clean-cut authority to go along with responsibility.

What has happened here is far more important than whether a Negro girl is admitted to the university. We have a breakdown of law and order, an abject surrender to what is expedient rather than a courageous stand for what is right.

Yes, there's peace on the university campus this morning. But what a price has been paid for it!

*1958*

# HARRY S. ASHMORE

for editorials on the Little Rock integration conflict

ALMOST a century had passed since a state had defied the federal government with troops, but in 1957 Governor Orval Faubus of Arkansas chose to do so. When nine black students attempted to enroll in Little Rock's Central High School under a federal court decision, Faubus chose not to accede but opted for a show of force. On September 2 he called out armed troops of the Arkansas National Guard to bar the students from entering. The *Arkansas Gazette*, one of the city's two daily papers, challenged the governor and the strong pro-segregation element of its city. Finally, on September 23, President Dwight Eisenhower moved federal troops into Little Rock to ensure the enrollment of the black students and to maintain order. The *Gazette*'s executive editor, Harry Ashmore, said he was never pro-segregation and saw the issue as one of the supremacy of the Constitution in all matters. Supported by the newspaper's 84-year-old editor and president, J.N. Heiskell, Ashmore unswervingly opposed the governor's actions and supported obedience to the law despite threats to the *Gazette*'s circulation and advertising. At one point, circulation fell 11,000, about 10 percent of its total. Anonymous letters, believed inspired by White Citizens Councils, threatened a "massive crusade" against stores advertising in the *Gazette*. The boycott of advertising and circulation cut total revenue by $2 million. Eventually, Ashmore vacated his position to alleviate some of the pressure on the paper. For the "forcefulness, dispassionate analysis and clarity of his editorials" during the integration crisis, he received the Pulitzer Prize. Below is the editorial, with its challenge to Arkansans to "decide what kind of people we are," most widely quoted from Ashmore's writings during that tense autumn.

# Reflections in a Hurricane's Eye

*Arkansas Gazette* • September 9, 1957

This is written in a moment of relative calm—something like the eye of the hurricane of emotion that has beset this city and this state for the past week and is due to resume in full force a few hours from now when Governor Faubus appears before a national television audience to explain his position and defend it if he can.

Sunday is a good day for calm reflection, and we hope Arkansans are so using it. Sunday is a good day, too, to be reminded that in the current crisis there are questions not only of law and of politics, but of morality.

Somehow, some time the present impasse between Mr. Faubus and the federal courts must be resolved. That is the problem, and it is an extraordinarily complex one, that faces the responsible leaders of the city, the state and the nation. We can assume that they are working on it, and we can pray that they will find a way out before the final show-down of force against force which Mr. Faubus has so far invited.

But it is also an inescapable problem for each one of us. Somehow, some time, every Arkansan is going to have to be counted. We are going to have to decide what kind of people we are—whether we obey the law only when we approve of it, or whether we obey it no matter how distasteful we may find it.

And this, finally, is the only issue before the people of Arkansas. It is quite true that most of us would have preferred to continue segregation in the public schools. But it is equally true that we cannot do so lawfully except with the voluntary consent of the Negro people whose children have been declared legally eligible for admission to schools heretofore reserved for whites.

It is important to remember that for the most part the Negroes of this community have volunteered not to exercise the new privilege guaranteed to them by federal law. They have accepted a plan of integration that involves only a tiny handful of members of their race. They have done so reluctantly on their side, but with good will—because they have recognized that the School Board of Little Rock was proceeding in good faith to work out the best practical solution to what all parties agree is a problem that cries out for time and patience.

This is the spirit in which the great majority of the white and colored people of this community accepted the School Board plan. Only a small and militant minority of whites urged upon Mr. Faubus the extreme course of interposing his state authority directly against the order of a United States Court.

We believe the great majority of whites supported the School Board last Tuesday—and still do despite the sensational events of recent days.

There are those, of course, who admire Mr. Faubus's courage, and in the calculated confusion of the hour have even come to believe that he may yet stand against the government of the United States.

There were also those, we suppose, who admired King Canute when he ordered the sea to turn back. But the sea did not turn back—and there is no indication that the federal government can or will abandon the authority of the United States Supreme Court.

The legal precedent is firm and clear. In the 1930's the governor of Texas called out the National Guard to prevent the enforcement of a federal law. The unanimous opinion written by Chief Justice Hughes concluded:

> If this extreme position could be deemed to be well taken, it is manifest that the fiat of a state Governor, and not the Constitution of the United States, would be the supreme law of the land; that the restrictions of the Federal Constitution upon the exercise of state power would be but impotent phrases, the futility of which the state may at any time disclose by the simple process of transferring powers of legislation to the Governor to be exercised by him, beyond control, upon his assertion of necessity. Under our system of government, such a conclusion is obviously untenable. There is no such avenue of escape from the paramount authority of the Federal Constitution.

This then is the law as interpreted by the Court whose voice on constitutional matters is final. It is the law that in the end will prevail—and on Sunday there must have been many who prayed that its enforcement will not increase the already heavy damage that has been done to the spirit of good will and brotherly love that prevailed before armed, uniformed men suddenly appeared unannounced on our quiet streets.

*1959*

# RALPH McGILL

for distinguished editorial writing

RALPH McGILL, editor of the *Atlanta Constitution*, spoke out against the bigotry and prejudice in his region of the nation with a boldness few other southern editors chose or dared to copy. One of his first acts when he became executive editor of the *Constitution* in 1938 was to require that the word "Negro" be spelled with a capital "N." It was a small gesture, but it made the paper perhaps the first in the South to adopt the practice. It also indicated something of McGill's attitudes. Throughout his career he opposed the Ku Klux Klan, bigoted politicians, and any others who used race to foment hatred. On a Sunday afternoon in October 1958 he returned home from a speaking trip in Georgia. His wife met him at the door to tell him that the Temple, Atlanta's largest Jewish synagogue, had been bombed. McGill, usually a gentle man except when confronting inhumanity, was furious. He went to his office and in 20 minutes of writing produced an editorial of indignation. He headed it "A Church, A School—" and it appeared on the *Constitution's* front page the next day. It was explicitly mentioned by the Pulitzer Board in its citation of McGill's work. This and other editorials about the bombing displayed McGill's style, sometimes angry, sometimes compassionate, sometimes poignant, humorous, lucid. For the editorials on the bombing and, in the official citation, "for his long, courageous and effective editorial leadership," McGill was awarded the 1959 Pulitzer.

# A Church, A School—

*Atlanta Constitution* • October 15, 1958

Dynamite in great quantity Sunday ripped a beautiful temple of worship in Atlanta. It followed hard on the heels of a like destruction of a handsome high school at Clinton, Tennessee.

The same rabid, mad-dog minds were, without question, behind both. They also are the source of previous bombings in Florida, Alabama and South Carolina. The school house and the church are the targets of diseased, hate-filled minds.

Let us face the facts.

This is a harvest. It is the crop of things sown.

It is the harvest of defiance of courts and the encouragement of citizens to defy law on the parts of many Southern politicians. It will be grimly humorous if certain state attorneys general issue statements of regret. And it will be quite a job for some editors, columnists and commentators, who have been saying that our courts have no jurisdiction and that the people should refuse to accept their authority, now to deplore.

It is not possible to preach lawlessness and restrict it.

To be sure, none said go bomb a Jewish temple or a school.

But let it be understood that when leadership in high places in any degree fails to support constituted authority. it opens the gates to all those who wish to take law into their hands.

There will be, to be sure, the customary act of the careful drawing aside of skirts on the part of those in high places.

"How awful," they will exclaim. "How terrible. Something must be done."

But the record stands. The extremists of the citizens' councils, the political leaders who in terms violent and inflammatory have repudiated their oaths and stood against due process of law have helped unloose this flood of hate and bombing.

This, too, is a harvest of those so-called Christian ministers who have chosen to preach hate instead of compassion. Let them now find pious words and raise their hands in deploring the bombing of a synagogue.

You do not preach and encourage hatred for the Negro and hope to restrict it to that field. It is an old, old story. It is one repeated over and over again in history. When the wolves of hate are loosed on one people, then no one is safe.

Hate and lawlessness by those who lead release the yellow rats and encourage the crazed and neurotic who print and distribute the hate pamphlets, who shrieked that Franklin Roosevelt was a Jew; who denounce the Supreme Court as being Communist and controlled by Jewish influences.

This series of bombings is the harvest, too, of something else.

One of those connected with the bombing telephoned a news

service early Sunday morning to say the job would be done. It was to be committed, he said. by the Confederate Underground.

The Confederacy and the men who led it are revered by millions. Its leaders returned to the Union and urged that the future be committed to building a stronger America. This was particularly true of General Robert E. Lee. Time after time he urged his students at Washington University to forget the War Between the States and to help build a greater and stronger union.

But for too many years now we have seen the Confederate flag and the emotions of that great war become the property of men not fit to tie the shoes of those who fought for it. Some of these have been merely childish and immature. Others have perverted and commercialized the flag by making the Stars and Bars, and the Confederacy itself, a symbol of hate and bombings.

For a long time now it has been needful for all Americans to stand up and be counted on the side of law and the due process of law even when to do so goes against personal beliefs and emotions. It is late. But there is yet time.

# LENOIR CHAMBERS

for a series on the school segregation problem in Virginia

THE racial difficulties the nation had faced in the 1950s were evident in the first Pulitzer Prize for editorial writing in the 1960s. Lenoir Chambers, editor of the *Norfolk Virginian-Pilot*, received the 1960 award for his editorials opposing resistance to integration of schools in his state. (Coincidentally, Chambers had been a journalism student at Columbia University the year the first Pulitzer Prizes were awarded.) Two editorials were cited specifically in the announcement of Chambers' prize. The first, which appears below, criticized state actions in shutting down nine schools to avoid court-ordered integration. In it, Chambers painfully decried the abandonment of the state's educational tradition. The second editorial, entitled "The Year Virginia Opened the Schools," was printed the last day of 1959 and applauded changing attitudes that finally had led to acceptance of integration. Following court decisions in January of that year, public and official reaction at first was defiant, as it had been to earlier orders. But gradually in Norfolk and most other parts of the state the acceptance of integration gained momentum and resistance finally grew scant. "Thus it came about," Chambers wrote on December 31, "that although the first half of the year found Virginia engrossed in immediate, complicated problems, the second half found the state moving calmly about its educational responsibilities."

# The Year Virginia Closed the Schools

*Norfolk Virginian-Pilot* • January 1, 1959

So far as the future histories of this state can be anticipated now, the year 1958 will be best known as the year Virginia closed the public schools.

This was the year when the automatic operation of Virginia law, moving precisely as the state's governmental leadership and its General Assembly had provided, reached out to shut and lock the doors of a Warren County high school in Front Royal, of two schools in Charlottesville, and of three junior high schools and three high schools in Norfolk.

By that same act the state denied nearly 13,000 boys and girls, some 10,000 of them in Norfolk, the kind of education which the people of Virginia had in mind when they wrote into their Constitution with wide approval and great confidence these words:

"The General Assembly shall establish and *maintain* an efficient system of public free schools *throughout the state*." (The italics are ours.)

Had anyone said a few years ago that the abandonment of this fundamental doctrine, which generations of Virginians regarded as a foundation of modern life itself, he would have been called foolish and irresponsible [*sic*]. Yet the year 1958 witnessed this blunt reversal of the educational course of democratic America in these three communities in Virginia and for these nearly 13,000 young Virginians.

That is what has made the year just ended unique in Virginia history and, save for another school-closing in Arkansas, unique in American history. That is the shame of 1958.

It is not enough to say, as the state has said in effect, that closing nine schools and kicking nearly 13,000 young people out of public education to shift for themselves is justified by the difficulties of obeying the law.

Of course the difficulties are there. Of course the changing of the customs of decades is painful. Of course perplexities exist and prejudices intrude. Of course law is a hard problem in enforcement and requires the most serious consideration when it runs counter to the deep wishes of majorities of people in a broad region of the country and of Virginia.

No one with knowledge of Southern life thinks there is anything easy about dealing with the situations that confront us all.

But the mark of Virginia's political shame is that in this confusion it found no better method than abandoning public education entirely rather than follow the courts' directions about admitting a few Negro children into all-white schools.

This is not a policy which Virginia can continue. It is so patently self-defeating that calmer judgment would find ways of getting rid of it even if it was not probable as governmental leaders acknowledge that the statutes for closing schools will be declared unconstitutional.

The punishment of innocent children is too severe. The desertion of a doctrine of education on which democracy itself rests runs too much against basic American convictions and beliefs, many of which originated or first found nobility of expression in Virginia. The damage in prestige is too grave. The loss in business, in commerce, in industry in a state which just begins to realize that it has lagged in new efforts in these respects is too costly even in prospect and in early results. It would be disastrous in the long run.

The year that has run out has carried Virginia, and especially Norfolk, where the penalty exacted has been the heaviest, far down a defeatist road. We cannot continue this way. The state is bound by every obligation of governmental principle and human dignity and decency and its own self-interest, to find a better policy than the one we live under.

That policy is collapsing before our eyes. But there will be small gain, or none at all, if in substitution the government of Virginia thinks it can stand still, or move backward in a changing age. It cannot. The question Virginians must ask themselves on this New Year's Day is what they can, and will, do in 1959 to recover from the tragedy of 1958.

# WILLIAM J. DORVILLIER

for editorials on clerical interference in an election

> WILLIAM DORVILLIER, editor and publisher of the *San Juan*
> (Puerto Rico) *Star*, won the 1961 Pulitzer for a series of 20 edito-
> rials on clerical influence in the 1960 gubernatorial election in
> Puerto Rico. He claimed Catholic bishops attempted to interfere
> in their parishioners' voting, and he called for their transfer by
> the church. The *Star* received a mountain of letters, protesting
> and supporting its stand, and kept its columns open fairly to all
> opinion. Governor Luis Muñoz Marin, overwhelmingly re-elected
> over the opposition of the bishops, wrote Dorvillier after the elec-
> tion: "To adopt such a strong and clear stand on so controversial
> an issue took great courage. It also set some valuable precedents
> in Puerto Rican journalism." "The Pastoral Letter" was the first
> of Dorvillier's editorials. It was indicative of the character and
> tone of the series.

## The Pastoral Letter

*San Juan* (Puerto Rico) *Star* • October 22, 1960

The Catholic bishops who signed the pastoral letter forbidding Catholics from voting for the Popular Democratic Party have
transgressed grievously against the people of Puerto Rico, against
their country and against the Catholic Church.

Archbishop James P. Davis, Bishops James McManus and
Luis Aponte Martinez have sinned against the people by making it
mandatory that they equate their religious faith with democratic
political convictions.

The bishops have sinned against their country by making
Puerto Rico the helpless pawn for bigots to use for their political
ends, and to injure the Catholic Church in the national campaign.

They have sinned against the Church by making it a temporary synonym for bitterness and hatred, instead of love, among a
people who know how to keep their worship and their politics sep-
arated.

The bishops have all the rights of citizens to express political
opinions and to urge support for their chosen candidates. But they
have no right to use their religion and the weight of spiritual
sanctions to intimidate faithful Catholics in the exercise of their
franchise at the polls.

This pastoral letter is more than an indiscretion. It is an action devoid of any virtue because it so obviously is a result of long
and thoughtful premeditation.

Because this pastoral letter is indefensible and inexpiable as
an affront to a people who have built a model democracy, we hope
Pope John XXIII will transfer the bishops to posts outside Puerto
Rico and that they will be replaced by representatives of Catholi-
cism who recognize the indispensability of the principle of separation of church and state in a democracy.

# THOMAS M. STORKE

for editorials on the John Birch Society

THE John Birch Society was formed in 1958. One of the first editors to attack it was Thomas M. Storke, 85-year-old editor and publisher of the *Santa Barbara* (Calif.) *News-Press*. In explaining his reasons for having his paper challenge the organization, an editorial stated, "His memory takes him back many years. ... He lived when conditions were rugged. When West was West and men were men. He lived during periods when if a man or a group of men openly by word of mouth, or the printed word, called our president ... and others at the head of our government, traitors, they were made to answer. Such slanders often called for a visit from a courageous and irate group which brought with them a barrel of tar and a few feathers. ... He lived when men were considered cowards when they hid behind their women's skirts and clothed their identity through anonymity." Storke's lead editorial on the Society, which appears below, struck this theme. The *News-Press'* coverage of the Society exposed it to Santa Barbara, and under the paper's leadership the community met the Society with a flood of opposition. Demand for the *News-Press* material about the Society was so great across the nation that the paper issued a special tabloid containing its stories and editorials.

# The John Birch Society: An Editorial

*Santa Barbara* (Calif.) *News-Press* • February 26, 1961

During recent weeks, the *News-Press* has sought to enlighten its readers about a semisecret organization called the John Birch Society.

We believe that the *News-Press* has performed a public service by bringing the activities of the society to the attention of the community. Hundreds of our readers have agreed. But a newspaper would be derelict in its duty if it did not express its opinion of the way the society is organized and the tactics it employs.

First, let there be no mistake about this: Communism must be opposed vigorously. Its gains throughout vast areas of the world are shocking. Every American must be alert for Red infiltration. But that does not lead logically to the conclusion that to fight Communism at home we must throw democratic principles and methods into the ashcan and adopt the techniques of the Communists themselves, as the John Birch leaders would have us do.

The *News-Press* condemns the destructive campaign of hate and vilification that the John Birch Society is waging against national leaders who deserve our respect and confidence.

How can anyone follow a leader absurd enough to call former President Eisenhower "a dedicated, conscious agent of the Communist conspiracy"? Those are the words of the national leader of the John Birch Society, Robert Welch, in a manuscript entitled "The Politician," of which photostatic copies are available.

The *News-Press* condemns the dictatorial, undemocratic structure of the society.

The *News-Press* condemns the tactics that have brought anonymous telephone calls of denunciation to Santa Barbarans in recent weeks from members of the John Birch Society or their sympathizers. Among victims of such cowardly diatribes have been educational leaders, including faculty members of the University of California at Santa Barbara, and even ministers of the Gospel.

The *News-Press* condemns the pressures on wealthy residents, who fear and abhor Communism, to contribute money to an organization whose leader has said that "for reasons you will understand, there can be no accounting of funds."

In the Blue Book, the society's "Bible," leader Welch said that the organization needed one million members. He also said that the dues are "whatever the member wants to make them, with a minimum of $24 per year for men and $12 for women."

One million members, divided equally between men and women, would bring him $18 million a year. Quite a sum to play with without accountability!

The *News-Press* challenges members of the society to come into the open and admit membership. A local enrollment "in the hundreds" is claimed, but so far only a few of those who have joined the organization have been unashamed enough to admit it.

The *News-Press* challenges the responsible local leaders of the society to make themselves known.

The *News-Press* challenges them to tell their fellow citizens exactly what they are up to and specifically what program they have in mind for Santa Barbara.

The John Birch Society already has done a grave disservice to Santa Barbara by arousing suspicions and mutual distrust among men of good will. The organization's adherents, sincere in their opposition to Communism, do not seem to understand the dangers of the totalitarian dynamite with which they are tampering.

The *News-Press* challenges them: Come up from underground.

And if they believe that in being challenged they have grounds for suit—let them sue. The *News-Press* would welcome a suit as a means of shedding more light on the John Birch Society.

*1963*

# IRA B. HARKEY, JR.

for editorials on an integration crisis in Mississippi

WHEN the courts ordered integration in the South in the 1950s
and 1960s, the reaction varied from place to place, but it often involved resistance. In Tuscaloosa, Alabama, mobs threatened a
university campus. In Little Rock, Arkansas, the governor called
out the National Guard. In most places, though, integration took
place with little incident. But in Mississippi, not only did integration result in mob violence and a calling out of federal troops;
there was even an attempt to close the state university. At the
center of the storm was James Meredith, who broke the color bar
and entered the University of Mississippi in 1962. Student mobs
grew violent, property was destroyed, people died, and troops
moved in to protect Meredith. Ira B. Harkey, Jr., editor of the
*Chronicle* in Pascagoula, defied the mob and Mississippi's authorities. For his "courageous editorials devoted to the processes of
law and reason" during the crisis, he was awarded the 1963
Pulitzer. Exemplary of his style and argumentation was "Perfectly Capable of Closing Ole Miss," a response to the suggestion
that the university be shut down to prevent its integration. But
his stand brought him more than a journalism award. Staunch
segregationists boycotted his paper, a bullet was fired through his
door, and he faced financial ruin. He eventually had to sell the
*Chronicle* and move out of state. In 1966 Meredith was shot while
demonstrating for civil rights in Mississippi. The Associated
Press photograph of the shooting won a Pulitzer Prize.

# Perfectly Capable of Closing Ole Miss

*Pascagoula* (Miss.) *Chronicle* • Date uncertain

Anywhere else in the United States, the suggestion that a
state university be closed down for any reason at all would not rise

to the level of public discussion. Such a suggestion could not origi-
nate outside a lunatic academy.

But in our state where the leaders for eight years led us to
believe we would not be required to obey the same laws that others
must obey, whose leaders called out the mobs to let blood in
senseless opposition to the will of the nation, where American GIs
and marshals are referred to in terms of hate formerly used only
for Huns who ravished Belgium in the World War and Japs who
tortured prisoners in World War II—in this state we had better
discuss the possibility. Now.

For the people who could do and say the things that have
been done and said in our state during the past six weeks have
proved themselves perfectly capable of closing down a university.

The suggestion has been made that Ole Miss be closed. It
has been offered by the same group of false prophets who deluded
the people for eight years into believing that we could maintain
school segregation in Mississippi while all about us other Southern
states were failing in their attempts to prevent integration.
Somehow, in the face of all that is sane, they managed to convince
most white people that they had a secret unknown to other
Southern leaders.

If we now let them convince us that it is proper to close Ole
Miss and destroy a century of cultural advancement, then maybe
we do not deserve any better than to be led by owners of grammar-
school intellects and of attitudes that most humans left behind
somewhere in history.

It is heartening to note a resurgence of manhood on the part
of the Ole Miss staff and faculty and the rallying of alumni support
to keep the institution going. All alumni, all parents of present
students, all Mississippians who care a hang about their state—we
will exclude moral and religious considerations here and mention
only the economic—all should also rally behind the university and
let our leaders know that we do not regard suicide as a solution.

*1964*

# HAZEL BRANNON SMITH

for steadfast adherence to editorial duty

WHEN Hazel Brannon Smith received her Pulitzer Prize, judges commended her for "steadfast adherence to her editorial duty in the face of great pressure and opposition." The statement was inadequate to describe her real dedication. Mrs. Smith's problems began in 1954 when she criticized a sheriff who shot a young black man. A local court awarded the sheriff a $10,000 libel verdict. Although an appeals court overturned the decision, pressure on Mrs. Smith began to mount. The White Citizens' Council encouraged an advertising boycott of her newspaper. Local residents were induced to drop their subscriptions. Opponents supported the founding of a competing paper. After opponents gained control of the local government, Mr. Smith was removed as administrator of the area hospital. The Smiths' financial situation grew critical. They drew from their savings to support their newspaper; they mortgaged their home and built up a debt of $80,000. Still, Mrs. Smith continued her attacks against racists, corrupt local politicians, slot machine operators, gamblers, and liquor racketeers. For her stands, she received the 1960 Elijah Lovejoy Award for Courage in Journalism and the 1963 Golden Quill Editorial Award from the International Conference of Weekly Newspaper Editors. When Mrs. Smith was given the 1964 Pulitzer, she described what she saw as her role as an editor: "All we have done here is try to meet honestly the issues as they arose. We did not ask for, nor run from this fight with the White Citizens' Councils. But we have given it all we have, nearly 10 years of our lives, loss of financial security and a big mortgage. We would do the same thing over, if necessary. ... I could not call myself an editor if I had gone along with the Citizens' Councils—feeling about them the way I do. My interest has been to print the truth and protect and defend the freedom of all Mississippians. It will continue." Included here is the editorial for which Mrs. Smith received the Golden Quill award, one of the editorials in her Pulitzer entry.

# Arrest of Bombing Victim
# Is Grave Disservice

*Lexington* (Miss.) *Advertiser* • May 16, 1963

> *It is not moral or just that any man should live in fear,*
> *or be compelled to sleep with a loaded gun by his bedside.*

Holmes County Deputy Sheriff Andrew P. Smith's action in arresting a 58-year-old Negro farmer, Hartman Turnbow, for fire bombing his own home has come as a numbing shock to the people of Holmes County.

It is a grave disservice to our county and all our people in these days of increasing racial tension and strife.

White and Negro citizens of Holmes County alike simply could not believe that something like this could happen in our county, that a man and his wife and 16-year-old daughter could be routed from sleep in the small hours of the morning and be forced to flee their home literally in terror, only to be shot at by intruders outside—then to have the head of the family jailed the same day for doing the dastardly deed by an officer sworn to uphold the law and protect all citizens.

The only evidence presented against the aged Negro man at the preliminary hearing was testimony given by Deputy Smith and that was only an account of the bombing and shooting incident, as reported by Turnbow, to him. Mr. Smith added his own opinions and suppositions, as did County Attorney Pat M. Barrett, who prosecuted the case. As a result the man was bound over under $500 bond for action by the Holmes County Grand Jury in October.

Mr. Barrett, who said he was "not a demolition expert," nevertheless told the Court that "it just couldn't have happened. There is no way on God's earth for that situation over there to have happened like he said it happened."

Four other Negroes, who had been arrested the same day in connection with the same case, were released for lack of evidence. Not one shred of evidence was presented against them. But they had been held in jail five days and five nights.

This kind of conduct on the part of our highest elected peace officer has done serious injury to relations between the races in Holmes County—where we must be able to live in peace and harmony, or not live at all.

It is distressing that no statement has come from Mr. Smith saying that he is continuing his investigation. Perhaps he is. We hope so.

But irreparable damage has been done, and let no one doubt it.

We have always taken pride in being able to manage our affairs ourselves. When we become derelict in our duty and do not faithfully execute our obligations, we may rest assured it will be done for us.

FBI agents and U.S. Justice officials have already made an exhaustive investigation of this bombing and shooting incident.

A suit has already been filed against Deputy Smith, Mr. Barrett and the District Attorney, stating these Negroes were arrested "on false and baseless charges," which were in effect an effort to coerce and intimidate Negro citizens of Holmes County and get them to cease voter registration activity. The Federal suit asks for a permanent injunction to prohibit these officers from interfering with voter registration activities, including the prosecution of the charges now filed against Turnbow, who attempted to register to vote here April 9, and Robert Moses, director of SNCC, a voter registration project.

This kind of situation would never have come about in Holmes County if we had honestly discharged our duties and obligations as citizens in the past; if we had demanded that all citizens be accorded equal treatment and protection under the law. This we have not done.

But if we think the present situation is serious, as indeed, it is, we should take a long, hard look at the future.

It can, and probably will, get infinitely worse—unless we have the necessary character and guts to do something about it—and change the things that need to be changed.

*1965*

# JOHN R. HARRISON

for a successful campaign for better housing

> CIVIC leaders in Gainesville, Florida, had been trying for 10 years to get a housing code adopted before John R. Harrison began his editorial campaign. Typical of Harrison's writing was "Memo to McKinney," published near the middle of the month-long campaign. Both descriptive and argumentative, the editorial began with a scene in one of Gainesville's inadequate housing areas and followed with a criticism of the city's mayor for dragging his feet on housing reform. Whether the quotation from Ralph Waldo Emerson in the final paragraph was the most appropriate way to close the editorial can be questioned, but borrowing statements from poets and novelists is not unusual among editorial writers. At the end of Harrison's campaign, Gainesville passed a housing code. When the Pulitzer Prize was awarded, judges commended Harrison for serving as a leader for citizens who were helpless by themselves to get the machinery of government to turn for them.

# Memo to McKinney

*Gainesville* (Fla.) *Sun* • November 20, 1964

The road was dusty, and the small Negro boy strained under the weight of the bucket he was carrying. He had brought it more than two blocks from the fountain that was provided "as a courtesy," the sign told us. Three to five times a week the child makes the trip.

The child lives in a house eighteen feet by twenty-four feet along with three other people.

On several of the open windows there are no screens.

There is no front door at all.

Sunlight comes through the roof in two places.

The child and his family share with another family the outhouse in the backyard.

Not only is there no lavatory in the house, there is no tub, shower or hot water supply.

The siding on the house had deteriorated, the chimney needed replacing, the foundation was out of level.

The water lapped over the side of the bucket as the child stepped up a concrete block into the house.

Now, Mayor McKinney, that's a third to a fifth of the family's weekly supply of water.

To drink.

And that family lives in the Northeast section, within the city limits, of Gainesville, Florida, and they pay $5 a week rent. That's Florida's "University City," Center of Science, Education and Medicine.

Now, tell us again, Mayor McKinney, as you have since last August, that a minimum housing code for Gainesville is unnecessary. Tell us again that you want more discussion of the minimum housing code as you did last week. After all, the League of Women Voters and the Citizens' Housing Association of Gainesville, Inc., have, since 1955, documented by studies housing in Gainesville that has no indoor plumbing or piped-in drinking water.

That's ten years, Mr. Mayor.

But tell the child that carries the drinking water down that dusty road that the minimum housing code is unnecessary.

In our mind's eye we'll try to console him with Emerson—"The dice of God are always loaded. For everything you have missed, you have gained something else. The world, turn it how you will, balances itself. ... Every secret is told, every virtue rewarded, every wrong redressed, in silence and certainty."

# ROBERT LASCH

for distinguished editorial writing

EARLY winners of the Pulitzer Prize were pro-American and nationalistic. Frank Simonds, Henry Watterson, and Frank O'Brien, winners from the World War I era, saw little to criticize in American policy. In the years of World War II winners such as Ronald Callvert, Bart Howard, and Geoffrey Parsons sang praise of the United States and called for unity against its enemies. Editorial winners in the era of the Vietnam War were different. They no longer lauded America. More frequently they criticized. In this vein were the editorials of Robert Lasch of the *St. Louis Post-Dispatch*. Their general theme was that American fortunes were poorly served by military involvement in South Vietnam, that force of arms was not an effective way to combat Communism, that national interests were stronger than ideological interests and would stop the spread of Marxism, and that the best way to contain Communism was to provide a better idea, the idea of freedom. Although the Pulitzer committee stated that the award went to Lasch for the whole of his writing during 1965, it was understood that his editorials taking issue with United States foreign policy impressed the committee. The *Post-Dispatch* said the committee specifically cited three editorials. One questioned American aims in Vietnam. Another asked if the United States, in its approach to China, were repeating its Cold War mistakes with the Soviet Union. The third, reprinted here, was remarkably prophetic in its forecast of our withdrawal from Vietnam and the future international climate.

# The Containment of Ideas

*St. Louis Post-Dispatch* • January 17, 1965

Coming events in South Viet Nam promise for many Americans a profound psychological shock, which a foresighted Administration would be preparing to offset. When the day comes for American forces to leave Viet Nam after 10 years of vain effort to build an anti-Communist bastion there, not only will our national pride be hurt, but some basic assumptions of our postwar foreign policy will be called into question. As fresh thinking is always more painful than mouthing shibboleths, this is going to cause a certain degree of anguish.

Unpleasant as it may be, the time for reappraisal has come, and thoughtful Americans should resolve to be realistic about it. The first step is to cast off the illusion of omnipotence, under the spell of which many of us have for years assumed that our mission in the world is to contain, roll back, destroy or otherwise combat Communism.

After World War II, the Soviet Union sought to expand its national power wherever possible. The United States, as the leader of the free world, was thoroughly justified in undertaking to contain that thrust, and it was contained. Only where the Red Army stood on land taken from the Nazis—which is to say, only in eastern Europe—were the Russians able to impose their national will on other peoples; and the passage of time has indicated that even there, subjugation is most likely temporary. National identities have survived and are persistently asserting themselves. There could be no better evidence that the Communists are not going to rule the world, and neither are we. Aspirations for independence, self-respect and self-government are too universal and too powerful to be subdued by any ideology.

In the meantime, however, American policy increasingly has tended to confuse the containment of Russian (and later Chinese) national power with the containment of Communism. We undertook to apply methods appropriate to a national power struggle— the methods of diplomatic maneuver, armed confrontation and in some cases war itself—in a realm where they are totally ineffective. Communism as an idea cannot be contained by such methods, but only by a better idea.

It is not the American function to combat revolution everywhere—to stand as the universal, all-embracing guardian of the status quo. This is an odd role, by the way, to be thrust upon a nation that was itself born of revolution less than two centuries ago. More important, it is a role that lies beyond the capabilities of any nation. Change is the law of life. Social change will sometimes take revolutionary forms in some countries, no matter what the United

States or any other nation thinks about it. A wise foreign policy begins with recognition of this fact.

American foreign policy is in deep trouble in Africa, in Asia, in Latin America precisely because we have let ourselves be pushed into a counter-revolutionary posture. Wherever oppressed masses struggle toward a better life millions of persons look upon the United States as their natural enemy, which means that they inevitably look elsewhere for friends.

Ours is not a revolutionary society, and we should not try to behave as if it were. But we can behave like a mature nation which knows that it has no right and no power to decide for the people of Cuba, Viet Nam or central Africa what form of revolution they should have. We can behave like a nation which is prepared to accept change, even in forms unpalatable to it, and is ready to work with peoples of any political faith for a peaceful world of diversity.

It is often said that we must hang on in Viet Nam, even to the point of an escalated war, because the effects of defeat there would be so damaging elsewhere in Asia and Africa.

Unfortunately it is true that if we got thrown out of Viet Nam, millions of people would be delighted. That is one reason why our Government would be wise to encourage a political settlement through negotiation before we are thrown out unless it is already too late. Whatever happens in Saigon, however, the American cause will not be damaged thereby half so much as it is already being damaged by the growing conviction that our power and influence are dedicated to the suppression of social revolution and political change wherever they occur.

We shall improve our position with the developing nations and the world at large not by proving that we can wage endless war in Viet Nam, but by showing, through actual conduct, that the CIA is not enfranchised to swagger around the world setting up governments and knocking them down; that we do not undertake to dictate the form and pace of political change anywhere; that we are prepared to accept revolutions even when we do not approve of them; and that we have enough faith in the ideas of freedom to entrust to them, rather than to arms, the task of containing the ideas of Communism.

*1967*

# EUGENE PATTERSON

for editorials during the year

> EUGENE PATTERSON, editor of the *Atlanta Constitution*, was one of
> the first to protest the Georgia legislature's attempt to refuse to
> seat Julian Bond. The refusal was not because of Bond's race; a
> number of Georgia legislators were black. Bond was a dissident, a
> critic of United States policy, a foe of the country's involvement in
> the Vietnam War and of the Selective Service law. In the editorial
> below, Patterson analyzed vividly the critical moment at which
> the legislature decided to disqualify Bond. As Patterson predicted
> in the editorial, Bond's case was taken to court. Although lower
> courts upheld the legislature's action, the U.S. Supreme Court
> held that Bond was entitled to his seat. At that time, Patterson
> wrote, "Net results of this controversy, which the Legislature
> should never have initiated, have been to make Julian Bond fa-
> mous, spread his views, revive the Student Nonviolent Coordinat-
> ing Committee and damage Georgia's claim to being a State of
> wisdom, justice or moderation. That was a mighty poor return on
> one day's blowoff in the Legislature."

# Julian Bond Got Used, Too

*Atlanta Constitution* • January 12, 1966

The breaking point in Monday's Bond drama came, it is now
plain, when Speaker George T. Smith asked Julian Bond to rise
and answer any concluding questions that members of the Georgia
House of Representatives might wish to ask him. The slight young
Negro rose and waited at the microphone.

He faced no questions. He faced a dead, absolute silence. The
Speaker told him he could sit down.

"I knew right then the House had made up its mind not to
seat him," said a senior observer. "Bond's statements already answered all the questions there were. The House did not want to

touch that fellow—didn't want anything in the world to do with him. It was all over."

Down the drain went all of the weekend's desperate biracial efforts to get the young representative seated at least, though censured.

The carefully selected contest committee did meet for a while. Until the day had worn on to the moment of heavy silence, this committee had been expected to recommend seating Bond, while censuring him. Such a recommendation might have passed, too. A large number of representatives were ready to vote for it, on the assumption that the censure motion might have enabled them to survive such a vote back home.

But something was expected of Julian Bond. Some modification, some clarification, some profession of faith in American motives that was not forthcoming as his testimony progressed.

Negro Senator Leroy Johnson and others had labored through the weekend seeking some face-saving formula for him and the House.

A guarded statement from Bond Monday morning seemed to qualify his support slightly for the SNCC statement he had previously endorsed—a statement that amounted to a bitterly cynical indictment not simply of United States policies, but of United States motives and basic honor. But James Foreman or Robert Zellner, the SNCC firebrands, were at Bond's elbow all day. And when he testified in the House chamber Monday afternoon, it was clear he did not mean to temper his position at all. With Bond trapped, SNCC could now trap the House (and seems now on the way to trapping Martin Luther King).

The faces of the House slowly froze. Here was a man who was not simply dissenting from U.S. policy, but was accusing his country of murder, deception, aggression; accusing it of being without respect for persons or law; accusing it of using the word freedom as "a hypocritical mask behind which it squashes national liberation movements"; and he was sympathizing with and supporting—even admiring the lawbreaking "courage" of—"men in this country who are unwilling to respond to a military draft."

As the day wore on and Bond hardened in such positions, the House hardened against him. Legal or not, it had decided not to seat him by the time he rose to answer final questions. There were none. Something very close to revulsion lay in the silence.

Bond is an elected representative and a court will probably order his seating, as the House in wisdom should have done. But the record may as well be kept straight. Bond was saying Tuesday that he was attacked because "I am dedicated to the cause of human rights." If that claim were true, it would be a derogation of the nine other Negro legislators and some whites who are also dedicated to the cause of human rights, but are seated with respect in the House and Senate.

# JOHN S. KNIGHT

for distinguished editorial writing

ONE of the press's earliest opponents of American involvement in Vietnam was John S. Knight. Born to money, a chain owner who ran his newspapers as a business, one of the most established of the establishment press publishers, Knight did not seem the type to challenge American foreign policy. He could not be called unpatriotic, un-American, or any of the other epithets thrown at opponents of the United States' part in the Vietnam War. Although his father, Charles L. Knight, had been a bitter opponent of U.S. participation in World War I, the son volunteered and served with the infantry in the front lines. During World War II he acted as a liaison between America's and Britain's war information offices. Even though John's oldest son was killed in the war, his youngest still attended a military academy. Besides, at age 72 Knight could not be mistaken for a college student in a protest demonstration. But since 1954, when the French were defeated in Indochina, he had been warning against our presence there. Knight reluctantly entered journalism on his father's paper and began writing editorials in the 1920s. "My father," he said, "to encourage me, told me some of them were good." Beginning in the 1930s he wrote his "Editor's Notebook," carried weekly in the newspapers in his chain. The long column might cover any of a wide range of topics in Knight's personalized style, which could be light or seriously analytical. His 1968 Pulitzer Prize was awarded for 10 of his columns on Vietnam. (In 1970 the Pulitzer Prize Board created a new category for criticism-commentary. In 1972 it split the category into two separate ones.) The editorial reprinted here demonstrates Knight's analytical, documented, persuasive approach.

# Our "Commitments" Open to Question

Knight Newspapers • May 7, 1967

The Senate Republican Policy Committee has issued a thoughtful and presumably well-documented study on the war in Vietnam.

Understandably, it credits the Eisenhower administration with making but a "limited commitment" to the South Vietnamese in 1954 while declaring that "under the Democrats, our commitment has become open ended."

This partisan study faithfully chronicles the mistakes of the Kennedy and Johnson administrations with respect to our involvement in Vietnam. It has caused the *Miami News* to comment that "the seeds of a meaningful dissent have been sown by the Republican party in the Senate."

True perhaps, but where were the dissenting Republicans several years ago when they could have questioned the wisdom of policies they now deplore?

Strangely silent, I submit. Did they fear being tarred as unpatriotic? Or were they coolly calculating that it was politically expedient to support the war while being critical of President Johnson's "mismanagement?"

Whatever the reasons for past GOP strategy, the Republican leadership stands indicted for failing to challenge the successive steps which have brought us to our present dilemma.

Only a handful of courageous Democrats rose in the Senate to pose the searching questions which might better have been advanced by a responsible minority party.

So when the Senate Republican Policy Committee comes now to inquire what our national interests are in Thailand, Cambodia, Vietnam and Laos and to what further lengths "are we prepared to go in support of this interest?" it is proper to ask why the Republicans have delayed so long in seeking this reappraisal.

Is it because their appetites are being whetted by the aroma of "meat a-cookin'" in 1968? Or to wear the mantle of statesmanship even as President Johnson appears to be losing stature?

The Republican Policy Committee, even though Senate minority leader Everett Dirksen looks askance at its report, has made a useful contribution to the debate on Vietnam notwithstanding its partisan approach.

What a pity it is that Senate Republicans did not accept the gauntlet when it was thrown down by the administration years ago.

They must, therefore, bear a goodly share of the responsibility for our growing involvement in Vietnam.

Their inaction—when the times called for courageous dissent—fell far short of the statesmanship to which they now aspire.

How often have we heard politicians intoning that hoary phrase, "we must live up to our commitments," or "the United States always honors its commitments?"

What are our commitments in Vietnam? Who made them? And when and why?

President Johnson says we have a "moral commitment," the same one as "the commitment made by President Eisenhower in 1954."

Secretary of State Dean Rusk assures us that it is a "binding legal commitment" as well.

Actually, three so-called "commitments" are involved. The first was the October 25, 1954, Eisenhower letter to Ngo Dinh Diem, then head of the Saigon government, promising American aid "provided your government is prepared to give assurances as to the standard of performance it would be able to maintain in the event such aid is supplied."

The second "commitment" turned on the SEATO treaty, a collective defense pact signed by the United States, Britain, France, Australia, New Zealand, the Philippines, Pakistan and Thailand.

Our third "commitment" was the Tonkin Gulf resolution as passed by Congress in 1964.

1—As seen in retrospect, the Eisenhower letter was not a commitment but a proposal to give economic aid to South Vietnam if certain conditions for self-help and reform were accepted. Incidentally, these terms were not met.

At no time did President Eisenhower intend to send U.S. military forces to Vietnam, a fact which he readily admits today. And as historian Henry Steele Commager has written, "even had

President Eisenhower intended his letter to be a kind of commitment, it would have had no binding force; the President cannot, by private letter, commit the United States to war or quasi-war."

2—The SEATO "commitment" is vague and legalistic, depending upon whether the parties thereto were dealing with "aggression" or "subversion."

The section dealing with aggression provides that whatever measures are taken "shall be immediately reported to the Security Council" of the United Nations.

This step was never taken, although a gesture was made in January of 1966—well after the fact.

The second section under which our "commitment" is defended provides for "collective consultation" in instances of subversion. The late John Foster Dulles, architect of SEATO, so interpreted this provision.

As Senator Walter George of the Foreign Relations Committee said at the time, "the treaty does not call for automatic action, it calls for consultation. All that we are obligated to do is to consult together."

Yet there was no consultation. Although Secretary Rusk talks about "the sanctity of our Pacific alliances," only SEATO members Australia, New Zealand, Thailand and the Philippines have made any contributions to the cause of South Vietnam. France openly opposes U.S. policy, Britain offers only sympathy, Pakistan is disenchanted. So as Commager says, "If our 'honor' is involved, why is not the honor of the other SEATO nations equally involved?"

The American Bar Association upholds our "commitment" in Vietnam on the ground that Article 52 of the United Nations Charter provides for regional agreements for the maintenance of international peace.

It does indeed, but such activities must be "consistent with the purposes and principles of the United Nations" and no enforcement "shall be taken ... without authorization of the Security Council."

So the question remains: Is the United States committed to unilateral action in Vietnam under the SEATO treaty?

It is my opinion, based upon extensive study of the subject, that we are not committed either legally or morally to our present course of action.

3—The Tonkin Gulf resolution was passed without debate

after the North Vietnamese had fired torpedoes at two American destroyers. The resolution pledged support to the President of the United States, as commander-in-chief, to "take all necessary measures to repel any armed attack against the forces of the United States and to prevent further aggression."

The question is now raised as to whether the North Vietnamese committed an act of aggression, since our destroyers were only 11 miles from shore in violation of the "international waters" understanding which is honored by most nations.

When North Vietnam asserted that we had violated her waters, Senator Gaylord Nelson asked on the floor of the Senate: "The patrolling (American destroyers) was for the purpose of demonstrating to the North Vietnamese that we did not recognize a 12-mile limit?" Senator J. W. Fulbright replied: "That was one reason given."

As Mr. Commager has written: "If the Tonkin Gulf affair was a clear case of aggression, why is it that the other members of SEATO have not rallied to our support, as is required by the treaty? If it was a clear case of aggression, why is it that we did not choose to follow the procedure laid down by the charter and submit it to the United Nations?"

Understandably, the American people have little patience with looking backward. One might well say: "Of what value are these facts now? We're in the war, aren't we?"

Yes, we are in the war but we can resent being told on the hour about "our commitments" which at best are but little more than the iterations and reiterations of the President, the Secretary of State and handyman Hubert Humphrey.

As Commager says, "These assertions have in themselves no more authority than had the assertion by the Emperor's tailors that his clothes were indeed regal."

The other argument runs that we have a factual commitment: "We are there whether we like it or not, whether we should be there or not."

Such honored generals as Matthew B. Ridgway, who commanded the UN army in Korea, and James M. Gavin, once Chief of Plans, think we should not be there.

And in the political campaign of 1964, President Lyndon Johnson thought we should not escalate the conflict as is shown by this one quotation from a speech delivered on August 29 of that year:

"I have had advice to load our planes with bombs and to drop them on certain areas that I think would enlarge the war and result in committing a good many American boys to fighting a war that I think ought to be fought by the boys of Asia to protect their own land. And for that reason I haven't chosen to enlarge the war."

When you reread remarks such as this and recall the pretentious predictions of early victory by Defense Secretary McNamara, General Maxwell Taylor and other functionaries, the American people cannot be blamed for their uneasiness over policies which they are unable to understand.

President Johnson does not impress them as a man of candor. He has failed to take them into his confidence, to explain why we are engaged in bloody conflict for objectives which remain obscure and uncertain.

It is not the dissent at home which is prolonging the war.

Rather, it is the determination of the man in the White House—entrapped by pride and circumstances—to bring about a victory or at least an accommodation with honor prior to the 1968 elections.

As history is being written, the possibilities of a wider struggle cannot be discounted.

Nor will our involvement in Vietnam be depicted as one of the glorious eras of American statesmanship.

*1969*

# PAUL GREENBERG

for editorials during 1968

LIKE the first Pulitzer winner of the 1960s, the last dealt with
race relations in the South. Paul Greenberg's editorials from the
*Pine Bluff* (Ark.) *Commercial* that were submitted for the Pulitzer
Prize were aimed at helping his community establish better relations between the races. Greenberg later described his editorials
as usually attacking local problems and even on national issues
discussing the local angles. He also attempts to begin with a news
peg for his editorial subject and then to "go into the broader issue." In deciding whether to write an editorial, he asks, "Is it
worth saying? Does it have originality of message? If the idea is
not original, is it worth repeating?" The editorial reprinted here,
written shortly before the 1968 presidential election, was a personalized attempt to persuade local residents not to vote for independent presidential candidate George Wallace.

# An Appeal to Reason

*Pine Bluff* (Ark.) *Commercial* • Date uncertain

We would like to address today's editorial column especially
to those readers who might be considering casting their ballot for
president of the United States in favor of George Wallace.

We would like them to consider the reason for the appeal of
Mr. Wallace.

Surely it cannot be any experience that George Wallace
brings to the great issues of war and peace, and to the awesome responsibilities that await the next president of the United States.
Far from claiming any background in foreign affairs, he seldom
ventures into the subject. When he does, it is in a primitive fashion. Like threatening to bring France back in line by demanding

payment of her war debt, a debt that no longer exists. Most of George Wallace's comments about foreign affairs, infrequent as they are, are no better grounded than this one. We cannot believe that the basis for supporting George Wallace is any widespread demand that the leadership of the United States and of the Western alliance in world affairs be entrusted to the wisdom of George C. Wallace.

It is, then, his stands on the numerous and complex domestic problems of these times? Surely not, since not many people really know where George Wallace stands on farm policy, taxation, the economy, labor, the cities. And not many really much care. Doesn't it say something alarming about George Wallace's appeal that so many people should be attracted on such narrow grounds? Is his one issue enough? It is enough for a talented demagogue, perhaps, but for a president of the United States?

Even when George Wallace talks about law-and-order, which is an issue for sure, the phrase turns cheap in his mouth. Because he is the same George Wallace who has pleaded guilty to contempt of court, who defied the supreme law of the land and threatened order, who only last week predicted a revolution if his demands were not met. Does this sound like a champion of law and order?

It might—if by law and order it meant ignoring the laws one doesn't like and ordering around anybody who gets in one's way. That's the kind of law-and-order that demagogues of both Left and Right always have preached, and preach today.

And there may be times when we are all susceptible to a base appeal. Before that first cup of coffee in the morning, one can almost understand the attraction of George Wallace. Or, if one is black, the attraction of some equal but opposite radical of the Negro race. The most likely explanation for the politics of rancour we are seeing today is that the whole, troubled country is in a bad mood.

Some may find it ironic, or anyway futile, to headline an editorial addressed to Wallace people An Appeal to Reason, since it is not reason but feeling, and often bad feeling at that, that accounts for so much of the Wallace boom. But one of the latest polls shows that something like 20 per cent of the American electorate is attracted to George Wallace; and we can't believe that 1 out of 5 American voters is immune to reason. Or even to second and better thoughts before November 5th is upon us.

Nor can we believe that so many Americans will, for very

long, equate George Wallace with the salvation of America. The idea of George Wallace as the man who is going to save the rule of law in America is grotesque; he is not its saviour but a symptom of the defiance that threatens it today.

George Wallace doesn't have a program for the country, only oratory. He says a lot, but what would he do? What could George Wallace do as president against Congress, the courts, the laws already on the books, the rights indelible and still developing in the Constitution, the whole tradition of equal justice before the law?

One of the most revealing, and hopeful, aspects of the Wallace vote is that many of those who plan to cast it don't feel very proud about it. At least not proud enough to argue that George Wallace really ought to be the next president of the United States. Instead, they explain their vote for him as a gesture of protest.

We wonder: Is it right to vote for a man you don't really believe is worthy of the office? Haven't we all been taught that a citizen has a solemn responsibility to cast his vote as if it were the deciding one? Is that principle now outmoded? Is the thrill of protest worth clogging up a venerable and suddenly endangered electoral system? Is this the honorable, the responsible, the patriotic course?

And finally, we wonder if a vote for George Wallace really is a meaningful protest against the unsettling trends that beset this country. Have you noticed how similar the extremes of Left and Right tend to be? George Wallace, for example, keeps talking about those left-wing anarchists who threaten American institutions. But isn't he threatening quite a few himself. Like the Supreme Court and the Electoral College and even the very principle that has been the key to maintaining law and order in this country— that the Constitution and the laws of the United States shall be the supreme law of the land.

Consider that the crucial fight in American politics is not between the extremes of Left and Right. But between the middle— with its sense of proportion and its tolerance of dissent—and both extremes, with their mutual intolerance for the rights of those they dislike. And so maybe the best way to stand up for America, for a nation conceived in liberty and dedicated to the proposition that all men are created equal, for a political system with justice and liberty for all, might be to reject the extremes. And to stick with still another old American institution that George Wallace threatens— the two-party system. Won't you consider it?

# PHILIP GEYELIN

for editorials during 1969

> ONE of the few Pulitzer winners in the 1970s to deal with non-local issues, Philip Geyelin concentrated on national politics. That seemed a natural subject, perhaps even a "local" one, for the editor of the *Washington Post*'s editorial page. In the editorial reprinted below, as Richard Nixon was about to succeed Lyndon Johnson as president, Geyelin attempted to tell the analytical "story of how Lyndon Johnson lost his majority." The editorial is laudable as an attempt to put contemporary events into historical perspective and as, in places, a lucid analysis. It does tend, however, to jump around from subject to subject with perhaps unnecessary details thrown in, and it leaves the impression that Geyelin simply tried to cover too wide a subject.

# Lyndon Johnson's Presidency

*Washington Post* • January 19, 1969

They have not been dull, the Johnson years. From the first crisis in Panama to Santo Domingo and South Vietnam, from the wild campaign of 1964 to the triumphs in Congress, the protests on the campus, the riots in the cities and the sudden abdication in 1968. And they have not been unproductive, in their rich yield of civil rights and social welfare legislation. More than anything, perhaps, they have been sad, in the sense that Franklin D. Roosevelt thought of Lincoln as a "sad man because he couldn't get it all at once—and nobody can."

Lyndon Johnson tried, you have to give him that. He brought more raw force and endless energy and craving for accomplishment to the office of President than anyone could ask. Where he succeeded, he succeeded big, in education and civil rights and all the rest. And while it can be said that he also failed big—by not being able to win his way in the war in his time, and by having to acknowledge such a division in the country that he could only carry on in his final year by foreswearing his candidacy for another term—not the least of his legacies to President Nixon is what he himself did to turn the war around and head it in the direction of a gradual American disengagement and a political settlement. Serious peace talking is to begin in Paris this coming week not so much because Lyndon Johnson halted the bombing of North Vietnam in October but because he stared down his generals last March and made the much more difficult decision to refuse them the massive reinforcement of American troops that they were asking for.

If this seems a somewhat negative legacy there are more than enough that are positive. The list of legislative accomplishments runs on and on from the 1964 Civil Rights Act to rent supplements, voting rights, model cities, medicare, control of water pollution, immigration reform, job training, educational aid. And while some of this was the finishing of unfinished business, well begun before his time, some of it broke new ground. A landmark aid to education act, for elementary and secondary schools, cracked a constitutional and political impasse over church-school relationships, and it was brought into being not by past momentum or by parliamentary manipulation, but through the innovation and sheer determination of the President.

And yet, for all of this, how history will judge him, in the main, is going to hang very heavily on how the war evolves and what it will be said, many years from now, was gained or lost in that conflict. It is sometimes argued that Vietnam wasn't everything, that the American commitment didn't begin with Lyndon Johnson anyway, that the great domestic problems probably would not have been dealt with, let alone disposed of, much differently if there had been no great expansion of the war in the Johnson years. Perhaps. But the fact remains that Vietnam was, of course, the thing that seemed to be the well-spring of dissent, the issue that shook public confidence, the great preoccupation of the top men of government, the spoiler of relationships with allies and antagonists abroad, and the crisis that brought Lyndon Johnson down. There were other sources of dissent, other spoilers; there would have been trouble anyway because there always is trouble

enough somewhere, growing out of something or other, for any
President. But it was always President Johnson's firm belief that a
Government which lost its mastery over Congress, and in the process lost the faith of the people, on one critical issue, was in grave
danger of losing its capacity to command support or trust in anything it touched. This, in a sense, is what happened to Lyndon
Johnson with Vietnam, and it happened because the President
never managed until much too late to reconcile what he was trying
to accomplish in the war, first with what the military men were
trying to accomplish, and then with what the public thought he
was trying to accomplish. He did not lead or educate or rally the
country until it was too late.

And so the dissent grew and the war dragged on and finally
it had to be conceded, if not acknowledged publicly, that pouring
on more pressure and projecting the possibility of an ever-widen-
ing, open-ended war was not going to compel the enemy to stop doing what it was doing, in Dean Rusk's phrase. Finally, it had to be
conceded that there were limits to this new thing called limited
war, and while this is progress of a kind it is not quite the same
thing as success.

It is often said of Mr. Johnson that his trouble came from
some incapacity to inspire, and thus to lead. He would say, on the
contrary, that he was unjustly victimized by Easterners and intellectuals and liberals and the Kennedy people who scorned him for
his regionalism and his roughness, his table manners and the
twang of his voice. There is truth to both, and also irony, because
the sad thing is that his origins are the best thing about him, the
thing he has going for him whenever he is himself, and he didn't
know it. Or maybe he just wasn't confident enough about it. Whatever it was, he tried to run the country in the way he ran the
United States Senate and it didn't work. He wheedled and cajoled
and high-pressured and over-sold, and seemed to be counting the
legislation passed not so much for its contents as its bulk, and this
wasn't what people were concerned about. They were worrying
about casualty figures and about how the combat troops got to
Vietnam in the first place and how they got involved in combat operations when the Secretaries of State and Defense had said they
weren't supposed to; they were worrying about how it was all going
to end and what it was doing to the country and whether it was
worth it, and by the time the Administration got around to leveling
a little more on the subject it was too late, because the confidence

was gone.

This isn't the whole story by any means but it was a big part of the story of how Lyndon Johnson lost his majority. If he was like Lincoln, a sad man, he didn't show it and he didn't let it slow him; he was forever driving. He wanted nothing more than to succeed— and he did, in many, many ways. But he wanted support for the war and money for a bigger antipoverty effort and safety in the streets and housing for the poor and education for all our children and medical care for all the elderly and the love and respect of all the people, and it wouldn't stretch. He wanted to get it all at once and Roosevelt was right: nobody can.

*1971*

# HORANCE G. DAVIS, JR.

for editorials supporting peaceful desegregation

> HORANCE "BUDDY" DAVIS, JR., said he wrote his Pulitzer-winning
> editorials "past midnight with two fingers on the typewriter." The
> prize was awarded for a campaign consisting of more than 30 edi-
> torials calling for peaceful desegregation of Florida's schools. The
> editorials argued that desegregation could be accomplished with-
> out violence. When violence did occur, Davis said, editorials in
> the *Gainesville* (Fla.) *Sun* "promptly deplored it." The focal point
> of editorial criticism was politicians who opposed busing whites to
> achieve racial balance in the schools. "We took the position that
> this was a lot of horseradish," Davis said, "and that we had been
> busing whites past Negro schools for years." The object of attack
> in the editorial below was Florida's Governor Claude Kirk.

# Do You, Governor Kirk?

*Gainesville* (Fla.) *Sun* • August 3, 1970

Governor Claude Kirk is due in Gainesville today, and we
want to pose a question.

Does he want re-election so badly that he will pull a George
Wallace and split Florida's people asunder?

It is a fair question, we think, because of Governor Kirk's
racial posture of the past few months. Early this year, he sought
extension of the deadline for school desegregation. This was not
unreasonable.

But what followed was contemptible. He descended into
Manatee County, twice suspended the School Board to keep it from
implementing court orders, and caused a confrontation with U.S.
marshals almost to the point of violence. Under threat of contempt
of court and $10,000 daily fine, Governor Kirk retreated while

muttering "victory" all the while.

Victory for whom? Certainly not law and order.

The governor's latest binge concerns private schools. He attacked the U.S. Revenue Service for removing their tax exemptions. Governor Kirk conveniently ignores that the IRS ruling clearly applies only to segregation academies.

Does Kirk approve of federal tax exemptions to schools created to avoid integration? "I don't know of any school that is actually doing what you're saying," he replied.

We can give some tips.

—While he's in Alachua County today, Governor Kirk might chat with County Commissioner Ralph Cellon, whose Rolling Green Academy out Alachua way was founded after school integration in February, has 100 students, a faculty of 7, and tuition of $450.

—He might also look into the explosive expansion of the Heritage Christian School out on North 34th Street, which intruded on public property to recruit students who had the necessary $575.

—He might ask about the embryonic Oak Hall Preparatory School founded by Dr. Billy Brashear and Dr. Harry L. Walker, open to all "without regard to race, creed or color"—with $1,100 tuition, of course.

These are not monumental and hardly worth pressing. More important is the state of Claude Kirk's mind. And we desire to address him directly.

Back in 1964 when passions ran hot, you said this, Governor Kirk: "I believe in equality before the law and equality of opportunity. ... We must put to an end the cultivated feeling of minorities and recognize that we are all Americans."

Back in 1967, you told the *Saturday Evening Post*: "I'm not one of those red-necked governors like Lester Maddox. ... I'm the only good guy in the South."

Later, when invited to a segregation conference in Alabama, you said: "We here in Florida ... cannot join in attempts to subvert or delay the law of the land as interpreted by the Supreme Court."

The important thing, Governor Kirk, is whether you have abandoned these high ideals and cast your political lot on the side of bigotry.

Do you, Governor Kirk, think so little of your people?

*1972*

# JOHN STROHMEYER

for editorials to reduce racial tension

IN August of 1970, Bethlehem, Pennsylvania, experienced the first episode in what became a continuing series of gang violence arising from racial tension. In the first outburst, a 14-year-old girl was killed and a 16-year-old boy seriously wounded at a neighborhood youth center. The city council ordered the youth center closed, and the mayor called for a police crackdown on youths congregating in the area. Confrontations resulted, and police beat a number of youths they considered troublemakers. The director of the youth center, blamed for the troubles by much of the city, was charged with conspiracy. In January of 1971, a young patrolman, John Stein, resigned and charged police with inviting confrontations and the chief of police with making a point of participating in one beating. The city council refused to investigate the charges. During all this time, John Strohmeyer, editor of the *Bethlehem* (Pa.) *Globe-Times*, questioned the actions of police and city government. In June the charges against the director of the youth center were dropped after a legal defense fund had been started for him. Eventually, the youth center was reopened, the police department took steps to correct its procedures, programs were begun to improve community relations, and the Junior Chamber of Commerce named the director of the youth center Bethlehem's Outstanding Young Man of the Year. Reprinted below is Strohmeyer's editorial challenging the city council's failure to investigate police beatings after the resignation of Patrolman Stein.

# Whitewash

*Bethlehem* (Pa.) *Globe-Times* • January 21, 1971

The vote of confidence passed by City Council to reaffirm its faith in the Bethlehem police force is about as meaningless as a vote for motherhood. It was an obvious attempt to apply a coat of whitewash on important issues raised by the concerns of former policeman John Stein.

Ex-officer Stein, who served on the force two and a half years, might have found it easier to step out silently and concentrate on his studies at Lehigh, where he is completing his fourth year. However, the cover-up of the role of high police officials in the station house beatings and the growing needless alienation between police and youth compelled him to state his views and risk the scorn of many of his former colleagues.

Only Councilmen William J. P. Collins and Walter Dealtrey seemed to understand the issues raised by Stein's account: (1) How could a departmental hearing which recommended a verbal reprimand really deal with the matter when, as it now develops, Public Safety Director Irvin Good was seen swinging at one of the youths corralled in the police station on the night of September 25? Was Good identified as a participant, and, if so, was he supposed to reprimand himself? (2) There have been many police arrests but few cases ever get to the prosecution stage: Why? As Councilman Collins asked, "I would like to know whether any of these alleged criminals have been given a license to commit crime?"

Council's blindness to these concerns was best expressed in the long harangue delivered by Councilman Ray Dietz who attempted to impugn the motives of John Stein, the *Globe-Times*, and apparently anyone else who would dare to question the operations of the Bethlehem police force. It never occurred to him that the motivations might have been public interest. Instead of recognizing his own public duty to clear the stigma, he chose to pour on platitudes about his pride in the police force. In the words of Mark Twain, Councilman Dietz showed only he would rather be popular than right.

A more proper way to "stand behind our police" is to ensure a responsible administration, to correct those abuses of police procedure which are letting so many arrest cases slip away, and to set standards for the vast majority of city policemen who want to do their duty above reproach.

By voting not to clear the air, City Council indicated that it either doubts its own ability to muster "a calm and serious approach" to the truth, or it is so certain of the outcome of an investigation that it fears the revelations.

*1973*

# ROGER B. LINSCOTT

for editorials during 1972

AN emphasis on local political and social issues was prominent in the Pulitzer awards for editorial writing in the 1970s. Roger Linscott of the *Berkshire Eagle* in Pittsfield, Massachusetts, wrote about local conditions in a way that prompted the Pulitzer personnel to remark that there "isn't anything very bland about [his] editorials." Employing a combination of sharp criticism, humor, irony, and sarcasm along with fact and analysis, Linscott focused on a number of targets—not without some effect. His editorials castigating two hospital boards for refusing to participate in a family-planning project resulted in one hospital changing its position. After several critical editorials on local bus service, the city council in Pittsfield set up a commission to study ways to improve the service. Included here is one of the editorials Linscott wrote opposing the wasteful spending of $213 million on local highways. In it, he contended that other needs were more important, even though they might take away federal money from his area. Following Linscott's criticism, the highway project was dropped.

# Our $213 Million Gift Horse

*Berkshire Eagle* (Pittsfield, Mass.) • March 17, 1972

When liberal academic types complain that this nation is suffering from a badly distorted sense of political priorities, the complaint is often cast in such abstract terms that it doesn't really register.

But we now have a concrete locally oriented example of what they're talking about, in the form of the state's proposal to allocate $213 million of interstate highway funds to a revamping of Routes 7 and 8 here in Berkshire County.

Nobody in these parts, of course, is likely to object very strenuously to such an outpouring of federal largesse. It would be nice to have a super-road to hustle transients through the area and to give all parts of the county speedier access to the Massachusetts Turnpike. And there is always the rationalization that if the Berkshires don't get the money some other area will.

Nonetheless, $213 million is a staggering sum of money. And at the risk of seeming to look a gift horse in the mouth, it is tempting to consider some of the other things that such a sum could buy.

For instance, with $213 million you could clean up the Housatonic River from its tributaries in Windsor to the Connecticut border, with probably enough left over to create recreational ponds and parks along its course.

Or you could build and equip enough schools to take care of all of the county's public educational needs for the next decade.

Or, if you wanted to dole out the $213 million to the cities and towns of the Berkshires as a revenue sharing device, it would be sufficient to permit a total moratorium on all local real estate taxes, throughout the county, for a period of about 10 years.

Or, to carry it from the sublime to the ridiculous, as a direct per capita hand-out it would be enough to provide a cash payment of nearly $3,000 apiece to every one of the county's 70,000-odd adult inhabitants.

But none of these purposes, worthy or otherwise, can have any claim on the federal money. The highway lobby has long since seen to that. The $213 million (more precisely, 90 per cent of it) would come from the federal Highway Trust Fund, which is lavishly nourished by the federal gas tax and is earmarked by law exclusively for highway purposes.

Indeed, as things now stand the Highway Trust Fund's multibillion dollar cornucopia can't even be applied to alternative forms of public transportation, despite the fact that a decent mass transit system in this country would serve to lighten the burden on our highways and save our cities from strangulation at the hands of the motor car. Just this week, Transportation Secretary John Volpe asked Congress for permission to spend a portion of the fund on mass transit in the coming fiscal year—and the best bet on Capitol Hill is that the answer will be no.

In the case of the Berkshires, the plan is to make available for Routes 7 and 8 most of the money the federal authorities had allocated to the Boston area but which isn't being spent there because of the governor's moratorium on new highway construction within the Route 128 circle. Because of the lower land-taking costs in the hinterlands, the state highway planners figure they can build 66 miles of super-road in the Berkshires for what a mere 4 miles would cost in the congested Boston area. This, they point out, is quite a bargain.

No doubt it is, if measured solely in miles of concrete. And no doubt, if the money has to be spent somewhere and can be spent on highway construction only we should welcome it. But there's no law against wishing for a system in which urgent social needs might be able to take fiscal priority over the inexhaustible demands of the automobile.

*1974*

# F. GILMAN SPENCER

for editorials on scandals in state government

IN 1973 the issue of government corruption came to a head. In Washington the presidential administration of Richard Nixon was mired in the Watergate scandal. Across the nation came charges of political impropriety. In New Jersey revelations of state officials' misdeeds piled up on top of each other. For years politicians had plundered the state. Finally, its secretary of state was convicted of bribery. Then its attorney general was accused of attempting to cover up the secretary's crime. When the State Investigations Commission exonerated the attorney general, it was charged with a whitewash. Numerous officials were accused of misuse of government equipment and corruption in campaign fund-raising. For the governor, William T. Cahill, the charges were especially damaging if for no other reason than the fact that in 1973 he was running for re-election. Continually focusing public attention on the scandals was F. Gilman Spencer, editor of the *Trentonian* in Trenton. His editorials are immediately distinguishable among Pulitzer winners for their free use of flippant phrasing. Of the suggestion that a legislative investigating committee be appointed, Spencer wrote: "Just the thought of Democrats and Republicans, many of whom couldn't care less about official corruption or personal reputation, joining in such an election year battle, is enough to send one into the streets, naked and screaming." Of one scandal he declared: "Even the most pious, biased, know-nothing Republican vegetable this side of Saturn should find it worthy of his attention." Another scandal was so "gorgeously simple that a reasonably alert farm animal would have little trouble grasping [its] significance." One government program, Spencer claimed, "could have been more competently conducted by a wayward garter snake than it was by the State of New Jersey." In time, a number of the state's officials were convicted of misdeeds, the State Investigations Commission was discredited, and Cahill lost his governorship to Democrat Brendan Byrne. In the editorial reprinted here, Spencer attempted to explain details of some of the corruption and point out their political significance.

# Mr. Cahill's Colleagues

*Trentonian* (Trenton, N.J.) • April 10, 1973

So-called political corruption scandals have a way of throwing a lot of semi-recognizable names at you and defying you to make one whit's worth of sense out of them or the incredibly complicated charges attached to them. Thus, the undoubtedly diminutive segment of the public that is struggling to understand the alleged Cahill election campaign financing scandal could be forgiven at this point if it were simply to throw up its hands and say to hell with it.

Even the most average of average New Jerseyans has a pretty good idea who Governor William T. Cahill is. But don't expect too much from Mr. Average when you start tossing out names like Paul Sherwin ... Bruce Mahon ... Eugene Mori ... William Colsey ... Joseph McCrane. And expect even less when those names are followed by the weirdo charge that untold thousands in Cahill campaign contribution checks were cashed at Garden State Park ... yes, that's right, at the race track.

That's why this particular editorial isn't directed at Mr. Average or even at Mr. Slightly Above Average. This editorial is for one man and one man alone—a man who will intimately appreciate the significance of the names and the allegations. His name is Cahill. His current objective is to get himself reelected. His problem is that a bunch of his good friends and close political associates keep popping up in the damndest places . . . like on the front pages of newspapers and smack in the middle of criminal investigations.

We are not going to waste our time repeating all the nice things we and others have said about many of the fine things Mr. Cahill has accomplished as Governor. Nor are we going to point out once again the disaster that could befall us all if the campaign thing or a couple of other dark episodes involving Cahill people were to result in the election of a Charley Sandman or a Ralph DeRose, neither of whom is fit to run a rat-judging contest, let alone the State of New Jersey. What must be said now, however, and said plainly, is that too many people too close to the Governor have been accused of doing too many things that have a way of destroying reputations of administrative purity.

We say this in full knowledge of the newness and incompleteness of the latest charges, which have yet to be confirmed by anyone really worth listening to. If the Garden State affair were the only thing to have called Cahill cohorts into question, we would be writing an entirely different sort of editorial or none at all.

But Mr. Cahill's number two man, Secretary of State Paul Sherwin, was convicted of bribery-conspiracy. A top GOP fund-raiser for the Cahill campaign, William Loughran, was also convicted in the same case. According to testimony at Sherwin's trial, a $10,000 kickback was handed to William Colsey, another Cahill fund-raiser, in the presence of New Jersey Treasurer Joseph McCrane, outside his State House office.

Mr. McCrane is the son-in-law of Eugene Mori, owner of Garden State Park race track. Mr. Mori is said to own a large tract of land adjacent to the huge new sports complex, proposed by the Cahill administration and now under construction in New Jersey. Mr. McCrane, a close personal friend of the Governor who recently resigned as State Treasurer, has allegedly been implicated in the campaign financing situation, as has another close political associate of the Governor, Bruce Mahon, Burlington County GOP figure and real estate broker, who, with Mr. Cahill, was blasted for land speculation deals by Democratic gubernatorial candidate Robert Meyner during the 1969 campaign. Cahill and Mahon denied the charges.

Another Cahill Administration official—Attorney General George Kugler—was recently absolved of attempting to cover-up the Sherwin case, but only after an investigation agency completely discounted the testimony of two top federal prosecutors.

Regardless of how one chooses to view all this, it is a fact that several top-echelon Cahill confederates have troubles the Governor doesn't need, particularly in an election year. It is also a fact that Mr. Cahill has not always reacted to charges involving men close to him in a way that fully inspires public confidence.

Obviously, there are ways to deal with the indelicate situation which now confronts him. But there are few ways he can deal with it without attacking his own. Whether Mr. Cahill will pay that price or can afford to is one of the largest questions to be asked in New Jersey in years.

*1975*

# JOHN DANIELL MAURICE

for editorials on a schoolbook controversy

WHEN the schools of Kanawha County, West Virginia, became the center of a public protest over textbooks, the county had an editor ably suited to explain the controversy. John Daniell Maurice, of the *Charleston* (W.Va.) *Daily Mail,* years before had won the Sigma Delta Chi editorial writing award for his opposition to the mayor's efforts to ban the book *Peyton Place* from the local library. The textbook dispute focused on works containing writings by such figures as the poet Allen Ginsberg and Black Panther Eldridge Cleaver. At one point, feelings ran so strong that attempts were made to force the closing of the public schools. Throughout the controversy, Maurice, generally disagreeing with the protestors, provided a keen analysis and remained admirably fair in his commentary. He felt the textbooks were simply a salient target for popular indignation over certain trends in education. The deeper complaints of protestors, Maurice suggested, were that schools no longer were teaching traditional values, that they had abandoned "patriotism" for "social change," and that they were not neutral but hostile toward religion. Perhaps because Maurice helped to provide a calmer atmosphere to study the problem, protestors agreed to have the courts settle the dispute, and the board of education, agreeing that protestors had not been allowed any input into the selection of textbooks, finally withdrew much of the objectionable material and set up new guidelines and procedures for selecting texts. Reprinted here are two editorials, from nearly 50 Maurice wrote during the controversy, demonstrating his balanced analysis of the fundamentals of the dispute.

# Where They Square Off

*Charleston* (W. Va.) *Daily Mail* • October 16, 1974

Most of the "fundamentalists" we talk to in this textbook controversy are utterly convincing on one point: They have no objection to the school curriculum which maintains toward religion, the churches and their spiritual and moral values a strict neutrality. In their dedication to the First Amendment, freedom of worship and separation of church and state, they are as respectful as anyone.

The "fundamentalist" objection is this: That in the guise of a benevolent neutrality toward faith and its religious expression, the public schools are imposing upon the young and the impressionable something called "humanism," which is not neutral at all. On the contrary, it is a counter-religion of its own which is often hostile to and even subversive of the traditional beliefs and values, and enjoys in this ageless struggle between faith and disbelief the overwhelming advantage of the political authority.

Most of the "humanists" we talk to in this textbook controversy are utterly blind and deaf to this objection. Like the "fundamentalists" in their faith, the "humanists" in their conviction cannot acknowledge as a fact or admit as a possibility that there is any antithesis. Let the churches teach one thing (on Sunday), the public schools everything else (Monday through Friday), and in this neat division of time and subject there is nothing to worry about.

The Roman Catholic Church knows better. Almost from the beginning, it has known that the schools which do not teach religion by design teach something else by default. It could be atheism, agnosticism, hedonism, scientism or, as the "fundamentalists" insist, "humanism," but in any case it is non- and potentially anti-religious.

Thus the Catholics have never readily conceded the possibility of education apart from the Church. "Pluralism," which currently enjoys a great vogue, is an invention of the "humanists." And where the church is not a full partner with the state in the education of the young, it does what it does in the United States. It exercises its constitutional option to maintain its own schools and teach and train as it pleases. Not at all incidentally, that option is also a "humanist" invention.

One word may illuminate the profound difference. For the true believer a miracle is no mystery. It is simply God's handiwork. For the "humanist" it is simply something science hasn't yet fully explained and surely will as soon as it gets around to it.

It is a genuine and enduring impasse in the controversy over texts and subject matter, and we describe it sketchily not from any knowledge of how it may be avoided or finessed. Rather it is to point out the probable consequences of persisting in the attack.

One is the destruction of the public school system as the American people have known it for more than a century. Another is the substitution of a conglomerate of private schools—as many as may be required to give full expression in education to the great variety of religious and anti-religious convictions.

# Washington, the Father or an Infamous Traitor?

*Charleston* (W. Va.) *Daily Mail* • December 7, 1974

Generally, there are two distinct philosophies on how to bring up the child so that in maturity he does not make a nuisance of himself.

The first and older of the two relies heavily upon training. Train the child. Train him so that when he grows up he will find his values, attitudes, even his habits ready-made for him. He will behave thereafter as he has been trained or indoctrinated to behave.

The second and more modern shifts the emphasis to education. Educate the child so that when he grows up he can think for himself and shape those values, attitudes and habits which serve him best in a rapidly changing environment.

Now this is a schematic distinction which clearly does not apply in the practice. The choice is not an "either-or." But one example, drawn from the textbook controversy, will suffice to illustrate the dispute over emphasis.

Most Americans have been brought up to esteem patriotism as the hallmark of their citizenship and good fortune. They were brought up, or trained, in this value because their parents and teachers wanted it that way. They wanted a generation of Americans conditioned to loyalty and duty. They did not want a generation educated to think freely about the conflicting values of patriotism and disloyalty and fall by error into the latter.

The mechanics of this indoctrination are familiar to everyone—the Pledge of Allegiance, the National Anthem, the salute to the flag. At this command decision, students are not educated to think it through and decide for themselves whether George Washington was, indeed, the Father of his Country or as millions of loyal Englishmen thought of him, the worst traitor to the crown since Oliver Cromwell. They learned the answer before they were old enough to think about it.

And at bottom, this is what the textbook wrangle is all about. Not to train the child in the values his parents have found enduring is to neglect him. Not to educate him is to condemn him to repetitious ignorance.

What is needed is an agreement upon the right mixture, and when this is reached the controversy will disappear.

*1976*

# PHILIP P. KERBY

for editorials against government secrecy and judicial censorship

FOR the fourth time in the history of the Pulitzer Prizes, the award for editorial writing in 1976 was given for editorials on freedom of the press. The subjects of attack for Phil Kerby of the *Los Angeles Times* were primarily legislation and judicial decisions restricting publication of information. (Coincidentally, the *Times'* first Pulitzer Prize for meritorious public service in 1942 was for a defense of freedom of the press.) The majority of Kerby's editorials dealt with press "gag orders" issued by trial judges and proposed federal legislation for stricter control over information relating to "national defense." Both topics were of major concern to the press in 1975. While Kerby provided some persuasive, clearly stated arguments against both restrictions, his reasoning was one-sided and his predictions sometimes exaggerated, not an unusual approach for journalists to take when discussing freedom of the press. In denouncing, for example, what he saw as a "radical trend in the courts toward censorship," he argued cogently that the "courts, agents of the people, have no proprietary right to dispense as little or as much news about their proceedings as they wish. Judges do not own the news." On the other hand, when the First and Fifth Amendments were both involved, there was little doubt in Kerby's editorials of which should take priority and no room for defenses of a right to a "fair" trial. In one editorial, Kerby even criticized courts for overturning criminal convictions because of prejudicial publicity. A small degree of inconsistency occasionally showed also from under the cloak of objective analysis. In one editorial, for example, Kerby criticized as an intrusion into privacy a law that opened information on bank accounts (without divulging depositors' names) to the Internal Revenue Service, while in another he denounced a privacy bill that would have shielded personal information from public disclosure by the press. Reprinted here is Kerby's most frequently mentioned editorial discussing the increasing tendency of judges to restrict more and more information. The thrust of the editorial, a prediction that the country was moving toward secret trials, has turned out to be inaccurate.

# Justice Is Blind—and Gagged

*Los Angeles Times* • November 26, 1975

This country may be moving toward secret trials. United States Supreme Court Justice Harry A. Blackmun's ruling in a Nebraska mass murder case points in that direction.

Justice Blackmun, upholding in part a "gag" order imposed by a Nebraska judge, decided that courts may forbid the news media to report confessions and other incriminating evidence before trial even though such information has been disclosed at a public hearing.

The original gag order by a Nebraska district court judge was comprehensive, but Blackmun's ruling went farther. The district court order prohibited the press from reporting details of the arrest of a suspect, the identity of a victim or victims who had been sexually assaulted, the results of ballistics and medical tests and the facts of a confession or the fact there had been a confession. Moreover, the court said "the exact nature of the limitations of publicity as entered by this order will not be reported," barring the media from reporting the extent of the censorship.

Justice Blackmun lifted the Nebraska judge's restrictions on reporting the details of the crime and the identities of the victims, but then reaffirmed the court's right to impose censorship by saying, "At the same time, I cannot and do not, at least on an application for a stay and at this distance, impose a prohibition upon the Nebraska courts from placing any restrictions at all upon what the media may report prior to trial."

Of more ominous significance, Justice Blackmun went on to lay down the procedures of censorship. He said, "The accused, and the prosecution if it joins him, bears the burden of showing that publicizing particular facts will irreparably impair the ability of those exposed to them to reach an independent and impartial judgment as to guilt."

This part of Blackmun's opinion is a transparent rationale for suppression, a mere admonition to the courts to go through a ritualistic exercise before imposing censorship. To say that a burden must be met is to say that it can be met and that prior restraint of publication can be imposed and backed by the use of the

contempt power. Prior restraint always has been regarded as repugnant to the First Amendment. Briefly imposed in the Pentagon
Papers case, it fell even though the government argued that publication would cause an immediate and irreparable threat to national security.

Blackmun accepted without reservation the theory that
prospective jurors must be delivered to a courtroom in pristine innocence. He phrased it this way: "A prospective juror who has read
or heard of the confession ... may well be unable to form an independent judgment as to guilt or innocence from the evidence ad-
duced at trial."

The presumption here is that once a prospective juror reads
or hears about a pending case, the juror instantly decides the guilt
or innocence of the defendant and becomes from then on an au-
tomaton. This view of jurors was expressed in a crescendo of con-
descending words by a defense attorney in a celebrated California
trial four years ago. He said, "Miss [Angela] Davis was presumed
guilty from the moment her name appeared in the press. ... One
would have to be blind, deaf, dumb and dishonest to say that the
articles I have quoted will not and have not affected the impartial-
ity of potential jurors."

This argument was marred only by one flaw. It was not true.
The jury returned a not-guilty verdict, and that has been the outcome of a series of trials in recent years in which jurors were said
to be predisposed toward conviction by publicity.

Blackmun said in the Nebraska case that once trial starts
restrictions on information should be removed, but it is only a step
from suppressing information in open, pretrial proceedings to cen-
soring the trial itself.

If this view is considered extreme, a look at the record shows
otherwise. At first the courts tested their powers by placing restrictions only on those within the system—prosecutors and defense attorneys—forbidding them to discuss prejudicial matters
outside the courtroom. Gag orders were then extended to the media. A Los Angeles judge, caught up in an excess of zeal, banned
comment about a case by the chief of police and the mayor. Another zealot on the Los Angeles bench ordered that nothing could
be reported about a murder case except information heard in court.
He was reversed, and so was a New York judge who banned the
public from an extortion trial and conducted it in secret, but the
trend in the courts toward secrecy is strong.

Secrecy was invoked in the New York case, as it is invoked in all court censorship, in behalf of a fair trial, but justice is not a private affair, and the best assurance of justice is to keep the courts, and all other public institutions, under public surveillance.

This issue is not between the courts and primarily the press. It is between censorious judges and the public. Secrecy lays no burden upon the press, which is only the intermediary, the messenger. The censorship that is imposed is censorship on the public. It is the public that the ministers of justice hold in contempt.

*1977*

# FOSTER CHURCH, NORMAN F. CARDOZA, WARREN L. LERUDE

for editorials challenging the power of a local brothel keeper

JOE CONFORTE opened his house of prostitution in the 1950s just across the county line from Reno, Nevada. From there he began to service metropolitan Reno. Because prostitution is legal in Nevada, Conforte's activities were accepted, and soon he was dropping money into the area's worthiest charities. A colorful character, he welcomed the national attention he received. His interests, though, were not limited to prostitution and charity. He clandestinely consorted with local politicians, passing out money and the services of his prostitutes, and gained favorable treatment in his real estate dealings. The *Nevada State Journal* (Reno) and the *Reno Evening Gazette* began to shed light on his political activities and the acceptance he had received from even such groups as the YMCA. As editorials by Warren Lerude, executive editor, Foster Church, editorial page editor of the *Journal*, and Norman Cardoza, *Gazette* editorial page editor, hit home, Conforte fought back with denunciations of the papers. Many readers criticized the editorial treatment of Conforte, claiming the newspapers were attempting to attract circulation by frequent use of the word "whorehouse" and page-one coverage of Conforte. The papers continued their assault. Eventually Conforte took on a low profile, politicians began avoiding him, and charities announced they would no longer accept his contributions. The editorials reprinted here criticized the notoriety Conforte had achieved.

# Conforte's Influence

by Foster Church
*Nevada State Journal* and *Reno Evening Gazette*• March 17, 1976

It is a measure of the times that Joe Conforte is one of the two or three best known citizens of Washoe County. Conforte has achieved a sort of folk character status since arriving in this area and opening his house of prostitution.

Several articles concerning Conforte have appeared in national publications. His personal style—vulgar and overstated—has made him highly visible whether he is seen driving his custom automobile or arriving at a sporting event, attired in expensive clothing and accompanied by women, reputedly prostitutes from his Mustang Ranch.

Popular literature and movies glorify the anti-hero. Conforte, who appears to have made his fortune by himself in an unconventional business, is regarded by some members of the community with a certain affection.

The report of the Washoe County Grand Jury that details the influence which Conforte has wielded over at least five public officials reveals the real Conforte: A man who is ambitious for power, influence and money, a man who does not hesitate to seduce public officials by offering them food, drink, money, airplane flights and the services of prostitutes. He is a man who, despite well-publicized gifts to the community, is intent on shrewd business deals and currying the influence of public officials to amass even more money.

The grand jury report details quite exhaustively Conforte's apparently successful attempts to make a killing on a land deal. Virtually nothing of Conforte's involvement in the deal was revealed to the public. Conforte worked behind the scenes. And if the Washoe County Convention Authority goes ahead with its plan to develop a golf course on property purchased from him, he could make more than $1 million.

It should be plain to anyone reading the report that Conforte, while he has done nothing illegal, has morally corrupted some public officials. And public officials appear to have profited in a variety of ways from their association with him.

The group that has obviously not profited by their association is the public which these officials promised to serve.

Reading the report, there are signs from the time the Capurro-Gault property was said to be for sale, that the public has lost out continuously to Conforte's manipulations.

In February of 1973, the Capurro-Gault land was for sale for $5,000 an acre. Sparks City Councilman Gordon Foote made a motion that the Sparks City Council go on record as being in favor of buying the land. Sparks Councilmen James Vernon and Pete Lemberes voted against the motion. A month later, the property was snapped up by Conforte.

Soon after the purchase, Vernon and Lemberes attempted to influence the city of Sparks to buy the land from Conforte and develop it as a golf course. Failing this, Vernon, Lemberes and Washoe County Commissioner Gerry Grow attempted to influence the Convention Authority to buy the land and develop it.

Shown that the Convention Authority would not be able to finance both the golf course and a proposed addition to Centennial Coliseum, Grow and Vernon proposed an increase in the room tax collected in the Reno-Sparks area.

And when it appeared the convention authority might be expanded to include four new members, then state Senator Stan Drakulich appeared before the convention authority to oppose the proposal. Drakulich had previously received $18,000 from Conforte as a real estate commission for the Capurro-Gault land transaction. He has acknowledged he did virtually nothing to earn the commission.

The increased room tax was approved with the support of Reno City Councilman Clyde Biglieri. Biglieri had already received a $20,000 commission from Conforte, according to the grand jury report, and could have profited handsomely by potential real estate sales when Conforte developed the land around the golf course.

And according to the grand jury report, while all this was taking place, Grow, Lemberes and Vernon were frequent visitors to Mustang Ranch. They discussed the public's business with Conforte. They were offered food, drink and the services of prostitutes. According to the report they even discussed getting rid of Reno Mayor Sam Dibitonto because he opposed the room tax increase.

The land transaction is only one example of Conforte's wide-ranging clandestine influence in area politics. According to the report, he was in a position to at least exert influence in the choice of a Reno police chief. And his political contributions, numerous and frequently large, have been accepted, and usually concealed by public officials ashamed of the associations with him.

When the veneer of the folk hero is stripped from Conforte, he becomes simply another man who desires to make large profits. He uses public officials to accomplish his ends. We see no indication that the public welfare enters his considerations.

Perhaps the public is partially at fault for having viewed Conforte with affection and amusement. But his influence, if it continues, should be open to public scrutiny.

Officials who became a part of his web of influence and have not yet been exposed should come forward now and admit it. They will probably be revealed eventually. The onus of being exposed later will be worse than voluntary disclosure.

No one can forbid an official to associate with Conforte but the association should not be clandestine. A secret meeting with a brothel owner cannot be in the public's interest. But as the grand jury report has shown, a brothel owner can profit handsomely by such dealings.

# Conforte Influence in Washoe County Is Shocking

by Norman F. Cardoza
*Nevada State Journal* and *Reno Evening Gazette* • March 17, 1976

Nevadans who believe that brothel operator Joe Conforte's influence in government affairs in this county have been blown out of proportion should read the county grand jury's new report on his relationship with various local officials.

It is flabbergasting. It confirms some of the rumors circulating for years that Conforte does indeed work hard and effectively at getting local and state officials into his influence.

It made many startling revelations, among them the following:

—That Conforte gave money to Washoe County Commissioner Gerry Grow for his election campaign, and offered Grow free services at the Conforte brothel.

—That Conforte also gave campaign money to Reno Mayor Carl Bogart and Councilman Clyde Biglieri. Other public officials received Conforte campaign money, too, the report intimates. They were not the object of this particular investigation and were not named.

—That Conforte lobbied various officials, some of whom he favored with campaign funds, to gather support for his golf course land deal near Sparks. This transaction, according to the jury testimony, stood to make him a million dollars.

—That he also lobbied officials to swing an increase in the county room tax in order to generate the public tax money necessary to bring the project to fruition.

—That he offered free food, drink and prostitute services to former Sparks Councilmen Pete Lemberes and Jim Vernon, both of whom were also in a position to help in boosting the golf course project.

—That he bought the 344 acres through the real estate firm owned by Biglieri and that Biglieri personally realized a $20,000 commission from the sale.

—That terms of sale dictated by Conforte awarded $18,000 of the $86,000 commission money to then state Senator Stan Drakulich for no reason that has been revealed.

—That he chartered a private plane to fly Grow back to Washoe County from Washington state, where he and his family were vacationing, in order for Grow to sign sale papers for a County Convention Authority golf course land purchase from Conforte.

—That he paid Grow's airline fare back to Washington and that he gave the commissioner $100 for his inconvenience.

—That he tried to have Councilman Lemberes's brother, Alex, appointed as Reno chief of police when a vacancy occurred.

—That he tried to talk former Reno Mayor Sam Dibitonto into accepting his choices for some Reno appointive positions. (Dibitonto, the jury found, refused to do so).

The most eye-opening aspect of the report is the indication that Conforte not only tried, but was successful, in drawing various elected officials into his seine of influence.

Under questioning, Biglieri admitted having taken Conforte campaign money. Biglieri's firm did handle the land deal and the councilman did get half its $40,000 commission, Biglieri did represent the tie-breaking vote on the council necessary to pass the room tax increase that in turn was necessary to make the golf course project possible.

Grow has admitted flying south to sign the papers, thus saving Conforte thousands of dollars in interest payments. He has admitted taking Conforte campaign money and the $100 gift. And he does not deny that he, Vernon and Lemberes met on several occasions to talk business with Conforte at his brothel.

Bogart has denied receiving Conforte campaign contributions, but the grand jury report claims he did receive the funds.

The grand jury notes that none of this has involved criminal conduct, so far as is known. The state's new conflict of interest law was not in effect when much of it was going on, and the law is now being challenged in the courts.

But it disproves any idea that Conforte is in reality a harmless character whose interest in civic affairs in this area in recent years is benevolent.

In fact the report clearly spells out Conforte's design to lure public officialdom into his influence for the purpose of personal gain.

Given a chance, we believe, he would try to control local government. Imagine how the rest of the country would react to the news of a brothel owner running government in this gaming community.

What is more, it would give Conforte the opportunity to legalize prostitution in this county and that, for reasons we needn't enumerate, would be a problem.

The report, we believe, should also be of grave concern to the citizens of this county because of the conduct of the public officials involved.

Not only were they foolish in the extreme in getting involved with Conforte, but they acted reprehensibly in doing it clandestinely.

There'll be no conflict charges. The state conflict of interest law is in a state of limbo. But the conflict is nonetheless clear.

The trust that the voters of this area put in the officials involved has been betrayed.

205

The citizens of Washoe County have a responsibility to read it all for themselves in the full jury report published in the *Gazette* on Tuesday.

It's not light reading. The Conforte influence web is complex and widespread. It takes some hard study to sort it all out.

But the reading is worth it. It's disgusting and deplorable. And it should arouse demands that the officials involved be called on the carpet.

The *Gazette* will make recommendations on such appropriate action in a subsequent editorial—to be published Thursday.


# Reno's Reputation

by Warren L. Lerude
*Nevada State Journal* and *Reno Evening Gazette* • March 25, 1976


For decades, Reno was known as the divorce capital of the world.

That's a reputation the citizenry at large, businessmen, in particular, and appreciators of the Truckee Meadows as a good place to live have tried to live down.

In recent times, divorce has gotten to be legally acceptable in many other states and Reno has matured as a pleasant family tourism center and sprouting business environment, through the likes of warehousing [and] light manufacturing.

Now, however, Reno faces a new reputation problem, created by the frequently national and sometimes international brothel promotion of Joe Conforte, coupled with the links some public officials have with him.

At the same time the community is trying to attract tourism and business by showing Reno to be a city of good values, Reno is becoming known as a whorehouse town, the kind of city that thinks it's great to have Joe's place called home.

Not long ago, a foreign film crew was in Reno. Were they excited about filming the beauty of Lake Tahoe, the cosmopolitan and free lifestyles of Reno, the excitement of the state's legal gambling?

What really excited this film crew from Japan was Joe Conforte's whorehouse. That's what they wished to film for the multitudes of tourists back in Japan who one day might visit Reno—the whorehouse town.

Over the weekend, a tragic shooting occurred at Mustang. A world famous boxer lay dead in a pool of blood a few feet from the fortress-like structure and its big fence and guard towers.

Around the world the story went on high-speed news teletypes. It's news when a world famous person dies in gunfire. And it's news where that takes place—the whorehouse, the one Joe Conforte runs, the one so many people around Reno have tolerated for so long as "just another business."

"Just another business?" Conforte? He who Washoe County sheriff's deputies say called them "dogs" and who was quoted by lawmen as pointing to the dead boxer's corpse and saying "It's just a dead man ... so what?"

If Reno wishes to continue to build the reputation it is getting as being home base for Joe Conforte and his brothel, a reputation the city deserves when some of its highest officials connect themselves with Conforte, the present course of action will continue.

Reno charities, organizations, politicians, businesses will continue to cater to Conforte.

But if Reno is to move forward now into a constructive and wholesome tourism future it should cast aside its relationships with Joe Conforte.

As this newspaper has stated before, if Conforte wishes to run a whorehouse, let him do it just as others do in Nevada without all the fanfare that is beginning to stigmatize Reno. The madams of the brothels are not the most widely known citizens of Elko, Winnemucca and Ely. It's about time Reno put Joe Conforte's ambitions in the same Nevada perspective.

It is time he got the message from a city too silent so far that Reno does not want him to ride in its parades, finance its bus lines, influence its politicians, be front row center as the gamblers celebrate him with the best show room tables.

As before, the question is: Who has guts enough in this city to declare Conforte persona non grata?

Harrah's?

Harolds?

John Ascuaga and his Sparks Nugget?

Charlie Mapes?

Public officials who don't have connections with Conforte?

The YMCA?

The Reno Rotary Club?

The United Way?

Service clubs?

The YWCA?

The Reno Service League?

St. Mary's Guild?

Any clergy person who might feel it inappropriate for his or her city to be known as a whorehouse town?

The Greater Reno Chamber of Commerce board of directors by name has had the courage to stand against Conforte's arrogance. The chamber backed up by the Washoe County Grand jury, which was critical of Conforte power.

Who, now, cares enough about Reno to stand with these business men and women?

The means is simple—a resolution declaring that Conforte's influence in local government is bad for this city. Get the resolution to this newspaper. We will report the news.

The word will begin to get around the country, just as has Conforte's promotion of prostitution, just as has the bad name public officials have brought the city because of the relationships with Conforte.

And maybe Reno can start living down the whorehouse reputation our silent citizens have allowed Conforte to build.

*1978*

# MEG GREENFIELD

for selected examples of her work

THE controversy over the selection of the 1978 winner of the
Pulitzer Prize received as much attention as the winner did. The
jury choice for the award was Paul Greenberg of the *Pine Bluff*
(Ark.) *Commercial,* winner of the 1969 Prize. Greenberg's exhibit
contained eight editorials on educational standards and quality in
the schools of Pine Bluff and Arkansas. The Advisory Board rejected Greenberg and selected Meg Greenfield of the *Washington
Post.* In the editorial reprinted below, Greenfield attempted to explain why a court ruling in favor of the press in a libel suit was
"useful and wise." The editorial is admirable for its calmness of
discussion about an area in which the press sometimes seems
loudly dogmatic. The opening and closing paragraphs are refreshing in their frankness. The body of the editorial, however, is little
more than a typically routine statement of press law known to
most college journalism students and verbatim quotation from
the court decision. A similar pedestrian quality marked the other
editorials in Greenfield's entry for the Pulitzer Prize. In 1979 the
United States Supreme Court overturned the Appeals Court decision praised here by Greenfield. Today, she is the *Post's* editorial
page editor.

# A Good Decision on Libel

*Washington Post* • November 9, 1977

We think we are not just being hypersensitive when we say
that there seems to be a pretty big difference these days between
the way the press responds to a court decision upholding its First
Amendment freedoms—and the way everyone else responds. Well,
almost everyone else. The point is that what looks to us like a

guarantee of the personal space required to do our job increasingly looks to others like a structure of special privileges, perks and exemptions that put the press beyond the reach of normal obligations and restraints. Another such decision—this one concerning libel— was reached by a Federal Appeals Court in New York on Monday. And on the theory that there may not be unanimity on this thing (there wasn't even unanimity on the bench, the decision being 2 to 1), we will try to explain why we think the ruling was useful and wise.

The libel suit had been brought against CBS by former Army Lieutenant Colonel Anthony Herbert; he was the subject of a CBS program called "The Selling of Colonel Herbert," which questioned the veracity of some of the charges the disaffected colonel had been making about the military with whom he served in Vietnam. The case itself still has not been settled. What has been settled, unless Colonel Herbert decides to appeal the ruling to the Supreme Court, is this: It is off-limits to the plaintiff in a libel case to inquire into a journalist-defendant's thoughts and opinions at the time he was putting together the offending story in order to establish the journalist's motives. The lower court judge said Colonel Herbert's attorneys could make such inquiries of a producer of "The Selling of Colonel Herbert." The Appeals Court said they could not.

The libel law, as it has been interpreted by the Supreme Court in its famous Sullivan decision and subsequent rulings, uses "malice" as the standard for determining liability. If you are a "public figure," as Colonel Herbert is, and you wish to establish that you have been libeled, you must prove that the defendant knew that a damaging statement was false or had reckless disregard for the truth or falsity of the statement—such as failing to try to verify the defamatory material in the face of serious doubts about its truthfulness. You must establish, in other words, that the defendant was acting in bad faith.

Clearly, then, on grounds of practicality and efficiency, there is an argument to be made for questioning the journalist-defendant about his motives. But there are strong reasons for ruling out this kind of inquiry and Judge Irving R. Kaufman, who wrote the Appeals Court's decision, made them. Judge Kaufman observed that the producer in question had provided a great deal of material for the plaintiff to review and had "answered innumerable questions about what he knew, or had seen; whom he had interviewed;

intimate details of his discussions with interviewees; and the form and frequency of his communications with sources." But he had drawn the line at "a small number of questions relating to his beliefs, opinions, intent and conclusions in preparing the program." In pronouncing this line to have been the correct one, Judge Kaufman said that a court ruling otherwise would have been "condoning judicial review of the editor's thought processes. Such an inquiry, which on its face would be virtually boundless, endangers a constitutionally protected realm, and unquestionably puts a freeze on the free interchange of ideas within the newsroom."

It is, we will readily grant, easier to be in favor of a free and untrammeled press than it is to love the journalists who constitute it. In fact, we suspect that a lot of people would find it easier to swallow Judge Kaufman's opinion if it didn't mean also swallowing a measure of freedom and ease for a noisy, pushy, growly press. But that, alas, has something to do with the democratic condition. Sometimes you have to make choices. And the New York Appeals Court made the right one.

*1979*

# EDWIN M. YODER

for selected examples of his work

EDWIN M. YODER was not the first choice of the Pulitzer nominating committee in 1979. He showed in his work, though, an intellectual depth on a wide range of topics. A Phi Beta Kappa graduate of the University of North Carolina, he was a Rhodes Scholar and received a degree in modern European political history and theory in 1958 from Oxford University. He joined the *Washington Star* as associate editor in 1975. Besides editorials, he wrote a weekly opinion column. (The *Star* having since folded, Yoder today is a syndicated columnist.) His 10 editorials submitted for the Pulitzer covered an array of topics, including an anti-smoking crusade by the secretary of the U.S. Department of Health, Education and Welfare, the retirement of a U.S. senator, and the visit to America of Israel's prime minister. The editorial included here, reacting to a speech by dissident Russian novelist Alexander Solzhenitsyn, was one that Yoder especially favored. The editorial is refreshing for its non-political subject matter and admirable for its depth of analysis. The most immediate criticism to be made of it regards the objectivity in Yoder's point of view. He implied that Solzhenitsyn's understanding of American thought was restricted by his limited contact with—his distance from—American life. The other side of the coin, apparently unrecognized by Yoder, is that the editorial writer's understanding of American thought may just as well have been obscured by his closeness to the society. One might also question whether Yoder actually answered as many of Solzhenitsyn's charges as he presumed he did.

# Solzhenitsyn at Harvard

*Washington Star* • June 11, 1978

It is probably a measure of their disquieting accuracy that Alexander Solzhenitsyn's periodic castigations of Western humanist values cry out for sharp rebuttal. He was back in the pulpit last week at the Harvard commencement; and the urge to respond sharply and defensively is, as usual, overpowering.

One's immediate instinct is to ask how much a Russian novelist living out his days behind a high fence, in an isolated Vermont village, really knows about the vibrant pluralistic society he finds so miserably deficient in spirituality. It is to recall that a cranky puritanism is the classic affliction of great Russian men of letters; that few of them, with the exception of Turgenev, have ever been of ironic, tolerant or self-critical temperament; that even Tolstoy, the greatest of all, ended his life in sour disgust with human variety and even with his own art, having concluded that all of it was vanity and frivolity.

Solzhenitsyn certainly needs placing in this tradition, for it explains quite a bit about his own jaundiced view of the world to which he came four years ago as an unwilling exile. Yet merely to establish the context of the matter is not to grapple responsibly with the matter itself.

What, to begin with, is he actually saying? The most familiar of his themes is, of course, that the liberal, skeptical pluralistic values of the West dangerously blind it to the relentlessness and evil of totalitarian ambitions—that we make fools of ourselves by attributing our own benevolent purposes to those who have very different ones. There is a disturbing truth in this; it is a worry that we must live with; but the remedy is never obvious. Is it not among the deadliest of many "totalitarian temptations" that free societies might adopt, in self-defense, the very character they set out to defend themselves against?

But politics and strategy are far from being the central feature of Mr. Solzhenitsyn's message. His prophecy isn't, in the strictest sense, political and in some respects is indeed anti-political. It belongs to other realms: historical, aesthetic, religious.

Historically, it is an attack on the fundamental shift of values which we traditionally associate with the Renaissance, in which the classical world's exalted estimate of the human personality was rediscovered and made the measure of things. Aesthetically, it is a keen and puritanical distaste for the frivolous and debased standards of popular culture—"TV stupor," as he calls it, and "intolerable music" and a pervasive commercialism that contaminates every purpose with a sales pitch of some kind. Religiously, it is the belief, quite pronounced in a sensitive Russian who has looked into the depths of the Stalinist hell, that the peoples of the West simply haven't suffered enough; that their dross is not sufficiently purged by misery.

These obsessions touch upon, but do not satisfactorily elaborate, complex truths about the West. They can't be dismissed with the mere protest that Mr. Solzhenitsyn dwells too much on the dark side and misses many concealed dimensions of seriousness—though that is also true.

In fact, in these highly subjective realms of perception, rebuttal as such is idle. There is no disputing spiritual perceptions, or tastes. Yet the great Russian prophet in our midst probably exaggerates Western decadence; and he certainly scants the the complex value of free political and economic systems.

Such systems cannot, in their nature, refine or even predictably direct the tastes and moral purposes to which they give free play. Regimentation, for good or ill, is not their purpose. What Mr. Solzhenitsyn sees as spiritual chaos and vulgarity is the inescapable consequence of our view that the state is not, and cannot be, the appointed teacher of people. That is a role we reserve for private institutions—the church, the school, the family. It is their strengths or weaknesses that are reflected in the decay and confusion Mr. Solzhenitsyn deplores; it is to their strengthening that free peoples look for "spiritual" regeneration.

The West, says Mr. Solzhenitsyn, is not today an appealing model for the spiritual rebirth of the totalitarian nations. To which the right answer is: Of course it isn't—and can't be. Those who are regimented in an evil and soul-destroying system will not find an alternative model of regimentation by looking West.

They will find, however, a system that affords human nature the opportunity to declare itself freely, in all its glory and sordidness.

*1980*

# ROBERT L. BARTLEY

for editorials on a variety of subjects

ROBERT L. BARTLEY, editor of the *Wall Street Journal* since 1979, was the newspaper's third Pulitzer Prize winner for editorial writing. He joined the paper in 1962 as a reporter and became editor of the editorial page in 1972. The title of editor had last been held by Vermont Royster, who won the editorial writing prize in 1953. William Grimes, editor from 1941 to 1958, won the 1947 prize. The following editorial by Bartley, one of 10 on a variety of subjects submitted for the Pulitzer, focused on the possible run by Edward Kennedy for the presidency. It recalled in a generally even-handed tone, and with a sympathetic lead, the shattering event (the death of Mary Jo Kopechne on Chappaquiddick Island a decade earlier) that many believe killed any chance the U.S. senator from Massachusetts may have had to become the second Kennedy to occupy the White House. The editorial was written at a time when Kennedy was seriously contemplating the presidential race. In a departure from traditional format, the editorial was buttressed with photographs illustrating the controversial route Kennedy took to plunge off the fatal Dyke Bridge. Kennedy quotations in 1969 and 1979 helped strengthen the reportage and point of view. The editorial spurred comment in many other publications. Many journalists considered it to be the most influential of Bartley's work during the year. The steady drumbeat of the paper's conservative stance in its frequently caustic and combative editorials often stirs the commentary pot. That doesn't bother Bartley. He was quoted in 1992 as saying, "I don't mind being the object of controversy. That's how I make my living."

# Chappaquiddick and Credibility

*Wall Street Journal* • November 6, 1979

The death of Mary Jo Kopechne on Chappaquiddick Island is a cross that Senator Edward Kennedy has borne for a decade, and in this he deserves the sympathy of any feeling man or woman. All of us have weaknesses and all of us make mistakes, and fate could turn many of them into ghastly tragedy, as it did for the Senator. The death is a private matter, and the rest of us need pass no judgment.

There is another aspect of the Chappaquiddick affair, though, on which we are fully entitled to pass judgment, indeed on which we are required to pass judgment as the Senator prepares to ask for the nation's highest office. For his ability to function as President depends no little on whether the nation feels he is a man it can trust to explain his actions fully and frankly. Without this trust national leadership is ultimately impossible, as more than one recent President has painfully learned. Voters forgive flaming personal misconduct forthrightly confessed, but are troubled by suspicious explanations. Rightly so, for the bonds of trust are always a legitimate issue.

So we find it disturbing that the Senator's account of the accident is so hard to believe. This difficulty is epitomized in the accompanying photographs, and in the accompanying extracts from Justice James Boyle's report on the inquest. [Not included in this anthology.]

Since the morning after the accident, the Senator has maintained that he mistakenly turned right instead of left at this intersection, and thus unknowingly headed over the fatal bridge. This requires us to believe that he turned off a paved road onto an unpaved one, over a banked corner, away from a painted line that is a bit obscured at the immediate intersection but leads clearly to it and away from it. We know of no independent observer who has visited this intersection who believes such a mistake is remotely conceivable. Justice Boyle entered a "presumption of fact" that the turn was intentional.

For ten years Mr. Kennedy has succeeded in avoiding hard questioning on this story. In granting interviews to three news organizations on the tenth anniversary of the accident this summer, he insisted on ground rules that banned recording equipment and allowed his staff to review the answers. Further explanation became necessary for the first time under Roger Mudd's questioning in the interview broadcast on CBS Sunday night. In explaining the turn, the Senator now asks us to believe that around Cape Cod paved and unpaved roads become "indistinguishable."

On the mistaken turn, it is almost impossible to attach credence to the Senator's explanation. And if you do not believe him on this key point, it reopens all of the rest of his account—the episode of his bolting away from friends and advisers Joseph Gargan and Paul Markham to swim fully clothed across the difficult channel to Edgartown, his testimony of having only two drinks before dinner, the whole notion of a ten-hour panic explaining the delayed accident report.

We expect that these questions will increasingly be pressed after the Senator formally announces his candidacy tomorrow. There is of course a natural and healthy hesitancy about reopening wounds that are so old, so personal and so tragic. Casting the first stone will not make you popular.

Since five books and numerous articles have been written about Chappaquiddick, too, there is a tendency to assume the whole story has been told. But those who attended the party have never yielded to public questioning. We have heard little even from men of independent stature—Robert McNamara, Theodore Sorensen, Burke Marshall—who advised the Senator.

This will come, as Mr. Mudd's searching interview suggests. The public and press are by now highly sensitized to the issue of credibility, having seen Lyndon Johnson and Richard Nixon forced out of office because their word was no longer believed. Even though the Chappaquiddick tragedy does not directly involve the conduct of public office, it will be hard for anyone to avoid the questions it raises about credibility, and beyond that about character.

Nor should these questions be avoided. For as Edward Kennedy announces for the presidency, voters will have to ask themselves whether they can believe his account of the major crisis of his life, and whether they could believe what he would tell them about any crisis of his presidency.

*1982*

# JACK ROSENTHAL

for editorials on a variety of concerns

> JACK ROSENTHAL, then deputy editorial page editor of the *New York Times* and now an assistant managing editor responsible for the *New York Times Magazine*, was the second *Times* editorialist to win the Pulitzer for editorial writing. The editorials submitted for judging were concerned with a variety of matters, including the federal budget and economic affairs; the inauguration of Ronald Reagan; immigration policy; parole for Sirhan Sirhan, Robert Kennedy's assassin; a baseball strike; and fat. The editorial published here, "The Pornography of Fat," is one of Rosenthal's favorites. It was presented as a signatured piece in "The Editorial Notebook" that appeared from time to time at the bottom of the space for institutional editorials and was considered an editorial rather than a column. Many of these signatured editorials were reflections on personal experiences. Rosenthal was only a few pounds overweight at the time he wrote the editorial. He approached this emotional topic—the sub-headline read "Which is Worse, Occasional Gluttony Or Relentless Puritanism?"—in a light but nonetheless serious tone that clearly answers the question and shames all of us who are intolerant of fat people. It makes for delicious reading. Editorial writers always hope that their work will spur results. In this case, Rosenthal was invited to speak to the National Association of Fat Americans.

# The Pornography of Fat

*New York Times* • May 29, 1981

Every era needs its own taboos, its own pornography. What is the pornography of modern America? Certainly not sex, not in a time when the most explicit devices and images are available over the counter or the television cable. But if our pornography is not sex, then what is?

Death, said Geoffrey Gorer, a British anthropologist, in the British magazine *Encounter* 25 years ago. Through the Victorian years, he wrote, sex was unmentionable—while death was unremarkable: "Children were encouraged to think about death. ... The cemetery was the centre of every old-established village." But gradually, as talk about sex became more open, death became unmentionable. Mr. Gorer could remember no modern novel or play with a deathbed scene of the kind familiar to Victorian and Edwardian authors.

At the time, the argument had the crystal ring of insight. Now, alas, one hears a dated clank. It may still be questionable to take children to funerals. But death has become wholly mentionable; as for deathbed scenes on stage, one quickly thinks of Tom Conti, or Mary Tyler Moore, in "Whose Life Is It, Anyway?"

If neither sex nor death constitutes the contemporary pornography, then what does? Anthropologists tell of primitive peoples who attach as much shame to eating as to excretion. There is reason to think our society does something similar—and that our pornography is fat.

A facet of it became evident in "Tom Jones," the 1963 movie. "In one incomparable scene," Bosley Crowther wrote in the *Times*, Joyce Redman and Albert Finney "make eating a meal an act so lewd, yet so utterly clever and unassailable, that it is one of the highlights of the film."

That, however, was only one facet. The pornography of fat offers a choice of pleasures. One can, with a racy sense of tasting forbidden fruit, plunge into gluttony. Or, resisting, one can become a modern puritan, telling others how unhealthy—*how repugnant*— it is to be fat.

This second pleasure seems to offer richer satisfaction. Indeed, if some of us sometimes feel a compulsion to eat, the rest of us seem to feel a constant compulsion to gloat. Society sends an unending stream of stern signals: A young Providence woman, 5 feet 1 inch and 210 pounds, is fired as a home health aide because of her weight ... the Los Angeles school board issues rules requiring weight loss among teachers ... Wisconsin officials halt an adoption because of overweight. How much? The husband, 6 feet 2 inches, weighs 215 pounds, and his wife, 5 feet 7 inches, weighs 210.

Such harsh moralizing may have reached its perverse ultimate a few years ago in the X-rated movie "Behind the Green
Door." Among the circus-related sexual acrobatics was a segment
in which an exceptionally gross circus fat lady was observed
writhing in explicit sexual pleasure. See, the movie was saying,
what's really disgusting is not sex, but fat.

The social pressure against obesity no doubt benefits the
general health. What's troublesome is that we are all so humorless
about it, so relentless, so determined to punish the overweight.
People who think of themselves as enlightened in every other respect become, on the subject of fat, every bit as blue-nosed as, say,
the Moral Majority.

Last winter Jack Kamerman, of the sociology faculty at Kean
College in New Jersey, told a *Times* reporter: "Not only are the
overweight the most stigmatized group in the United States, but
fat people are expected to participate in their own degradation by
agreeing with others who taunt them."

He's right; and his observation exposes in us all an intolerance more obscene and far more damaging than any form of
pornography.

# EDITORIAL BOARD, *MIAMI HERALD*

(Jim Hampton, editor; Joanna Wragg, associate editor; Robert A. Rankin, Joe Oglesby and Robert F. Sanchez, editorial writers; and Jim Morin, editorial cartoonist)

---

for editorials against the detention of illegal immigrants

THE Pulitzer entry for the *Miami Herald* in 1983 included seven editorials and four cartoons. Editorial cartoons as a separate Pulitzer category dates to 1922. The inclusion of cartoons in writing and reporting exhibits is a recent phenomenon. Cartoons were submitted with stories in at least two winning entries in the meritorious public service category: the *Washington Post* in 1973 for its Watergate coverage and the *Charlotte* (N.C.) *Observer* in 1981. On occasion, other entries have contained graphic material. The editorials and cartoons in the *Herald*'s 1983 entry hammered away against President Ronald Reagan's policy of detaining illegal Haitian immigrants in a sterile, barbed-wire camp in the city of Miami. The editorial presented here was the first of the entry package. Its strength was a clear lead, followed by a description of the compound that has the reader sensing the sights, sounds, and smells of a truly desolate place. Editorial board members visited the site, interviewed federal officials, and marshalled local support for their viewpoint. In June of 1982, a federal judge ordered the Justice Department to free Haitians at Krome and other detention centers.

# The Shame of Krome

---

*Miami Herald* • January 9, 1982

The barbed-wire detention center run by the U.S. Government out on Krome Avenue is, as civil-rights leader Jesse Jackson

says, nothing less than an ugly scar on the face of American
democracy. The Reagan Administration's lackadaisical tolerance of
conditions there remains utterly unacceptable.

Today some 600-plus Haitians who came in search of freedom remain confined there. They are segregated by sex in separate
compounds. The Government provides them shelter, meals, and
medical care. It provides rows of bunk beds in stark but reasonably
clean concrete-block houses. It provides each compound one television, several pay telephones, one soft-drink machine, one snack
machine, and one cigaret machine. Within the fences, large rock-
encrusted dirt fields are open to the use of detainees. Nothing else
is provided.

Some Haitians are in their seventh month of languishing
behind the barbed wire; most have been there at least several
months. Each day inside passes in crushing boredom. No
organized social activity—recreation, education, work—is offered.
Donated playing cards, dominoes, and Creole Bibles provide
distraction for some. Most of the imprisoned appear sunken into
deepest anomie, however. They sit. They stare. They sleep. They
wait.

The Government has no choice but to insist upon orderly legal immigration. The nation's borders cannot simply be thrown
open. Illegal entrants regrettably must be refused admission.
Those hard but unavoidable facts are not disputed here.

The outrage stems from the Government's inhumanity even
as Washington discharges its legal obligations. Each Haitian is entitled to a legal hearing. Those fleeing political persecution are entitled to asylum.

The hearing process remains intolerably slow: The Government blames the Haitians' few lawyers for intentionally exploiting
systemic delays by being obstructive. Doubtless there is truth to
the allegation. Nevertheless, the U.S. Government is morally obligated to speed the process. Nothing excuses the inhumanity of im-
prisoning hopeful refugees behind barbed wire for month after
endless month. The treatment of the Haitians is a very real measure of American justice and civilization. By that measure now,
Krome North humiliates this nation.

Recently the Dade Bar Association asked all local lawyers to
voluntarily help expedite the Haitians' processing. That is a most
positive step. Volunteers are needed. The obligation nevertheless
remains on the Government to do more. This week's decision to

assign four more judges to Haitian hearings is a welcome, though cruelly belated, recognition of that.

Illegal immigrants surely will continue to arrive in South Florida. Regrettably, that necessitates a permanent Federal facility to house them while their status is determined. The facility must be permanent, but the time endured within it by any immigrant must not be permitted to last longer than a few days.

The Justice Department this week at last promised to improve the physical quality of Krome North. Recreational and educational programs at last are pledged, though no one can say precisely when they will begin. They should be instituted permanently without delay; indeed, they should have been provided all along.

*1984*

# ALBERT SCARDINO

for editorials on various matters

WANT to own a weekly and raise Cain? Following in the tradition
of many hard-charging weeklies that practice some of America's
most aggressive and outspoken journalism, Albert Scardino, editor of the *Georgia Gazette* in Savannah, won his Pulitzer for editorials on a wide range of state and local issues, often dealing
with corruption. One of his favorite targets was Sam Caldwell,
Georgia's labor commissioner. The editorial reprinted here followed Caldwell's indictment on corruption charges. The tone was
direct and clear and exemplified the outrage that was typical of
many of Scardino's editorials. The Herman Talmadge he mentioned is a former governor and United States senator who was
part of a Georgia political dynasty. But even a Pulitzer couldn't
help rescue a newspaper in financial trouble. The *Gazette*, which
he co-founded in 1978 in Savannah and produced with his publisher and lawyer wife Marjorie M. Scardino, reached a peak
4,000 circulation. It folded the year after Scardino won the
Pulitzer, deeply in debt. A veteran wire service and daily newspaper journalist, Scardino hooked up with the *New York Times*
and later became press secretary to New York City Mayor David
Dinkins. The Scardinos left for London in 1993, Albert to free-
lance and Marjorie to become chief executive officer of the
*Economist*, a publication that doesn't shy away from editorializ-
ing. In the book *Winning Pulitzers*, published in 1991, Scardino
reflected on the life and times of the *Gazette*: "Would I do it
again? It depends where. But the answer's yes, in about twenty
seconds. I don't think Marjorie feels the same way, though. I
think she feels it's something you outgrow. I would love to do it
again. You cannot enjoy telling stories and not break out in a big
smile at the thought of being able to do that. But it would have to
be for a purpose. Our paper had that and I consider it to have
been a great success. For seven years it changed the way life existed for 200,000 people."

# Moldy Department

*Georgia Gazette* • November 3-9, 1983

Corruption in government grows like a mold. Give it something to live on and provide just the right conditions for growth and it will spread until it covers everything in sight.

Sam Caldwell turned our state Dept. of Labor into a perfect medium for growing corruption. For 16 years he built an empire insulated from what few checks and balances existed in our state government. But Caldwell could never have extended his power as far as he did by himself. He needed help.

Some of that help came from Herman Talmadge. Caldwell served as a puppet for the larger corruption that flourished under Talmadge, and for most of his tenure in office, Caldwell's manipulation of public affairs couldn't hold a candle to that of the Talmadge clan. But Caldwell followed the Talmadge theory of government to the letter—exploit the weak and cater to the powerful.

Among the weakest that he exploited were his own employees. They owed their jobs to him, and he never let them forget it. Over and over again he extorted campaign contributions, sexual favors and private services on public time.

The state merit system was supposed to protect these workers against just this kind of corruption, but Caldwell managed to give those who controlled the merit system just enough favors to stay out of his department's affairs. As a result, none of the rules was ever followed.

Under state regulations, when a job comes open, it must be advertised within the department so that those who are already on the payroll have a chance at advancement. Time and again, the better jobs were filled by a Caldwell crony from a small, rural county who had no understanding of what to do and no qualifications for the job, much less any experience in the state Dept. of Labor.

For the most senior level executive jobs, Caldwell picked ex-convicts, owners of topless go-go bars and political hacks who couldn't find an honest job anywhere. At best, they were incompetent. At worst, they were crooks and thugs—and judging by the number of them who have already been convicted of felonies this year, there were more of the latter than the former.

Even as Caldwell prepares to face trial himself, more of his supervisors are being indicted. By most accounts, another 50 to 60 officials will face criminal charges before we have cleaned this one department. And then we have the Dept. of Transportation's problems with bid rigging, and what about the hints of corruption in the Dept. of Agriculture and the State Comptroller's office?

We have a long way to go to reform the government of Georgia. If we stop with the Dept. of Labor, the mold will grow back as soon as we turn off the lights.

*1985*

# RICHARD AREGOOD

for editorials on a variety of subjects

RICHARD AREGOOD'S editorials were noted for their slashing and uncompromising point of view and tone. They were blunt and forceful. Sometimes they were witty. They were often brief. They were always readable. The editorial selected for this anthology was about gun control, one of the domestic issues that have dominated the American scene for years. The lead and conclusion were typical of Aregood's punchy writing. He didn't mince verbs. He raised rebuttals in advance and answered them. In truth, however, Aregood may be best remembered for a November 21, 1975, 122-word editorial that never made it to a Pulitzer jury. It was headlined: "Yes, the Chair." The lead: "It's about time for Leonard Edwards to take the Hot Squat." The conclusion: "Fry him." You get the point. Aregood joined the *Philadelphia Daily News* in 1966 and became an editorial writer in 1974 and editorial page editor in 1980. Reflecting on a question by an interviewer for *Best Newspaper Writing 1985*, published by the American Society of Newspaper Editors, he said, "A big thing missing in lots of editorial pages is passion; I have this feeling that many people writing about stuff don't really care about it. Some don't have the passion. The way most journalists think about editorial pages now, it's kind of a bloodless thing, even a committee thing." And about his writing in general? "Tone and timing," he said, "are the secrets in any kind of writing."

# We Must Be Crazy

*Philadelphia Daily News* • July 23, 1984

We must indeed be crazy.

We Americans have sat by for years taking casualties because some people like to fire off guns and don't want to put up with any hassle when they buy them.

We're not alone in the world for lunacy—the Germans get downright surly whenever anyone threatens their sacred right to drive at 130 miles per hour on the autobahn. But we stand pretty much alone in pretending that our country is still some kind of frontier where a citizen needs a few pieces in his home in case of surprise attack.

James Oliver Huberty is not unique. But he is an excellent example of why gun laws must be tightened. He was a surly, resentful man who hated almost everyone. Both he and his wife had a history of waving firearms at people with whom they had had minor squabbles.

Why Huberty—or anyone—should have a legitimate need for an Uzi assault rifle is something nobody can justify, although the gun nuts will try. Why Huberty—or anyone—should have armor-piercing ammunition is equally unjustifiable.

But he did. And he also had the 12-gauge shotgun and 9mm pistol with which he walked into a California McDonald's restaurant last week. With them, he killed 20 people and wounded 19 before a policeman put a well-deserved rifle bullet through his chest. Pity he didn't suffer.

How many surly sociopaths are there out there thumbing through *Soldier of Fortune* magazine and fondling their Uzis? How many kids can buy a handgun on the street about as easily as they can buy a hot dog? Doesn't that frighten you?

In their own defense, the gun lovers will tell you that the Constitution allows them their deadly pleasures, although they customarily leave out the part about a "well-regulated militia." That means organizations like the National Guard, although the gun lovers will tell you all of them automatially qualify.

They will say that cars also kill people, forgetting that you need a driver's license and auto registration to buy and operate a car. They will say that kitchen knives can also kill, although they choose not to talk about how one could go about slaughtering an entire McDonald's with a kitchen knife.

They will also say that they like to collect weapons, as if that were some kind of constitutionally protected pleasure. It doesn't matter to them that burglars just love to rob gun collectors and peddle their swag to any criminal who will buy them. Would the country be as understanding of some nut who liked to collect various strains of anthrax?

The defenses are so much bull----.

What legtimate purpose is served for hunters or target shooters by assault rifles, machine guns and heavy handguns that aren't accurate enough to shoot at target distances? Those weapons are good only for killing people or playing soldier. And what legitimate purposes are served by permitting anyone, even a whacked-out head case like Huberty, to walk in and buy any kind of deadly weapon he pleases?

Sixty Americans die every day—*every day*—in this country from handguns. Is it worth it?

There is no good reason why this country cannot ban the sale of military weapons to civilians. There is no good reason why handgun sales cannot be severely limited to target shooters and those with other good reasons to own them and their resale tightly regulated. There is no good reason why the majority of people in this country who favor controls have to be cowed by the minority that likes to play with guns.

There is only one reason, in fact, that makes any sense.

We must be nuts.

*1986*

# JACK FULLER

for editorials on constitutional issues

> ABORTION is one of the most hotly debated issues in America.
> Jack Fuller, a lawyer and former Washington correspondent
> turned editorial page editor for the *Chicago Tribune*, engaged in
> this contentious public policy debate in one of 11 editorials sub-
> mitted for the Pulitzer in 1985. His editorials centered on a broad
> range of constitutional issues, none of which has been more ex-
> plosive than the Supreme Court's *Roe v. Wade* decision in 1973
> addressed by the piece reprinted here. The editorial's point of
> view, summed up in its headline, was carefully and clearly devel-
> oped. The editorial avoided the often overly emotional rhetoric
> espoused by both sides. Fuller suggested a solution, like it or not,
> based on his view of constitutional decision making. Toward the
> end, however, the editorial's tone became more tentative, with
> some "oughts" and "perhapses." Today, the abortion debate con-
> tinues with ever-increasing emotion by a Supreme Court with
> new members, by an increasingly combative and restless public,
> and by divided editorial writers and columnists.

# Too Far Too Fast on Abortion

*Chicago Tribune* • July 26, 1985

Twelve years ago the U.S. Supreme Court pre-empted the
national debate over the legality of abortion. The Constitution, it
said, left the choice largely to the private conscience of women and
their physicians, with very limited guidance from the states. A
dozen years later it has become painfully clear that the court went
too far too fast.

Now the Reagan administration has asked the justices to
admit they were utterly wrong and to give the states back the

power to determine when human life begins.

No matter how the court had ruled on abortion, it would have been controversial. This was and is a matter of life and death. It touches the most intimate issues of individual control of one's body and the obligation human society owes to generations yet unborn. It involves deep realms of personal integrity where the authority of the state never has the final say.

And yet in 1973 the Supreme Court attempted to decide the whole agonizing question in one bold stroke. Its majority opinion was deeply flawed, and time has not cured its defects. It was an exercise in judicial arrogance, the most stunning example in the latter half of the century.

Drawing more on medical textbooks than on constitutional precedent, the court divided pregnancy into three-month intervals and set varying rules for state policy during each period. Even legal scholars who favor legal abortion have trouble justifying this decision, because the court in effect convened itself as a legislature of nine and in one bold and foolish stroke wrote a new statute for the country covering one of the most difficult moral dilemmas of the day.

Since 1973, advances in medical technology have rendered the court's assumptions out of date. Abortions today deliver fetuses that doctors can sustain alive outside the womb. The whole idea of when a fetus is viable has changed. The country has begun to define the legal end of life in terms of brain activity, and that does not square with the Supreme Court's definition of the legal beginning of life.

The intellectual underpinning of the court's 1973 ruling was weak to begin with, and the passage of time has eroded it to the point that the question now is not whether the court will have to change its position on abortion, but rather how it should go about the task.

Anti-abortion groups hope President Reagan will fill enough vacancies on the court to swing the balance of power their way. Even one appointment might do it if Chief Justice Warren Burger, who has never been comfortable with the court's position, were to change his vote.

But an abrupt turnaround would be nearly as irresponsible as the original ruling. The message to the public would be cynical and would undermine the legitimacy of the court. A sweeping reversal would suggest that all that matters in constitutional cases is a count of heads.

The Supreme Court has a special role in this country. Its power does not derive directly from the consent of the governed exercised at the ballot box. But it does depend on a different sort of consent. The Supreme Court can stand against the political majorities to protect constitutional principles only to the extent that it has the general and widespread respect of the people. It must not squander this precious asset.

Having failed miserably in 1973 to put forward a defensible position on abortion and having failed to lead the country to some rough consensus then or since, the court now has a duty to retreat from the discredited rule in a way that re-establishes the legitimacy of constitutional decision making and repairs the damage a decade of bitter controversy has done.

Instead of sweeping away the old rule, it ought to proceed case by case in small steps, which is a matter befitting a court. It ought to try to find a new position that it can intellectually sustain and that can win general respect, if not agreement.

Perhaps in the end the justices will have to determine that the federal courts have no business in the field at all, that abortion policy should be left to the states. Perhaps they will discover some other line short of this that preserves a right to abortion under certain circumstances.

The point here is not where the line should be but rather the way the court should go about discovering it, this time with a humility, statesmanship and sense of principle that it sorely lacked in 1973. It should make certain its retreat is an orderly one that does not go too far too fast once again.

*1987*

# JONATHAN FREEDMAN

for editorials urging immigration reform

THE United States' immigration policy has long been the target of editorialists. The *Miami Herald* won a Pulitzer Prize in 1983 for editorials about illegal Haitian immigrants. In 1987, Jonathan Freedman, writing from a West Coast perspective, won the award for editorials concerning Mexican illegals. At the time, the first major immigration reform legislation in 34 years was being debated in the U.S. Congress. Freedman was no stranger to the Pulitzer Prize process; he was a finalist in editorial writing in 1983 and 1984. His editorials written in 1986 perhaps captured the Pulitzer board's attention because of the compelling detailed description and intimacy, unusual for many editorials, represented in the piece that follows. The tone was engrossing. It was mournful and sad in many places but never lost sight of the theme. Much of the piece was based on quotations from the individuals involved and on facts of the event that helped propel the point of view. The legislation passed after rousing debate in the House and Senate.

# Easter Sunrise on the Border Ends in Trauma

*San Diego Tribune* • April 3, 1986

The night before Easter, three compañeros crawled through a hole in the chainlink fence—into America. The border where they crossed is a no-man's land. But in the spring, yellow flowers bloom waist-high beside the torn fence.

The compañeros stopped to rest. Tomorrow was Domingo Santo, the holy day when the crucified Jesus rose from his tomb.

They laid a blanket under the flowers near a dirt track. They lay down and nestled together.

In the darkness, the fence was silhouetted against the garish lights of the Zona Norte, the red-light district of Tijuana. Pieces of clothing caught in the fence fluttered in the wind. As the moon crossed the heavens, it was possible, perhaps, to imagine the fence was a cross. And the clothing was the body of the Señor, crying out, "Porque me olvidaste?"

But that was on Good Friday. This was Domingo Santo—the resurrection. Today was the promise of rebirth, a new life in this land of work, America.

Before he slept, one compañero closed his eyes and put his hands to his forehead.

"I prayed for my little mother and my brothers," he said later, lying in a hospital room. "I prayed for myself. I was afraid of bandidos who assault us."

As he prayed, he thought of his mother and father and eight brothers back in Guanajuato. Their home was roofed with tin, and the floor was dirt. His father, a cobbler, earned 6,000 pesos ($12) a week: "Not enough to pay for the light and water and for schooling. There were times when we went hungry. I'm the oldest brother, so I came here to work."

It was the second time. Last year, he dug ditches to build a road in Encinitas. He worked for an American. "His name was hard to pronounce. But he paid me $250 a week."

He slept in a van during the rains in Encinitas. He was better off than many illegal aliens in the North Country, who shivered in ravines and in spider holes.

"I wanted to go back to work for the man in Encinitas," he said.

But after the long journey from Guanajuato, he fell asleep in the flowers. In the darkness came others from Mexico and Central America and other parts of the world, countless as the chain links in the fence. The Border Patrol driving Ram Chargers chased them along the fence, down paths between the flowers, catching some and letting others escape to El Norte.

Sometime in the early morning, when sunrise services were going on in San Diego, one of the Ram Chargers turned down the dirt path near the fence.

"I woke up screaming," the 20-year-old remembered, his eyes filling with tears in the hospital room, where he had no family or friends. "The migra ran over us with the van. My compañero was crying."

The Border Patrol agent called for help. A Life Flight helicopter landed and carried the aliens to the trauma hospital.

One was released with minor injuries. The second suffered bruises on his legs and was released in a wheelchair, to be taken back to the border to be held for deportation. Two floors below the room where the second told his story, the third compañero lay unconscious in the trauma unit. He was surrounded by tubes. Doctors said he had a chance of recovering. But he had lost his spleen.

As the second youth was rolled away to the Border Patrol sedan in his tire-marked jeans and dirty sweatshirt, he asked: "Where is my money? Where are my shoes? How am I going to work?"

Far away from the border, it is cherry blossom time in Washington. There, the House of Representatives is taking up immigration-law reform once again.

Immigration law, like the fence on the border, is riddled with holes. And each loophole in the law is defended by a lobbyist, paid to keep that loophole open. Business interests want to keep the aliens coming through the fence, to work for cheap wages. Organized labor wants to stop the illegal aliens, but it does not want to provide an organized program of guest workers.

Those claiming to speak for the illegal aliens represent Hispanic-Americans, who have their own suffering and fears of discrimination. Nativists, who want to stir up opposition to all immigration, exaggerate the danger of the illegal-alien "invasion" of America.

As the factions in the House Judiciary Committee fight over the remnants of previous immigration reform bills, the harsh reality on the border is as hidden as the three compañeros sleeping under the flowers.

The courts must determine whether the Border Patrol agent who ran over the aliens was negligent.

But the truck that drove over bodies was driven by us, the American people. We make the immigration laws, and we hire the aliens who must cross the border like hunted animals to build our roads, harvest our crops, clean our hotels and serve dinner to the politicians banqueting in Washington.

Congress, remove our guilt. Halt the crucifixion of illegal aliens on the border.

*1988*

# JANE HEALY

for editorials protesting urban overdevelopment

A PUBLIC policy issue that received the attention of recent editorial writers is urban sprawl and the devastating consequences of mismanaged growth plans. Jane Healy, associate editor of the *Orlando* (Fla.) *Sentinel*, had been a finalist in the editorial writing category in 1985. In 1987, she tackled the matter of unfettered urban growth in a series of 10 hard-hitting editorials entitled "Florida's Shame." Six editorials took on Orange County commissioners for allowing profit-hungry land speculators and real estate developers to virtually dictate growth policy in an area with an exploding population at the expense of adequate schools, fire protection, roads, and other services. Four editorials concerned saving the Wekiva River, "a treasure," Healy wrote, "in a sea of subdivisions, strip shopping centers and office buildings—the things that make up so much of Central Florida." The tough and scathing editorial presented here was the first of the series, a biting, informational piece that set the forward-march, no-retreat direction and tone of those that followed. The editorial led to a punchy conclusion that emphasized the series' title. All editorials in the series were enhanced by the use of maps, charts, and photographs to illustrate key points.

# An Orange Going Sour

*Orlando* (Fla.) *Sentinel* • November 1, 1987

How would you like to live in a place where:
- **(A)** Some elementary school children must eat lunch at 10:30 a.m. because the cafeteria is too crowded to seat everyone during normal lunch hours.
- **(B)** All but one high school is overcrowded. Some academic

classes have to be held in the school gym or, worse, the gym's storage room.

• **(C)** Cars jam up bumper to bumper on dozens and dozens of roads, and the worst is ahead. A place where in just seven years half of the major roads will be carrying more cars than the roads were built for.

• **(D)** Parks rank so low on priority lists that total park acreage must increase by 60 percent just to meet state standards.

• **(E)** All of the above.

Welcome to Orange County, Fla., the 13th fastest-growing area in the country, where you never have to choose between the rotten fruits of unmanaged growth. In Orange County, the answer is always **(E)**, "All of the above."

The Sun Boom? No question, Orange County is right in the thick of it. The economic statistics look jim-dandy on paper, but kids don't go to school on paper. Nor do roads and parks get built on it. Beneath all those rosy data-bank projections, Orange County is being sold out for a quick buck. It's a county in crisis.

Mind you, Seminole, Osceola, Lake and Volusia counties have serious problems as well. But that's a subject for another day. In this series of editorials, we'll concentrate on Orange County, a place still hanging a "For Sale" sign at its border, a quick-buck, bottom-line piece of real estate that's selling its future for a pittance.

Is it the same tired Florida story? To some extent, sure. Taking the real-estate money and running may be the oldest profession in the Sunshine State. And elected officials here have been managed by quick-buck speculators, instead of managing them, since time immemorial, or so it often seems. But, no, the Great Florida Land Grab of the 1980s isn't the land boom of the 1920s.

Then, developers and land speculators used up Florida for their own purposes and headed back up North to enjoy life. Today's developers and land speculators use up Florida for their own purposes and head to North Carolina to retire.

Then, developers and land speculators stuck the communities they pillaged with all the bills for necessary services. Today's developers share in the cost of growth by helping build roads and sewer systems, but don't worry, they still can meet the Mercedes payments. Oh, yes, today's developments also look prettier, sit back farther from the road and might even have smaller signs.

But, face it, that's window dressing. The land grab continues.

And when all is said and developed, the people who live here still
are the ones left to fight the traffic, pay most of the bills and live
with the eyesore.

Maybe worst of all, the all-consuming greed back in the
1920s was out in the open, where just about everyone who cared to
look could see it for what it was. Today's greed gets to hide behind
the illusion that Florida finally is serious about managing its
growth.

The illusion? The tough new law the Legislature passed two
years ago, the one that said services must go hand in hand with
growth.

The reality? In the Orlando area, the law won't go into effect
for at least three more years. That's a year later than originally
scheduled. Too much paperwork for everyone, the state says. The
rest of us can only wonder how many more times this deadline will
be delayed.

This means at least three more years of business as usual in
Orange County. Hold on to your steering wheel.

As for that thick, serious-sounding growth management plan
Orange County has, yes, it exists. But try to get a majority of Orange County commissioners to treat it as anything other than an
annoyance. Just look at the pitiful record:

**August 1985**—Orange County updates its 5-year-old plan
for growth, leaving enough land in urban areas to accommodate
developers for the next 20 to 30 years. In other words, the county
says it won't be necessary to leapfrog out to rural areas and waste
money building roads, utility lines and schools all over the place.
Commissioners even agree that developers won't be able to ask for
changes to the plan every time they walk in the door. They now
can ask for changes only twice a year. Hallelujah, a new day.

Or perhaps we should say, it looked like a new day. Turns
out most of these commissioners are leapfrogging fools.

**Spring 1986**—County commissioners grab at the first
chance they can to leap 5 miles into the woods. They allow an industrial park in rural southeast Orange County that will employ
40,000 people. That's 5,000 more than work in downtown Orlando
now.

**Summer 1986**—Commissioners allow 525 more rural acres
to be developed at urban densities, this time on the west side.

**Spring 1987**—Commissioners open 3,790 acres southeast of

Orlando International Airport to city-like development. They also open 1,200 acres near Windermere to such development.

**Fall 1987**—Commissioners say "go ahead" to urban development on another 300 rural acres east of Windermere.

By now you must be wondering how much of Orange County isn't on the verge of urban development. Good question. The answer is: not much.

Who benefits from this contempt for limiting urban densities to urban areas? Certainly not the typical Orange County resident. Such development only further strains the county's ability to provide adequate schools, roads and parks elsewhere.

No, the people who benefit from all this are the same folks who have been pillaging the Sunshine State for most of this century—the speculators and developers who get rich quick whenever land becomes urban overnight. How? Easy. Land costs a lot less in the rural area, but once the county commission declares it urban, values skyrocket. A developer can build at least four times as many homes in urban areas because lots can be smaller.

Sadly, the county commission still refuses to say, "Enough. We won't be stomped on anymore for a quick buck." That is Florida's Shame.

# LOIS WILLE

for editorials on local issues

LOIS WILLE was a veteran of the Pulitzer Prize competition and Chicago journalism by the time she won the editorial writing award in 1989 for the *Chicago Tribune*, where she was editorial page editor. In 1962 she was the reporter on a series of articles in the now-defunct *Chicago Daily News* calling attention to birth control services. That series won the Pulitzer Prize for meritorious public service. She also was a finalist for the 1984 editorial writing award while working for the *Chicago Sun-Times*. The withering, uncompromising, and often scathing tone of the 10 editorials submitted for the 1989 award no doubt caught the eyes and ears of the Pulitzer board. The editorials were a forthright reflection on Chicago and Illinois politics. Wille articulated the theme of the entries when she was quoted as saying, "I owe it all to the state of politics in Chicago, which is a constant inspiration." Politicians beware. Typical of her wonderfully caustic style is the lead and conclusion of the editorial published here.

# Election Board Caves In to a Swindle

*Chicago Tribune* • April 7, 1988

Just when it seems that some Chicago public official has sunk to the very limits of disgusting behavior, another one or two or three prove there are still new depths to be plumbed.

What, for example, could be worse than Ald. Timothy Evans blocking construction in his ward of 900 units of scattered low-rise public housing to replace 900 units in rundown high-rise buildings that are miserable places to live, but popular with politicians who think it's easier to control votes when they're stacked in concentration-camp settings?

What could be worse than Ald. William Henry stamping out job-creating development opportunities in his desperately poor North Lawndale ward because he wanted to be part of the deals.

Difficult as it may seem to surpass such foul deeds, Chicago's Board of Election Commissioners has managed to do it.

• • •

The three commissioners are supposed to make certain Chicago elections are run honestly and fairly. Does it have to be spelled out to them in big, easy-to-read letters that they also are supposed to make certain the city has elections in the first place? Apparently so. This trio, bending under pressures from various political masters and their own spinelessness, decided on Tuesday that they can't decide whether Chicago must have a mayoral election in the spring of 1989.

The state law, they said, simply doesn't give them enough guidance.

That's garbage. The law is abundantly clear. Its new-found "ambiguity" is so obviously phony it's amazing that Gov. James Thompson and Sheriff James O'Grady and House Speaker Michael Madigan and Cook County Board President George Dunne and the crew propping up Mayor Eugene Sawyer think they can get away with mouthing it. Didn't it ever occur to them that some people might actually look up the state law and see what it says?

The relevant passage in the Illinois Cities and Villages Act— the only passage relevant to Chicago's mayoral situation—states that "if a vacancy occurs in the office of the mayor of a city with a 4-year term, and there remains an unexpired portion of the term of at least 28 months, and the vacancy occurs at least 130 days before the general municipal election next scheduled under the general election law, the vacancy shall be filled at that general municipal election."

Mayor Harold Washington died with at least 28 months remaining in his term, and at least 130 days before the state's next general municipal election. Those elections, as the Illinois election code specifies, occur "in odd-numbered years ... on the first Tuesday in April."

A general municipal election is scheduled in Illinois on April 4, 1989, as the law provides. A city that normally would not elect a mayor until the 1991 general municipal election is required, by

Illinois law, to elect one on April 4, 1989, if its mayor died as early
in his term as did Harold Washington.

If Gov. Thompson, Mike Madigan, George Dunne, and the
rest of the "ambiguity" crowd are correct, the law can be
interpreted to mean that a city can stick by its own election cycle
no matter when its mayor departed. Then why even bother to have
a law concerning mayoral vacancies? According to the newly
minted interpretation by Thompson et. al., no vacant mayoral
term ever would be filled by voters. A mayor could die the hour
after taking the oath and not be replaced with a duly elected
mayor for another four years.

The ambiguity boys know the state law was never intended
to be interpreted that way. Each of them has another reason for
not wanting the people of Chicago to elect a mayor for several
more years.

• Speaker Madigan wants no distractions, particularly in
fundraising, from his own campaign for County Board chairman in
1990.

• Gov. Thompson wants anything that Mike Madigan wants,
if that is the price for the speaker's support of a state tax increase.

• Sheriff O'Grady and his Republican backers want time to
build an O'Grady mayoral campaign, and the longer Eugene
Sawyer is in office embarrassing himself and his supporters, the
better for them.

• George Dunne wants what he thinks the committeemen
who reinstated him as county Democratic chairman want, and
right now the majority of Chicago's Democratic committeemen are
too gleeful about the prospects of cleaning up under Eugene
Sawyer to risk giving it up next spring.

• As for Acting Mayor Sawyer, the people who run him saw
what happened to a few of their crowd in last month's primary.
They were chopped down. They are not about to let their meal
ticket go before the voters if there is any way they can prevent it.

•  •  •

With heavies from both parties pushing at them to abrogate
their responsibility to schedule a mayoral election next spring, the
three Chicago election commissioners obligingly caved in.

Michael Hamblet, a Democrat, said don't look at me, it's up
to the city clerk to set the next election. Utter nonsense. James

Nolan, a Republican, said gee I don't know what to do; it's up to the state election commissioners to advise me. Nikki Zollar, a Democrat, thought the Nolan copout sounded good to her and seconded it.

Chicago has endured more than its share of political corruption and irresponsibility in its 150 years. But this is the first time it has been burdened with a set of politicians—of both parties—arrogant enough to try to swindle the city out of an election.

*1990*

# THOMAS J. HYLTON

for editorials on a local bond issue

POTTSTOWN, Pennsylvania, is not as well-known as the large cities of most of the newspapers whose editorial writers won the Pulitzer in the 1980s. In October of 1989, however, Thomas Hylton of the *Pottstown Mercury* wrote a series of editorials that resembled the theme of the editorials for which Jane Healy won the 1988 award with her attack on rampant urban development in Orlando, Florida. In his case, Hylton's concerns centered on the preservation of farmland and other open spaces in the Quaker State's Chester County, which is in the paper's circulation area. The tone was gentler than Healy's, but just as effective. The *Mercury* advocated a non-binding $50 million bond referendum to, as Hylton wrote in the conclusion of the final editorial of the series, "protect what we have left." Hylton first proposed the bond issue in a 1988 editorial. Presented here are two editorials from the 1989 series, both of which appeared on October 23. The first laid out the paper's reasons for endorsing the referendum. The second strengthened the argument using an anecdotal appeal buttressed with additional facts and argumentation. Cartoons appeared with most of the editorials in the series. The series also had a logo that showed the silhouette of a high-rise city on the horizon encroaching on a tranquil farm landscape in the foreground. The bond issue passed on November 7, 1990. In 1993 the campaign was gaining speed in Montgomery County, home of the *Mercury*, joining in with other bond issues in behalf of open spaces.

# Bond Issue Is Essential To Protect Chester County's Future

*Pottstown* (Pa.) *Mercury* • October 23, 1990

The Chester County commissioners have placed a non-binding referendum on the November 7 ballot asking if $50 million in bonds should be issued during the next four years to preserve farmland and open space.

The *Mercury* wholeheartedly endorses the bond issue. We urge every resident to vote *yes* on the question, which the commissioners are using to gauge public support for conserving open space.

Each day this week, we will discuss a different aspect of the bond proposal. We hope to show why it is vitally important, not only to the future of Chester County, but to all of southeastern Pennsylvania.

The referendum is crucial for two reasons:

First, the bond money is desperately needed to preserve open land against the unprecedented tide of development that has been engulfing Chester County in the last three years.

Second, the referendum itself is a watershed event.

If the people vote overwhelmingly in favor of the bond issue, it will clearly signal a change in public attitude about the management of our most precious natural resource—our land.

It will give our elected officials confidence to explore changes in the tragically misguided land-use policies that have ravaged southeastern Pennsylvania for three decades.

If we act in time, perhaps the magnificent countryside—some of the richest farmland in the world—can be saved for future generations. Perhaps we will temper development, accommodating growth without needlessly diminishing open space.

But if the referendum fails—or passes only by a narrow margin—then Chester County will be doomed to the same congestion that strangles much of metropolitan America.

Although we are squarely in the center of the densely populated corridor between Washington and New York, the suburbanization of Chester County is not inevitable.

There are ways for the millions to live in harmony with farms and woodlands. The English, the Belgians, the Dutch, and the Germans have been doing it for years. We can adapt their methods to our needs; we need only the will to do so.

Time is of the essence. Political reality says it will take years to change Pennsylvania's antiquated land-development laws to allow Chester County to control its own destiny.

We don't have those years to wait. We must begin immediately to protect our most endangered land before it's too late.

The bond issue is the crucial first step.

# Rampant Development May Doom Chester County's Farm Industry

*Pottstown* (Pa.) *Mercury* • October 23, 1990

This is the last fall harvest for Horace Mowrer.

"It's no longer farming country," said Mowrer, an East Vincent Township supervisor. Development has taken over.

The first Mowrers came to Chester County from Germany in the 1740s. For six generations, the family tilled Chester County soil. Mowrer has worked his own 104-acre farm and planted several hundred acres rented from neighbors.

Mowrer's son, Michael, will continue the tradition. But not in Chester County. The Mowrers have bought two farms, of 348 acres and 202 acres, in central Pennsylvania.

"The main reason I'd say I'm looking forward to getting out of here is the traffic situation," Mowrer said. "With all the building going on, traffic's going to get heavier." The Mowrers considered another spot in Chester County, but "we couldn't afford anything in this area here."

The Mowrers are not alone. Between 1982 and 1987, Chester County lost 252 farms and 30,037 acres of farmland, not to mention thousands of acres of woodlands and other open space. All went to development.

Aside from a few rural counties with small populations,

Chester County is the fastest growing county in Pennsylvania. Lancaster and Bucks counties are close behind.

The urban megalopolis is surging down the Route 202 "high-tech" corridor from King of Prussia into the very heart of the county. Strip malls and luxury-class Levittowns are elbowing into the Brandywine Valley from Delaware. Development spatters from the new Route 422 expressway onto the northern townships.

Last year, 32,400 acres—an area one third the size of Philadelphia—was approved for commercial and residential development.

The Chester County Planning Commission expects the county's population to grow from 340,000 in 1987 to about 400,000 in the year 2000—an increase of 60,000 people in just 13 years. But the planning commission has underestimated growth in the past.

According to existing zoning laws, there is room for more than one million people in Chester County.

This proliferating growth is coming at the expense of Chester County's number one industry—agriculture. Last year, Chester County's 1,800 farms employed about 14,000 people, more than any other industry. With $290 million in cash receipts last year, Chester County ranks second in agricultural output among Pennsylvania's 67 counties, and 11th among the 1,566 counties east of the Mississippi River.

Not only does Chester County have soil that is as fertile as any in the world, a stable climate, and a solid agricultural support industry, it is conveniently adjacent to the fourth largest metropolitan marketplace in the United States.

Does it make sense to destroy the farms to accommodate suburban sprawl?

"Every year we lose 2 to 5 percent of our dairy farms," said Richard Breckbill, president of the Chester/Delaware County Farmers Association. Unless something is done, he said, "there're not going to be any left in 10 or 15 years."

Something *you* can do to ensure there will be farms in Chester County a decade from now is vote *yes* on the $50 million bond issue for farmland and open space preservation.

*1991*

# RON CASEY, JOEY KENNEDY, AND HAROLD JACKSON

for editorials about the Alabama tax system

UNDER the logo "What they won't tell you about our taxes," the *Birmingham* (Ala.) *News* hammered away at an issue near and dear to every reader's heart. In a series that ran for one week during August and September 1990, the *News* fulfilled a pledge that, if a state-sponsored blue-ribbon tax reform study commission did not make a promised report by the last week in August, then the paper would pick up the baton. The newspaper obviously did not believe the commission would meet the deadline. According to publisher Victor H. Hanson, II, Ron Casey, the editorial page editor, and writers Harold Jackson and Joey Kennedy "worked for almost three months, examining history books, studies and tax documents and interviewing dozens of experts to produce the week-long series informing voters about what is wrong with Alabama's tax system and how it became so contorted." Their penetrating editorials examined with great depth and clarity the state's system of taxing income, property, and merchandise sales. In effect, Casey was quoted as saying, Alabama's tax system "historically worked as a Robin Hood in reverse." Historical analysis gave great depth to the plain-spoken writing. The series is an example of how editorial writers can make a complex subject understandable without sliding into oversimplification.

# The Bubbling Caldron

by Ron Casey
*Birmingham* (Ala.) *News* • August 26, 1990

The first thing they won't tell you about your taxes concerns the caldron of poverty, exploitation and rotten politics from which they bubbled.

Outgrowths of our thorny history still hold us back. They germinated in the uprootings of farm families from the fields to the smokestacks after the close of the Civil War.

Auburn University history professor Dr. Wayne Flynt and other historians have outlined a long, slow slide into deprivation.

Many were on the precipice of poverty before the war began. Four years of missing manpower, bad crops and destruction pushed them over the edge.

Thousands lost their land. More than 85 percent of the state's white residents owned property before the war. Over the decades, that figure continued to fall until by 1930, 65 percent of Alabama's farmers had to farm soil owned by someone else.

The landless blacks and whites searched for something better than tenant farming or the cyclical bondage of sharecropping.

Lumber became a major industry here and around the Southeast after timber companies used and abused homestead laws to gain control of thousands of acres of federal lands. Textile mills, coal mines and blast furnaces grew up in the foreground of a rural landscape.

Near the turn of the century, former subsistence farmers could make a dollar a day at a sawmill; earn $3 for a week of 12-hour days in a textile plant; or earn 50 cents for every ton of coal scratched from some of the most dangerous mines in the country. Alabama miners died on the average of 10 per month between 1900 and 1910.

Instead of helping the struggling, our Legislature went in another direction.

In 1888, for instance, a five-year tax exemption for small family farms was turned down. But tax laws were revised that same year to help big planters.

Following Mississippi, South Carolina, Louisiana and North Carolina, in 1901 Alabama adopted a new constitution aimed at barring blacks from voting. But its insidious features, like the cumulative poll tax due weeks ahead of an election, kept low-income whites away from the ballot box also.

The year 1901 marked another milestone. It was the last time the Alabama Legislature altered its representation for more than 60 years.

Instead of redrawing its House and Senate districts based on the state's population after each census, the Legislature stood still.

No matter what shifts in population took place, the same counties got the same number of lawmakers.

In 1960, Jefferson County had a population of 634,864. Yet it had one senator, just like 12,917-person Lowndes County.

Control of state government remained in the hands of the big planter counties in the Black Belt in collusion with unscrupulous industrialists.

Though most of the state's residents, wealth and revenues were supplied by north Alabama, the Black Belt's grip remained in place until federal courts ordered redistricting in the early 1960s.

The Great Depression devastated Alabama. Employment plummeted here like nowhere else in the South. In 1935, Franklin Roosevelt called Birmingham "the worst hit town in the country."

Even with so many strikes against it, Alabama was on the verge of making a comeback after World War II. Federal dollars and federal jobs poured in. Alabama lured new industries with tax incentives and promises of cheap labor.

By the 1960s, the state was embroiled in one racial confrontation after another as the walls of segregation fell and the doors to the voting booths opened. The turmoil ended an abhorrent system, but it also saw continuing damage to the state's ability to lure out-of-state businesses.

The federal money began drying up in the 1970s and 1980s, and the economy turned global. Textile jobs went to even cheaper labor in the Far East. Coal came pouring in from South America. Steel jobs went to Japan.

With an undereducated work force, bargain-basement services and a reputation for racial turmoil, Alabama withered in the shadows of Sun Belt growth.

One 1984 estimate said as many as 25 percent of its people could qualify for food stamps.

The political diseases of the hard-scrabble years plague us still:

• We live in a state with no tradition of strong financial support for public education. The children went to work.

In 1900, 59 percent of Alabama's boys and 31.4 percent of her girls between the ages of 10 and 15 held a job. By 1910 the percentages increased to 61.9 percent and 41.3 percent.

Many mills, mines and factories calculated pay on "family wages," or how much more to pay for new sons and daughters at the plant.

The poor saw little value in a high school or college educa-tion. That attitude passed from one generation to the next. In the 1980 census, 43.5 percent of Alabama's people above the age of 25 did not have a high school diploma.

Alabama ranked 51st in the nation in state and local revenue per-person for schools in a 1987 census update.

• We live in a state where the people have a gut-level dis-trust of their government. Demagoguery has been more in vogue than democracy; corruption more prevalent than compassion.

Yet the structures erected to guard against abuse of the pub-lic trust hamstring our elected officials. So much of the state's money is locked into outdated earmarking systems, we can't make revenues match needs. We can't deal with debilitating problems.

• We live in a state where officials have paid more attention to protecting big-land interests than people.

For decades, we have bent over backward to make sure the large landholders, timber companies and corporate land barons who controlled Montgomery paid next to nothing in taxes.

• We live in a state where the poor, black and white, who were kept away from the ballot box for decades have seen a shame-fully unfair burden of taxes laid on their backs.

Little wonder they don't want you to know about the tax sys-tem which bubbled up from such a vile brew.

# Nickels and Dimes

by Joey Kennedy
*Birmingham* (Ala.) *News* • August 29, 1990

Alabama nickels and dimes its people to death. And its sales tax hits the poor and middle class hardest.

Tax breaks that should lighten their burden instead go to in-terest groups with the most clout in Montgomery.

We tax formula for babies. We don't tax formula for calves.

The guy who buys a new car gets a sales tax break. The guy

who buys a pair of work boots does not.

Food for the elderly is fully taxed. Food for chickens isn't taxed at all.

We let so many off with special treatment, we have to raise the sales tax on the rest of us to make up the difference.

In proportion to income, sales and excise taxes place seven times the burden on poor families they place on wealthy families. They place four times the burden on middle-class families.

A much larger slice of the income of people on the lower end of the economic ladder is eaten up by food, clothing and other bills subject to the tax.

On its face, Alabama's basic 4 percent sales tax rate compares favorably to other Southeastern states. Georgia's sales tax is 3 percent, Tennessee's rate is 5.5 percent and Mississippi and Florida each charge 6 percent.

But looks are deceiving. Because Alabama's local governments have such a hard time raising other taxes, hiking the sales tax is a convenient and often-used revenue enhancer. No legislative authority or public vote is needed.

As a result, some Alabamians pay as much as 9 cents on the dollar—or more than double the state's basic rate.

In the end, only three states in the Southeast have a higher effective state and local sales tax rate than Alabama—Tennessee, Mississippi and Louisiana.

The way the tax is applied in Alabama makes it clearly unfair. But, while no tax can be classified as popular, the sales tax is probably one of the least objectionable, anyway.

Governments like sales taxes because they generate a lot of money for the collection effort they involve. Non-residents pay just like residents, which makes sales taxes especially popular for tourist states such as Florida.

Residents prefer sales taxes over others because there are no forms to fill out or separate checks to write. An increase in the sales tax is counted only pennies at a time, making it appear, deceptively, as a low-impact tax.

The major drawback to the tax is its regressive nature, the way it hits the poor and middle class hardest.

And the regressive impact of Alabama's sales tax is amplified because our state has a much higher rate of poverty than many others.

If exemptions and rate deductions truly offset the uneven

burden of sales taxes, Alabamians would be celebrating. Alabama has exemptions—plenty of them—but most of them work against poor and middle-income families instead of for them.

If you buy a carton of milk, you pay sales tax. If you buy a "Flight Simulator" home computer program, you don't.

Many items—fertilizer, computer software, food for livestock, chicken litter, and boxes, twine and stakes used in tomato growing—are not taxed at all.

Others—heavy machinery, automobiles and food from vending machines, for instance—are taxed at lower rates.

Alabama's sales tax regulations are so complex and loaded with so many favors and rate breaks they go on and on, page after page after page, for better than 300 pages.

In all, special exemptions and lower rates cost Alabama nearly $600 million in sales tax revenue last year. While some exemptions are necessary to prevent double taxation, or (like food stamps) are required by federal law, many are simply the result of one strong lobby or another having its way with the Alabama Legislature.

While some states exempt food and over-the-counter drugs from their sales taxes to give poorer families a break, Alabama doesn't.

It might cost $123 million a year to exempt food, but that much and more could be raised by getting rid of the tax break for automobiles and taxing exempt retail services, like haircuts and dry cleaning. The Alabama Department of Revenue estimates that a sales tax applied to retail services alone would raise nearly $160 million.

As Alabama shifts from a manufacturing to service economy, there will be more pressure to apply the sales tax to retail services.

And why not? Why charge a sales tax for a meal consumed in a restaurant, but not for a haircut and manicure given at a beauty shop?

A sales tax on services, while still regressive, has a lighter impact on Alabama's poorer families. A poor family has to buy milk and bread, but seldom pays somebody else to launder its clothes.

Any equitable tax reform in our state has to target the sales tax. Exemptions should be made for sound economic reasons, not as favors.

A genuine effort must be made to relieve Alabama's families

of some of their sales tax burden. That's especially true now that Uncle Sam has stopped allowing taxpayers to deduct state sales taxes from their federal returns.

The state has to stop panhandling its poor and middle-class families to death.

# Handcuffing Money

by Harold Jackson
*Birmingham* (Ala.) *News* • August 31, 1990

Alabama handcuffs more of its tax money than any other state.

"Earmarking" a tax means it can only be spent on a specific program or agency. Alabama earmarks nearly 90 percent of its revenue. The national average is only about 28 percent.

Too much earmarking is one reason "fiscal crises" are so common in Alabama. When an emergency requiring more money arises, most of the tax revenue we collect can't be shifted around to solve the problem.

Even the day-to-day providing of essential services the public expects is hampered by earmarking because the state can't spend money where it's needed the most.

Alabama has one of the highest infant death rates of any state in the nation. That demands that we spend more on prenatal services for poor pregnant women.

But the amount of money available to save sick babies' lives in Alabama is limited by the excessive amount of earmarking we do.

The money we earmark is not being spent frivolously. Yet this state has greater or equal needs that are not benefiting from its rigid spending schemes.

And earmarking turns the tax system on its head. Instead of deciding what is the fairest tax and then how it should be allocated, we decide what we want to fund first and then pick the easiest way to squeeze out some money for it.

Reducing the amount of earmarking will mean placing more

trust in the Legislature and governor to make wise spending decisions.

Alabamians have been loath to do that because they don't trust their elected officials. Also, education in this state benefits from earmarking. Though they may not fund it with the same tax effort of other states, Alabamians do care about educating their children.

We earmark money for education because politicians throughout our history have not shown a strong commitment to schools.

In 1927, Gov. Bibb Graves convinced Alabamians that if they raised "nuisance taxes" on telephones, telegraphs, etc., the money would be spent on education. And Graves kept his word.

But the Great Depression bankrupted Alabama, and by 1932 the state had no money for its schools.

So it followed the advice of the Brookings Institution and considered education a non-essential service that didn't have to be included in the budget.

An income tax was created and earmarked to pay off the state's bonded indebtedness, but still no money was set aside for schools.

Everyone had it rough during the Depression, but teachers were particularly hard hit in Alabama.

If they got paid at all it was usually with promissory notes or "scrip" worth only 10 cents on the dollar.

Finally, in 1936 a sales tax was imposed and earmarked for teachers' salaries.

And in 1947, with the state's indebtedness paid off, Alabamians approved a constitutional amendment re-earmarking the income tax for teacher salaries as well.

Post-war Alabama, flooded with returning veterans exempt from the poll tax and anxious to make life better than in the Depression years they grew up in, was showing a stronger commitment to public education.

Politicians continued showing their equal willingness to make education a sacrificial lamb.

They used fear of the Supreme Court's 1954 school desegregation decision to get an amendment enacted in 1956 that removed all references in the state constitution implying Alabama had an obligation to fund public education.

With politicians having gone on record twice saying education was a service the state had no obligation to provide, it's easy to see why teachers and others have opposed past attempts to reduce earmarking in Alabama.

But they must understand that earmarking tax dollars is not enough to make public education what it should be.

Teachers understand the link between other problems affecting children—poverty, health care, crime—and the jobs they try to do.

Alabama can't solve those other problems unless it has the flexibility to aim more of its tax money at them.

Earmarking affects not only education's money, but dozens and dozens of taxes in Alabama.

It has made Alabama like the poor man with an overcoat that's too short and only has two buttons left.

That poor man needs to open his eyes and admit his coat isn't what it was; it's gotten old and frayed and no longer provides the protection it once did.

And unless he makes some repairs, moves some buttons around and adds some, it will be of little service.

Alabama must open its eyes and see that this state must have the flexibility to spend the meager revenue it collects where it is most needed.

Alabamians must have faith in ourselves that we can use our power as voters to get rid of politicians who don't spend our tax money where we want it spent—on education and other important, essential programs.

If we use our power at the polls,we will never have to rely so heavily on handcuffs again.

*1992*

# MARIA HENSON

for editorials about battered women

MARIA HENSON worked 16 months researching and writing editorials published in the *Lexington* (Ky.) *Herald-Leader* under the title "To Have and to Harm, Kentucky's Failure to Protect Women From the Men who Beat Them." The series ran for over a year. It prompted political and judicial leaders in Kentucky to pass legislation, open records of domestic violence complaints for the first time, and make other improvements to the hearing process. Still, Henson is a realist about the lasting impact of editorials no matter how powerful. "We're not naive enough to think that we're going to change everything, because what we're dealing with is attitudes," she said after being notified of the Pulitzer award. The *Herald-Leader* has come close in the Pulitzer process before and after Henson's win. Editorial writers for the paper were finalists in 1989 and 1993, although in the latter year no award was given. Henson's powerful editorials were dramatic in their use of real cases to illustrate the physical and emotional devastation that women suffer at the hands of batterers. The editorial reprinted here exemplified the tone and descriptive writing of the series in telling of the chilling consequences of senseless beatings and the state's seeming indifference. It was accompanied by "before" and "after" photographs that graphically illustrated the results of the beating. It illustrated the determination of one victim to demand justice on her own, which is clear in the conclusion of this piece. Henson, the paper's assistant state editor, received a Nieman Fellowship to study at Harvard in 1993-94.

# A Victim No More

*Lexington* (Ky.) *Herald-Leader* • February 3, 1991

Lynn Milam has five metal plates in her head to remind her of the night her former boyfriend nearly beat her to death.

The assault left her unconscious in a Frankfort street. Her face was fractured in several places. Three of her teeth lay on the pavement. Her assailant's footprint was stomped onto her chest.

Lynn survived that beating. She went on to see that the man who beat her was punished for his actions. But before justice was done, she learned a hard lesson: To avoid becoming a victim again, a beaten woman often must fight for justice.

Had two things been different in Kentucky, Lynn might never have had to learn that lesson.

• Kentucky's law against wife-beating should apply to all unmarried couples, but it now applies only to those who have a child in common. So when the man with whom she lived for six months first began to beat her, Lynn could not turn to the courts for a protective order.

• Every Kentucky prosecutor's office should employ victims' advocates to follow the cases of beaten women through the courts. Such advocates help remind prosecutors and judges that the public is watching how they handle the cases of beaten women. But prosecutors in Franklin and most other Kentucky counties don't have the money to hire advocates.

So Lynn, unprotected and on her own, had no choice. To see justice done, she had to become her own advocate.

Lynn began to realize that in September of 1989, about three weeks after she was assaulted.

She was at a Frankfort shopping center one evening when she saw something that shocked and terrified her. David Brantley, the man who had beaten her, was in a store renting movies and a VCR. Lynn knew David was supposed to be in jail awaiting trial.

Up until then, Lynn thought that she could concentrate on recovering physically and emotionally while civilization held David responsible for his actions.

But when she saw her assailant renting movies when he was supposed to be in jail, Lynn realized that civilization might turn its back on her.

Determined not to become a victim again, she set to work on her own behalf.

Lynn began by calling the Franklin County jail and complaining that David was abusing his work-release privileges. When she saw him out again at unusual hours, she called and complained again.

She learned that since the night of the assault, the State Police had not interviewed witnesses, including the two men who were the first to see her after she was beaten. Lynn went to the State Police to demand more attention to her case.

She wanted to make sure that David received a fitting punishment for his crime. So she went to the law library in the state Capitol and began studying what had happened in other assault cases. She copied the cases and showed them to prosecutors.

But what really sent Lynn into action was the news that prosecutors were considering a plea bargain in David's case. He was charged with second-degree assault, a felony that carries a maximum sentence of 10 years. Lynn recalls that prosecutors were considering letting him off with the minimum sentence, five years.

That was unacceptable to Lynn. With the assistance of Allie Hendricks, a therapist on contract with the Lexington spouse abuse shelter, she contacted Travis Fritsch, a victim's advocate in the state attorney general's office, and Sherry Currens, head of the Kentucky Domestic Violence Association.

The four women got together and paid a visit to Franklin County Assistant Commonwealth's Attorney Larry Cleveland. They wanted to make sure the prosecutor understood how serious Lynn's case was.

Cleveland got the message.

"I will say this about the case—because (they) were so interested in it, it probably got a little more of my attention than it would have otherwise," he says. "I mean, otherwise I would have said, 'Look, OK.' I would have cut a deal. ... The guy probably wouldn't have gotten as much time."

Eventually, in Cleveland's words, "The guy got his butt kicked." David agreed to a plea bargain calling for seven years in prison.

In the end, Lynn felt that of all the officials who had handled her case, only Cleveland had understood its importance. "Larry Cleveland was the only one that gave me any support at all," she says.

The experience taught Cleveland something. "You don't mess with a whole roomful of women that looked as serious about this as they did," he says.

• • •

Two simple changes can help keep other women from going through what Lynn experienced.

First, the legislature should extend the state's wife-beating law to protect unmarried women from violent men with whom they live or have lived. Unmarried women are as much in danger as married women and just as deserving of the law's protection.

Second, there should be victims' advocates in all prosecutors' offices throughout the state. Making that a reality won't be easy, but it can be done.

There's no reason, after all, that the victims of violent men should have to act as their own advocates. And beaten women surely should not have to assemble a roomful of angry women to remind prosecutors of their responsibility as protectors of those who live in a civilized society.

*1994*

# R. BRUCE DOLD

for editorials aimed at helping reform Illinois' child protection
system

R. Bruce Dold, the *Chicago Tribune*'s editorial page editor, submitted for the Pulitzer Prize ten editorials published between
April 21, 1993, and October 29, 1993, under the logo *Killing Our
Children*. The editorials ran concurrently with a year-long series
of news articles using the same logo. Both the stories and the editorials were all published on Page One. In all, some sixty children
who had come into contact with government child-protection agencies nevertheless had died. Dold's series focused on the death of a
three-year-old boy, Joseph Wallace, and the failure of the juvenile
court and child welfare system to save him. In the first editorial,
Dold wrote that the boy's mother had been hospitalized "for mental problems off and on for a dozen years. She abused her body in
grotesque ways, even set herself on fire. She seriously injured a
worker at a mental health center. She was a clear threat to herself
and her two children." Young Joseph was taken away from his
mother three times, but circuit court judges and various children
and family-services welfare agencies ultimately returned him to
her custody. She later hanged the boy using an electrical cord after watching him wave good-bye. The editorials smolder with angry indignation. Indicative of the tone is the editorial published
here, the longest of the ten. On receiving the Pulitzer Prize, Dold
said, "I don't think these editorials were all that hard to write. It
was the kind of thing where the anger came pretty naturally. Anybody who knew anything about this case had to be angry about it.
I just had to put it in print." The total editorial campaign contributed to the passage of a number of fundamental legislative
changes profoundly affecting the state's juvenile courts and child-
welfare system. Among them were a doubling of the number of juvenile judges in a system that had long been considered a dump-
ing ground for weak judges and a tripling of the number of case
workers assigned to investigate and follow the progress of children
in state care. With the changes, Dold said, many judges sought to
come into the system and it had become a "top place" to dispense
justice. He summed up the results as developing a firm belief, that
took a long time in developing among readers and the courts, that
the "best interests of the child come before anything else."

# The System Is the Scapegoat

*Chicago Tribune* • October 29, 1993

*"The committee is charged with trying to find out where the system failed, because it is clear that it did fail."*

With that directive, Chief Judge Harry Comerford impaneled three attorneys last spring to investigate how the Cook County Circuit Court allowed 3-year-old Joseph Wallace to be returned to his mother—and to his death. Amanda Wallace allegedly tied an electrical cord around Joseph's neck, strung the cord over a transom, and watched him wave good-bye just before she hanged him.

Six months later, that committee has completed its work. It has reviewed every court transcript and document that it could find. It has interviewed judges, attorneys, doctors and social workers, and compiled a shocking record of callow disregard for Joseph's life.

And with that revolting record before it, the committee has reached the most feckless possible conclusion. In the words of the report, "the system itself is responsible for the human error . . . the juvenile justice system surely consigned Joseph to his death."

Of course! Why didn't we think of that? It was "the system's" fault. "The system," which can't be fired, suspended or reprimanded. "The system," which can't speak in its own defense.

Nonsense.

• • •

The attorneys on the committee won't say it. Judge Comerford won't say it. Both, perhaps, are acting out of professional courtesy. We feel no need to extend such courtesies; so we'll say it.

The actions of several judges in the Joseph Wallace case were negligent. They contributed mightily to Joseph's death.

For Comerford and the others to attempt to shield the judges from responsibility for their terrible mistakes is to invite the cries of "whitewash."

Judge Walter Williams, the first judge to come in contact with the Wallace family, had ample evidence that Amanda Wallace was highly unstable and dangerous to herself and her child.

Yet he neglected the evidence, rejected the arguments of an assistant public guardian and an assistant state's attorney, and ordered Joseph returned to Amanda Wallace. In the words of the report, "there was the absolute certainty that Joseph would have grown up being cared for by a suicidal, anti-social pyromaniac."

Judges Daniel Gillespie and Allen Goldberg made crucial decisions based on incomplete knowledge of the Wallace situation. Goldberg made, perhaps, the most understandable mistake. He relied on the lawyers in the case to tell him the whole truth, and they did not. Such uncritical scrutiny led to uninformed decisions.

In its strained efforts to excuse the judges, the report says they are "captive" to the system, constrained by the capabilities of the lawyers who present them with evidence, burdened by the workloads that push them to move on to the next case.

Captive? The judge is timekeeper, referee and final arbiter. He has ultimate power and responsibility in the courtroom. If he does not exercise it, these matters of life and death might just as well be settled by majority vote of the lawyers, psychologists and social workers gathered around his bench.

• • •

It is tempting to dismiss this report. What saves it is the fact that it is as perceptive in its revelations as it is puzzling in its conclusions.

It reveals key problems in logistics—such as the failure to transfer files between jurisdictions—that contributed to the misguided decisions. The logistical problems should be the easiest to cure, and, indeed, Comerford has begun to address them.

But the report's most important finding is this: from the moment Joseph was taken from his mother in August 1989 to the moment she ultimately won custody of him in February 1993, the only concern of the court was what *she* had to accomplish to get him back.

The issue should have been whether it was in the best interest of Joseph to be in the unsupervised custody of Amanda Wallace. The answer couldn't come from the system. It had to come from the people charged with protecting Joseph. The answer should have been obvious. The answer was no.

• • •

Changes are coming in Cook County juvenile justice. Next month, the number of judges hearing abuse and neglect cases will grow to 26, about double the number that were doing so at the time of Joseph's final court hearing.

Procedural reforms recommended by two previous investigations of the Cook County Juvenile Court have been put in place. The Illinois Department of Children and Family Services is greatly reducing caseloads so social workers can give more attention to each child. One important action taken by Comerford in response to this report will provide judges with a source of independent psychologists and psychiatrists who can make unbiased determinations of a parent's fitness.

The General Assembly should approve another recommendation for hearing officers to assist the juvenile judges. Such officers could make sure that all critical information and witnesses are prepared and available before a case goes to the judge.

More changes must come, chief among them the recognition that the young clients in juvenile court depend more than anyone else in the judicial system on the wisdom and mercy of the court. It's not clear that everyone in the system recognizes that.

Amanda Wallace inhabited two distinct worlds. Outside the court, she was an immensely disturbed woman who mutilated herself, attempted suicide through drug overdoses, threatened to kill her children, attacked other people, set fires, and slipped in and out of mental institutions. Inside the court, she was a mother who wanted her children and would get them if she just went to the right classes and said the right things. The failure of anyone to recognize the great chasm between those two worlds was appalling—and for Joseph, fatal.

*1995*

# JEFFREY GOOD

for editorials urging reform of Florida's probate system

Jeffrey Good, now managing editor of the *Valley News* in Lebanon, New Hampshire, was a news reporter for more than a decade before he became an opinion writer. During that time he investigated problems with Florida's probate system. So it was natural that after becoming an editorial writer he should continue his crusade. He convinced his editor, Philip Gailey, that the effort was worth undertaking. Gailey told Good that if he pulled off the project, he would win a Pulitzer. Good said that the only way to persuade the state legislature about the need for reform was to have the full weight of the newspaper behind the effort. The legislature made changes; and, most gratifying to the editorialists, readers praised the paper for giving them tools to protect themselves and their loved ones. Good and Gailey decided on blending investigative reporting and editorial writing in a lengthy series spread over four consecutive weeks that appeared on the front page of the "Sunday Perspective" section. Gailey, said Good, had the "guts to take a big chance." Good was detached from regular duty for eight months to pursue the subject, which he determined was too large and complex to fit the traditional mold. The piece reprinted here—important with its focus on a human face—was the first and introduced many practical and explanatory components, as did the entire series, with the prominent note that this was a "Different Kind of Editorial." The introduction to the series explained, "Today and for the next three Sundays, the *Times* is publishing a different kind of editorial. Final Indignities is an examination of the estate system, based on months of research and writing by editorial staff member Jeffrey Good. It appears on the front page of this section to convey its importance. Floridians should be able to face death trusting the legal system to carry out their last wishes. But we have found that, too often, the trust is broken. We invite you to educate yourselves and join our call for reform." Attorney Lauren Sill, the lawyer mentioned in the editorial, went to jail. Although now a news editor, Good is on the editorial board and continues to write an editorial once a week for the family-owned 18,500 circulation *Valley News* in a location dear to his and his wife's family roots. He said he is happy to have found a smaller paper with the same spirit of feisty independence that inspired him at the *St. Petersburg Times*.

# Broken Promises

*St. Petersburg Times* • August 28, 1994

Joe Thomas wanted to end his life as he lived it: with quiet dignity. In Florida, that was too much to ask.

For most of his nine decades, Thomas had made do without the help of others. He paid his bills on a parks department salary, saving pennies by sprinkling warm water on his cereal. He lived alone, retiring to a modest boarding hotel where he bothered no one and even made his own funeral plans.

But there was one job Thomas could not do alone: leave a final gift to 32 beloved grandnieces and grandnephews. He wrote a will asking Florida's probate courts to carry out his wish.

When Thomas died in 1988, he left enough for each beneficiary to inherit about $8,500. The heirs made earthy plans for Uncle Joe's bequest: help a child through college, put money down on a house in a safer neighborhood, weather a spell of joblessness.

A judge appointed St. Petersburg lawyer Lauren Sill to serve as executor of the Thomas estate. Although she was supposed to begin distributing the inheritances within one year, the courts let her keep the cash for nearly five.

By the time a judge asked Sill what had become of the money, it was too late. She had stolen $270,000, nearly all the dead man's savings. With help from Florida's probate court, she had stolen something else: Joe Thomas' final dignity.

Each year, more than 140,000 people die in Florida. Many are like Joe Thomas: They work for decades and retire to this place in the sun. As the end nears, they write wills leaving a final gift to friends, family, a favorite charity. Somewhere along the way, a lawyer says, "Don't worry. The courts will take care of your last wish."

We face death believing this promise, trusting that our passing will be marked with a final measure of dignity. Too often, the trust is broken.

Make no mistake: Most estates are administered honestly and well. But these successes come not because the system demands it, but because individual executors, lawyers and court officials choose to do the right thing.

Florida's probate system is designed to be "self-administering," that is, the courts generally don't get involved unless someone raises a red flag. That system works fine when estate administrators are honest, efficient and open about their work.

But in other cases, the system's loose oversight opens the door to wrongdoing. Trusted executors loot estates, while court officials look the other way. Wrongdoers receive light punishments, while victims get an empty promise of repayment. And as the probate horror stories mount, elderly Floridians take refuge in living-trust plans that leave them even more vulnerable to exploitation.

The probate system is not intrinsically evil. Run properly, it is a fine way for people to pass wealth from one generation to the next. Assets are gathered, bills are paid and bequests are passed to the rightful heirs—all under the court's watchful eye.

But the system is no better than the law that governs it, or the people who run it. Today, in the first of a series of editorials on Florida's estate system, the Times explores how probate court fails the people it is designed to protect.

Too often, the people who take advantage are the ones in whom the courts—and the public—place the greatest trust: lawyers.

### Broken Deadlines

Would you give someone a one-year deadline for distributing $283,000, and then wait five years to ask what had become of the money? That's exactly what Pinellas County judges did with Joe Thomas' life savings.

Florida law gives nearly unchecked power over estates to the executors—also known as "personal representatives"—appointed to administer them. In return, executors are supposed to begin distributing inheritances within a year, or provide a good reason why they have not.

That time limit is written into law, but court officials don't always enforce it. As Sill blew off deadline after deadline, the judges granted her extension after extension. Sill celebrated by writing herself fresh checks from Joe Thomas' bank account. After Circuit Judge Helen Hansel gave Sill a 60-day extension in 1992, for instance, Sill stole nearly $97,000.

Last year, after Sill had enjoyed eleven deadline extensions, Hansel finally called her bluff. Sill was summoned to court and asked: Where is the cash?

"In the bank," Sill replied.

All $283,000?

"That's correct," said Sill.

Then an amazing thing happened. After five years of lies, someone thought to check up on Sill. Five minutes later, he reported, "Your Honor, I have been advised by the Chase Bank that the balance in the estate account at this time is $3,611."

Five minutes and a phone call. That's all it took to expose Sill as a thief and a disgrace to the probate system. That's more than the courts had been willing to do—until it was too late.

Earlier this year, Sill was convicted of stealing money from four estates, including Joe Thomas'. She was sentenced to two and a half years in prison. While the delays in her case were extreme, they are far from unusual.

As of March 31—the most recent date for which statistics are available—nearly half of all Florida estates were open past the one-year limit. The percentage of overdue estates varied widely among counties. For instance, Pinellas had 31 percent over deadline, while Hillsborough had 49 percent and Palm Beach a whopping 86 percent. (These figures are for estates under $600,000 that don't involve a legal contest; more complicated estates have longer deadlines.)

In recent years, court officials have done a good job sending out warnings on delinquent cases. But they need to do more. They need to demand proof that executors are not delaying estates to drain them.

The system failed when it didn't demand that proof of Lauren Sill. Joe Thomas, 1901–1988, deserved better.

## Cozy deals

Overseeing an estate isn't always as simple as calling the bank. Many people die leaving not only cash, but also antiques, art, jewelry and rare stamps.

Florida law gives estate administrators vast power to sell such valuables and distribute the proceeds to heirs. In a logical world, the law would require the administrators to prove they had conducted these sales honestly and in the best interest of the estate.

But this isn't a logical world. It's Florida.

State law does not require executors to obtain objective, professional appraisals. Because of this loophole, the courts don't know if executors are protecting estates—or looting them.

Consider the case of Margaret Fiala.

Mrs. Fiala was a widow who died in Pasco County, leaving her life's treasures to two grown children. Because the heirs lived out-of-state and could not properly administer the estate, a judge appointed Pasco lawyer David C. Gilmore to carry out Mrs. Fiala's final wishes.

Gilmore needed to sell the estate's stamp collection and distribute the proceeds to Mrs. Fiala's children. While not required by law, an appraisal was important; the untrained eye can't distinguish between a 10-cent stamp and a $10,000 one. So, Gilmore hired a professional appraiser.

The appraiser, Pasco Coins & Jewelry owner Tim Carr, set the collection's value at nearly $5,000. Did Gilmore then use that appraisal to guide him as he put the stamps on the market, seeking the highest price? No. Gilmore simply turned around and sold the stamps to Carr for $5,000—without seeking any other bids.

Gilmore and Carr insist that was a fair price. One of the heirs, Diane Fiala, has her doubts. Fiala has obtained professional estimates setting the stamps' value as high as $100,000—20 times Gilmore's sales price.

Fiala initially approved Carr's hiring. But now she wonders if Gilmore and the appraiser struck a deal to get the stamps cheap and then resell them at a profit, a suspicion both men vehemently deny. What is the truth? That's the $95,000 question—one the courts can't answer, because they didn't require Gilmore to prove he had sold the stamps at arm's length. In fact, Gilmore didn't even have to tell court officials who had appraised and purchased the stamps.

Pasco Circuit Judge Lynn Tepper, who oversaw Gilmore's work, refused to answer questions from the Times. But a veteran probate judge not involved in the case said selling property to an appraiser raises serious questions. Pinellas-Pasco Circuit Judge Thomas E. Penick Jr. said, "That's loose operations."

It's also an insult to a woman who put her faith in the courts. Margaret Fiala, 1911–1985, deserved better.

**Protection lost**

Diane Fiala might never have known how much the stamps in her mother's estate had sold for, if she had done what too many beneficiaries do: waive her right to a final accounting.

The law requires executors to submit a detailed financial report before closing an estate, unless they get a waiver from the beneficiaries. Many lawyers urge their clients to sign away this important protection, saying, You can trust me.

Really? Consider the case of the red Mercedes. After Esther Specht died, Tampa lawyer Karl Stevens Jr. administered her estate and asked the beneficiaries to waive a final accounting. Not suspecting any skullduggery, they signed the forms. No longer accountable, Stevens bled the estate, taking a $16,400 "loan" to treat himself to a Mercedes-Benz convertible. The color: Sunset Red.

Normally, Stevens' cash grab would have gone undetected; a judge would have seen the waivers and closed the estate. Luckily, though, Stevens' secretary had a conscience and tipped off the Florida Bar.

After he was caught, Stevens repaid the money and pleaded guilty to grand theft and related crimes. But his case reveals a serious flaw in the probate system: While beneficiaries expect the court to be protecting them, officials expect beneficiaries to be savvy enough to protect themselves. In the canyon between those expectations, deceit flourishes.

Even in cases where accountings are completed, court officials do little more than stuff the documents in a forgotten file. A survey of court officials in six estate-heavy counties—Pinellas, Hillsborough, Broward, Palm Beach, Orange and Pasco—found that none routinely audits accountings.

Said Orange County probate manager Robert Herndon: "If they (beneficiaries) have no objections to how the funds are managed, or mismanaged, then the court has no concern."

Herndon is right, and the system couldn't be more wrong.

In many cases, beneficiaries live out of state, are unfamiliar with probate law, or lack the financial knowledge to police an estate administrator. They count on the courts for that protection.

People facing death have a right to expect that their money will go to chosen beneficiaries, not to a crook in a convertible. Esther Specht, 1909–1987, deserved better.

### Uncaring courts

When problems do surface in estates, judges have the power to ask the tough questions and make things right.

Judges can order estate administrators to court and put them under oath. They can demand documentation of bank balances and estate sales. In the worst cases, they can appoint investigators and throw errant administrators off the case or into jail.

Used judiciously, these powers allow judges to ferret out wrongdoers and strike fear in potential villains. Yet, some judges seem ridiculously reluctant to use them.

In the Thomas estate, court officials issued warning after warning to attorney Sill, but didn't back them up until it was too late. In the Fiala estate, the judge seemed more interested in making excuses for attorney Gilmore than in investigating legitimate questions about his work.

Probate is a cozy club. The same judges see the same lawyers every day inside the courtroom, and often outside. When the lawyers say something is so, the judges tend to believe them.

Diane Fiala was like many beneficiaries of Florida estates. She lived a thousand miles away, didn't understand Florida law and could only communicate with the court by letters, phone or an occasional visit.

Gilmore says Fiala has no right to complain now, because she didn't protest the stamp sale when it was done. But court records show that while Diane Fiala did not specifically object to the appraiser buying the stamps for $5,000, she did tell court officials that a stamp club president said her parents owned "very good stamps, worth over $25,000." And in a formal objection to Gilmore's financial accounting, Ms. Fiala protested that Gilmore "has failed to properly account for the true value of the personal property of the Decedent."

That objection forced Pasco court officials to address her concerns. But when they did, Ms. Fiala didn't have a friend in the right place.

Probate judges often rely on court clerks to watchdog problem files. In the Fiala case, that job fell to Pasco deputy clerk Lisa A. Peters—who had worked nearly three years as Gilmore's probate secretary before she began examining his work on the Fiala estate.

Neither Peters, her bosses, nor Judge Tepper would answer questions about how that past relationship affected the court's actions. They don't have to; Peters' conflict-of-interest clearly disqualified her from being an objective overseer.

When Fiala raised questions about Gilmore's actions on the stamps and other estate issues, the judge should have appointed an independent investigator, sometimes known as an administrator ad litem. Instead, Tepper brushed off the protests and closed the estate—leaving questions that have hounded Fiala and Gilmore through years of legal feuding.

Diane Fiala once trusted Florida's legal system, but now she is justifiably bitter. "The people who are supposed to uphold the trust are more geared to their personal networks," says Fiala. "It isn't a system of checks and balances. It's more like a good ol' boy network."

We all deserve better.

*1996*

# ROBERT B. SEMPLE, JR.

for his editorials on environmental issues

The *New York Times'* long and robust tradition of writing about the environment was revived in the late 1980s with the arrival on the editorial board of Robert B. Semple, Jr., who had already had a long career at the newspaper, starting as a general assignments reporter in the Washington bureau in 1963. He later became White House correspondent during the first Nixon term. He went on to become deputy national editor, London bureau chief, foreign editor, and Op Ed-page editor. Semple joined the editorial board as associate editor in 1988, mainly to write about politics, but soon was encouraged to write also about environmental and energy matters, first by Jack Rosenthal, his first editor, and later by Howell Raines, who succeeded Rosenthal in 1993 and is now *Times* executive editor. Read an editorial on those subjects today in the newspaper and Semple probably will have written it. Raines, an avid fly fisherman and outdoors enthusiast, "took an interest of mine, environmental questions, and really made it flourish," Semple said when the award was announced. Raines, he added, "gave me a whole lot of support and took it to a whole other level. That's what really made it flourish." The editorial reprinted here was the first of a series spanning the year of 1995 and set the tone for what was to follow. Semple said this piece took weeks to research, as did the entire series, and that he enjoyed getting back to reporting and digging for information in a complex and contentious area of public affairs in order to make grounded opinion. Eventually, the gold mine that was the focus of the editorial was blocked, partly because of the combination of Semple's editorials and the dedication of environmentalists. Secretary of the Interior Bruce Babbitt had developed a keen interest in the matter and enlisted President Bill Clinton in the battle that saw the land preserved.

# Stopping the Yellowstone Mine

*New York Times* • March 27, 1995

Congress is in a mood to abandon the preservation of America's ecological heritage. It is therefore imperative that the Clinton Administration muster its resolve and its executive powers to block at least one monumental and irreversible environmental catastrophe. This disaster-in-waiting is a proposed gold mine in the upper reaches of Montana's Henderson Mountain, less than three miles from Yellowstone National Park.

The mine and its lethal wastes threaten not only the original crown jewel of the national park system, but one of the most beautiful and fragile wilderness areas in the country. So grave are those risks that this page suggested last year that Congress appropriate the necessary funds, about $35 million, to compensate Noranda Inc., the Canadian conglomerate that owns the site, for its exploratory expenses and then ask the company to go away.

That is still the best course of action for saving the great national park established by President Ulysses S. Grant. But it is unlikely that the Republican Congress will spend the necessary money or pay attention to various creative strategies offered by opponents of the mine. These include a proposal by Representative Bill Richardson, Democrat of New Mexico, to put the area off limits to mining by declaring it a national recreation area.

But the battle is far from lost. Under the 1872 Mining Law, the Federal Government cannot simply seize claims to which Noranda has already taken lawful title. It can, however, use existing statutes and its regulatory machinery to break Noranda's resolve. This is a company that persists in building a mine that few others want. Washington has enough legal authority, if the White House will wake up, to prevent the desecration of an American treasure by a foreign corporation.

Under the 1972 Clean Water Act, for example, the Environmental Protection Agency, through the Army Corps of Engineers, can prohibit development on wetlands. This is an important power because Noranda proposes to dig out 56 acres of wetlands high on the mountain. There it would build what it calls a "state of the art" impoundment site for storing acid wastes—a deep reservoir the size of 70 football fields. Reputable geologists say that any such structure, no matter how beautifully engineered, is bound to crack at some point given the region's extreme weather and its history of earthquakes. That will send poisons directly into the surrounding watershed, which includes two of the nation's important wild rivers.

If the E.P.A. and the Corps deny Noranda the necessary permits, the company will have to look elsewhere to store its toxic material. Alternative sites could be prohibitively expensive. But even if the two agencies duck what is an obvious moral obligation, there are other weapons available.

Noranda's 200-acre mine site is in the Gallatin National Forest, which is under the jurisdiction of the Agriculture Department's Forest Service. Noranda owns most of this land but does not yet have clear title to 27 acres that sit directly above a portion of the mother lode of gold, valued by Noranda at $500 million. Environmental lawyers believe that Secretary of the Interior Bruce Babbitt, following a formal request from the Forest Service, has the power under the 1976 Land Policy and Management Act to take permanent title to these acres on behalf of the Federal Government.

If these experts are right, then the Forest Service should promptly ask Mr. Babbitt to declare these acres off limits and the Secretary should rapidly comply. Deprived of some of its potential riches, Noranda might fold its tent.

Two environmental groups—American Rivers and Trout Unlimited—have suggested yet another approach to those pivotal 27 acres. They argue that a close reading of the 1872 Mining Law and a handful of court cases suggest that Mr. Babbitt can deny Noranda's claim if he can show that the land has greater value in an undisturbed state than it does as a mine. They also argue that even the $500 million in estimated deposits cannot begin to compare to the ecological and recreational values of Yellowstone and its adjoining ecosystem.

Mr. Babbitt may have trouble quantifying those values, but of course American Rivers and Trout Unlimited are right. The numbers are not important. As a nation, we have to draw a line and announce that some places are simply too valuable and too sacred to our history to be put at risk.

*1997*

# MICHAEL GARTNER

for editorials affecting the lives of people in his community

In early 1996, the *Daily Tribune* in Ames, Iowa, received a letter from a woman who was worried that a piece of church-owned land long used as a neighborhood playground had been sold to a developer. If she could raise the money, the developer told her, he'd carve out the acres the children had been using and keep it as a park. Michael Gartner, the *Tribune*'s editor and co-owner, opened the letter and, instead of running it, called the woman. He'd buy the land and give it to the city, he said, if they'd name the park after his late son Christopher Carl Gartner. The city agreed, and the park was built. Christopher was the older son of Michael and Barbara Gartner. On June 30, 1994, he died at age 17 of an initial attack of juvenile diabetes. "He was a healthy, robust boy on Tuesday. He got sick on Wednesday. He died on Thursday," Michael Gartner wrote in a column at the time. He often stopped by the park, and he wrote about it, about his son, and about families in an editorial that appeared just before Christmas of 1996. He was trying to "direct sadness into something positive," he explained. The Pulitzer he won was for "common sense editorials about issues affecting the daily lives of people of his community." The editorial reprinted below jumped to the top of the heap, one judge said. Readers liked it, too, and Gartner ran it each Christmas until he and his partners sold the 9,200-circulation *Tribune* in 1999. His first comment on Christopher, whom Gartner described as a "gentle giant, everyone's best friend, and the world's leading expert—on everything," was published as a column in *USA Today* and the *Tribune* on July 5, 1994. The letter response was immense. Michael Gartner had a long and varied career as Page One Editor of the *Wall Street Journal*, editor and president of the *Des Moines Register*, general news executive of Gannett Co. and *USA Today*, editor of the *Courier-Journal* and *Louisville Times*, and president of NBC News. He is a former president of the American Society of Newspaper Editors and a former member and chairman of the Pulitzer Prize Board. Today he is the "boss," as his informal note pads declare, of the Iowa Cubs, the triple-A farm club of the Chicago Cubs, and 50 percent owner of a small daily in Nebraska and weeklies in Nebraska, Colorado, and West Virginia. The editorial published here was intended to reflect on Christopher's life

and on the purpose of the park, which, wrote Gartner, was "to provide joy unbounded—joy for little kids, joy for their parents, joy for
their dogs. For Christopher Gartner was the most joyous boy that
ever lived." Years ago, the great Kansas editor William Allen
White, who won a Pulitzer for editorial writing in 1923, locked
himself in his office and quickly and expertly wrote a long editorial tribute about his young daughter, Mary, who died after being
thrown from a horse. One long-time editorial critic called the es-
say a masterpiece of American literature. Writing a detached but
loving tribute about the death of a child can be tough duty, but
here's another classic that all writers should contemplate if such a
terrible duty calls.

# Holiday Message Tucked Away in Park

*The Daily Tribune, Ames, Iowa* • December 23, 1996

We have more than a passing interest, of course, in Christopher Gartner Memorial Park in west Ames. We stopped by,
throughout the fall, and watched the children playing on the little
playground or romping on the two acres of lawn. We smiled when
we saw a mother or father with a youngster—pushing a swing, perhaps, or tossing a ball, or just sitting and watching. We grinned, especially, the day we saw a little boy with a big dog, each watching
out for the other. We laughed out loud when we saw two little boys
getting into harmless mischief.

The park, just a few months old, is already serving its purpose, we thought.

That purpose is to provide joy unbounded—joy for little kids,
joy for their parents, joy for their dogs.

For Christopher Carl Gartner was the most joyous boy that
ever lived.

He was born grinning, and the grin only got bigger as he
grew—and grew and grew and grew. He laughed at everything—
when he was little, at his grandpa's wild stories; when he was big-

ger, at his pals' wild escapades. By the time he was 15, he was an exuberant story-teller, regaling his pals with the latest funny thing his friend Andrew said, the latest crazy thing his friend Joey did. His grin and his laughter were infectious. Life for him was fun, and he wanted his friends and his mom and his dad and his grandparents to have fun, too. (He was genuinely kind, as well as cheerful, and early on he figured out that was an advantage. "You know," he once clued in his little brother, "if you're nice to your teachers you don't have to study nearly as hard," something he liked because being nice was a lot easier for him than studying.)

Life for him was love, too. By his early teens, he was a bear of a boy, probably six-feet three-inches or so, and he would almost have to bend over double to kiss his tiny grandma, whom he stopped by to see almost every day. But he never had that reticence or shyness that boys sometimes develop. He was an unabashed hugger from the day he was born in 1976 till the day he died in 1994. His last words to his father, as he lay in the hospital early in the morning of the summer day he died so suddenly and unexpectedly, were, "I love you too, dad."

We tell you this today, with more joy than sadness, for a couple of reasons. The first is just a technical one. The deed to the park was turned over to the city the other evening, so Christopher Gartner Memorial Park is now an official city park, and we just thought we'd tell you a bit about the boy the park is named after. (We could tell you much more—about how he goofily learned to walk with the help of a big unruly dog, who cushioned every fall; about how he drove his mother's new convertible into a tree the very day he got his driver's license—it was the tree's fault, he laughingly argued; about how he'd wake his parents at midnight to report in—and then tell them funny stories of what happened at the game or the party or wherever he'd been. All those or the million other happy memories that vie for space against the grieving a hundred times a day.)

The second reason we tell all this is because this is the Christmas season, the time of joy and of families and of fun and of love. We thought there was no better way to wish you a merry Christmas than to tell you the story of a boy who embodied laughter and love and giving, a boy who brought so much joy to so many people in just 17 years.

Our purpose surely is evident: to urge you to have fun this holiday season with your kids or your parents—or both. To urge you to sit around and tell family stories as two or three or sometimes four generations gather at the table—to share in the laughter. And to urge you to tell one another, the young and the old and the very old, that your family is a pretty nice family—to share in the love.

Finally, if it's a nice day tomorrow, you might want to wander over to Christopher Gartner Park—it's tucked away at the dead end of Abraham Drive—and toss a ball around or romp with a dog or push a swing. And think nice thoughts about the cheerful boy who has lent it his name.

It's too bad you never knew him.

You'd have loved his laugh.

You'd have loved him.

*1998*

# BERNARD L. STEIN

for his gracefully written editorials on politics and other issues affecting New York City residents

Bernard Stein, editor of a feisty 14,000-circulation weekly newspaper, was used to winning prizes. The *Riverdale Press* had been recognized as the best weekly in New York State eight times and had won more than 300 state and national awards, all destroyed when the paper was firebombed in 1989 for an editorial defending author Salman Rushdie and the public's right to read his controversial novel *The Satanic Verses*. Even today, he remains wary over what he considers a live issue. "I seldom think that I'm being stalked because of an editorial I write," he explained. Nevertheless, he added, "When I come to the office and I'm the first one here, I look carefully around before I open the door." He continued running Rushdie editorials for ten years thereafter, including one in the submission of ten for the 1998 Pulitzer Prize. He had been a finalist for the editorial writing award in 1987 and 1988. The 1998 award brought a surge of pride among residents of the closely knit community who deluged the paper with hundreds of letters and phone calls of congratulations. Said Stein in reaction to the response, "It was the kind of feeling that no metro journalist can have because he doesn't have the intimate connection with his readers that we have. Our readers feel there is a mutual interplay with the paper and how they are living their lives." Stein's father founded the paper in 1950. Bernard Stein is fierce in his deep belief in the quality of the reporting and writing in community journalism, which he feels is too often consigned to the minor leagues of the profession. He took on former *New York Times* editorial page editor (and later executive editor) Max Frankel, who had written in a column that there should be a separate Pulitzer category for small newspapers. "There are very talented people working for community newspapers," Stein said. "One reason I enter contests is to get our name known in the profession. Our reporters are young, and we pay them miserable salaries. We know they are going to move on. When we win an award like the Pulitzer, we hope editors out there are going to say 'Hey, they must have had good training.'" The editorial featured here is a bit of a departure from the hard-hitting essays he often writes. He reflected on the topic when he was unsure about what to write about one day. "I walked the site. What's good about this editorial is the concrete description and the discovery that it's not a pretty place. It's a dry patch, but the Warblers bring it alive. I enjoyed using my eyes instead of being chained to my desk. This piece gets to a central issue of how the land is to be used and preserved in my community."

# Learning from 'the Fieldston Warblers'

*Riverdale (N.Y.) Press* • January 2, 1997

One of the things Peter Mott's students learn in his biology class at Fieldston School is that he thinks numbers are important. He's been known to have them count the number of fallen leaves on a particular patch of ground.

For many years, Mr. Mott himself has been counting birds on the Fieldston campus. That's hardly surprising, since he is also the president of the New York Audubon Society. His observations form the basis of a recently completed scientific paper, and also of his column in the January-February issue of The Urban Audubon, the Society's newsletter.

They lead him to a surprising conclusion, one that can help illuminate this area's perennial battle to preserve green and open space and demonstrate that what's at stake are neither selfish nor parochial concerns.

As he walked to work along Riverdale Avenue one morning in May, 1985, Mr. Mott recalls in his Urban Audubon column, he heard the distinctive song of the parula warbler coming from a tree on the Fieldston campus. For 11 years thereafter, he watched the five-acre area behind the school library during the migratory season.

Between April 25 and June 5 of those years, he observed 25 species of warbler, including the mourning warbler, a somberly fledged bird spotted infrequently enough to cause John Kieran to exclaim over sightings in Van Cortlandt Park 40 years ago. Nine species have come to Fieldston every year; another six have missed only a year or two; and all of them have visited for at least two years. "If you come to visit on the busiest day of migration, day 130, you could expect to find up to eleven species," Mr. Mott reports.

The plot he surveilled constitutes no urban Eden. It's a rather shabby patch of ground concealing a small parking lot from which a rutted track leads to well-tended tennis courts and to abandoned older courts that have fallen into ruin.

The trees that dot the landscape are scruffy. Most are thin and some are twisted; they are remarkable more for what they say about nature's tenacity than its beauty. A pair has pushed through the asphalt to grow in the doubles alley of a disused tennis court. Another, struggling to find sun, has bent through a chain link fence, and has burst the links as it continued to grow.

But Beth Robinson, one of Mr. Mott's students, established the importance of these slatternly trees to the bird life they shelter and nourish. True to her teacher's methods, she counted the trees in the little woodland. There are 400 of them, and 69 percent are oaks, the warblers' favorite tree. They spent 92 percent of their time in the oaks, she found.

She also noted that different species used different portions of the trees for cover. The mourning warblers favored the underbrush, as did the yellowthroats and five other species. All but two species spent time in the suckers that are trimmed away by landscapers and home gardeners concerned with the appearance of specimen trees.

"The 'Fieldston Warblers' are a delight," Mr. Mott writes. "They please and they raise another questions. How important are these patches? How many of these pockets are there in the city? What will happen if they go?"

Can they, he wonders, be as important cumulatively as the larger oases being classified as Important Bird Areas, places like Jamaica Bay and Central Park? Should they, he asks, be identified and protected in the same way?

Isn't this just another way of sounding the same warning the Riverdale Nature Preservancy sounded when it found that if Riverdale's institutions, including Fieldston School, expanded to the maximum allowed by their acreage they would add more than 8.6 million square feet of buildings? Isn't it just another way of saying what opponents of building a massive filtration plant in the Jerome Park Reservoir have been saying?

For decades, Riverdalians have struggled to strike a balance between development and open space. For decades, their instincts have told them what Mr. Mott's study tells him: how valuable, how nourishing a patch of green is, and how much it contributes to the human endeavors in its midst.

*1999*

# EDITORIAL BOARD, *NEW YORK DAILY NEWS*

(Brian Kates, Alex Storozynski, Karen Hunter, Michael Goodwin,
Karen Zautyk, Jonathan Capehart and Michael Aronson)

for the paper's effective campaign to rescue Harlem's famed Apollo
Theater from the financial mismanagement that threatened the
landmark's survival

The *New York Daily News'* series of editorials about the Apollo
Theater, a Harlem icon, was developed by the *News'* editorial
board and not the newsroom. "There was lots of original reporting
on our part," said Michael Goodwin, then editorial page editor and
now the paper's executive editor. The board concept gave the staff
the luxury to detach editorial writers for independent observation
and reporting. They would come together at the end of the day to
sort out the clearest and strongest revelations to bolster the point
of view. The ten editorials the *News* submitted for the Pulitzer
Prize reflected on major events concerning the Apollo story, starting in April of 1998 and ending on December 30. The editorial
reprinted here, the second in the series, moves quickly and deci-
sively to the point of view and hammers away at the leadership of
U.S. Rep. Charles Rangel, a long-time congressman and chairman
of the Apollo Theatre Foundation who "has allowed the Apollo to
fall into sad disrepair and be sapped of its vast economic and cultural potential," the central theme of the editorial campaign. It
focused unrelentingly on Rangel's seeming indifference and the
deterioration of the Apollo. To be sure, there were sideshows, including Rangel's attempt to play the race card. At one point, in a
conference call, he said he had never known a black who had
worked for the *News*. Well, said African-American editorial writer
Jonathan Capehart, in a totally deflating comment, "You're talking to one." Capehart and another key writer, Michael Aronson,
praised the editorship of Goodwin. "He told us to develop our own
stories," said Capehart. Rangel no longer heads the foundation.
Meanwhile, the *News'* editorial board continues to follow the story
closely.

# Give Theater Board the Hook

*New York Daily News* • April 27, 1998

No one symbolizes the power of Harlem more than Rep. Charles Rangel. With 28 years on Capitol Hill, he is the dean of the state's congressional delegation. And he has put his clout to good use, with the $300 million Upper Manhattan Empowerment Zone being the most visible sign.

But as chairman for seven years of the Apollo Theatre Foundation, the nonprofit corporation entrusted with the crown jewel of 125th St., Rangel has been woefully ineffective. He has allowed the Apollo to fall into sad disrepair and be sapped of its vast economic and cultural potential.

The first, and most crucial, step toward restoring the Apollo's legacy must be for Rangel to sever his link to the theater. During his reign, the Apollo has become a physical eyesore. It sits dark most of the week. And its modern recording studio and sound stage remain underused.

Only on Wednesdays does the theater come alive—for the popular Amateur Night, where new talent has been hailed, hooted and hooked since the 1930s. The show proves the theater's lure is magical—if properly presented.

Then there is the popular syndicated TV show "It's Showtime at the Apollo," whose producer, powerbroker Percy Sutton, is Rangel's life-long friend and ally. Thanks to a five-year-old sweetheart licensing deal, the Apollo—and all its trademarks—essentially have become Sutton's exclusive domain.

That lopsided deal has been compounded by the failure of Rangel and his board to enforce the contract terms. Late last year, with Sutton owing what some insiders estimated at more than $3 million, a board panel accepted a mere $145,000 as full payment. It is not clear whether the full board has ratified that settlement and whether any money has actually been paid.

Rangel claims to know nothing about the settlement. And therein lies the problem: Rangel's absentee leadership. He has entrusted the theater to Sutton and an insular board that bears the taint of the Harlem Urban Development Corp.

Rangel and HUDC formed the Apollo foundation in 1991— four years before HUDC was disbanded amid allegations of corruption and fiscal chicanery. Apollo board members Eugene McCabe, Richard Greene and the Rev. William James all served with Rangel on the HUDC board. Of the 11 founding foundation board members, eight remain. As McCabe said, half in jest, in an interview, serving on the Apollo board is a "lifetime appointment." That must change.

In a telephone interview, Rangel said, "The Apollo is very dear and near to me and probably deserves better than me." He's right. Rangel has left the theater begging for money, while his pal Sutton continues to enjoy its fruits.

Until the Apollo Theatre Foundation has a leader with vision, expertise and the fiscal sense to spend wisely, the organization's campaign to raise $30 million for renovations and a stabilizing endowment must be halted. Under current leadership, donors would be throwing good money after bad.

The board must be reconstituted—sans Rangel and his cronies—with a mandate to renegotiate the "It's Showtime at the Apollo" deal. The current agreement with Sutton expired in December but has been extended temporarily. A new agreement must not be signed until the board can demonstrate it has collected all the money Sutton owes. Even then, the board, despite hiring a respected law firm to guide it, has forfeited all trust that it can properly run the theater.

Under inspired new leadership, the Apollo could take advantage of the Harlem tourism boom. A lucrative gift shop and cafe— dreams of executive director Grace Blake—could become a reality under an energized, creative board.

If business (or lack thereof) as usual continues under Rangel, the state, the owner of the Apollo, must step in. Its lease requires the foundation to maintain the theater in good condition and to provide quarterly financial reports. The foundation has done neither— ample justification for turning the operation over to a more responsible group.

Also, under state law, Attorney General Dennis Vacco or a board member can petition the court to remove Rangel or dissolve the entire body. All that's required is evidence of a breach of fiduciary duties. Although no government agency has ever audited the foundation, there is evidence aplenty—as this page has shown today and yesterday.

When the Apollo Theatre Foundation was created, the goal was to insure that the legendary theater would remain a haven of dreams, ambition and talent. Rangel can now put it back on that path. By stepping down gracefully.

*2000*

# JOHN C. BERSIA

for his passionate editorial campaign attacking predatory lending practices in the state, which prompted changes in local lending regulations

John Bersia joined the *Sentinel* editorial board in 1985 after years as an analyst and writer on international affairs. He was to focus on international relations, national affairs and business and economic issues. He later took on the loan-sharking business in Florida in a no-holds-barred fashion that named victims and legal perpetrators, particularly the car title lenders and payday advance businesses. Today, some of those lenders still exist but under tighter restriction that the state legislature imposed. Still, Bersia said, the problem is global. The editorial reprinted here was the first of the ten he submitted for the Pulitzer Prize. Overall he wrote more than 150 on the topic. The editorial is typical of the hard-hitting point of view exemplified in those that followed. They were unrelenting in their condemnation. In the editorial here, starting with the italicized one-sentence introduction that sums up the point of view, Bersia details the outrage, legal though the lending practice was, and quickly moves to the state legislative leaders who looked aside. The tone is scathing. The concluding sentence offers the solution. Today, Bersia is a part-time opinion writer for the *Orlando Sentinel*, crafting a weekly column exclusively on international affairs. It falls in line with his day job as special assistant to the president for global perspectives and university professor at the University of Central Florida, his undergraduate alma mater. He holds advanced degrees in international relations and political science, government and public information administration.

# Legal Loan Sharking

*Orlando Sentinel* • March 28, 1999

*Whether lawmakers want to admit it or not, Florida has legalized loan-sharking.*

Consider:

A Sanford woman who's going through a divorce has only her car to her name. She turns to a title-loan company for a paltry, $250 loan. In return, she is charged interest and fees totaling 264 percent a year—plus the company keeps an extra set of keys to her car, just in case she doesn't pay up.

It's all perfectly legal.

A homeless Orlando couple with too little money to maintain a bank account must pay a fee and forfeit 3 percent of their meager earnings simply to cash a paycheck. Then, to pay their bills, they have to shell out even more to buy money orders because they can't write a check.

It's all perfectly legal.

A Winter Springs woman needs $100 for car repairs. She goes to a store where she gets an advance on her paycheck—for what amounts to a triple-digit annual interest rate. Still struggling to pay her bills, in the next two and a half years, she will wind up borrowing nearly $2,500 and paying back more than $6,500. And still she will be in debt.

Again, it's all perfectly legal.

Title-loan companies that require you to put up your car for collateral, check-cashers that can take a huge cut from people too poor to open an account at a regular bank, stores that give you an advance on your paycheck at absurd interest rates—those businesses all prey on the working poor, the elderly on fixed incomes and others desperate for money. And they do so with the state's blessing.

In Florida, the law treats the poor and financially strapped differently from those who have money. And the shameful truth is that the poor pay more than the rich. Though state law limits the interest rate that banks and Florida-based credit-card companies can charge to 18 percent a year, predatory businesses on the financial fringe are flourishing. They are devouring the meager assets of hundreds of thousands of Floridians who live payday to payday—the very people who can least afford to be exploited.

No knee-caps get broken, but—in a manner of speaking—lots of backs do. The charges are more than the poor can bear.

Florida's booming tourism industry, which has brought comfortable salaries to those at the top, has spawned a huge population of minimum-wage workers. Unfortunately, banks have had little desire to busy themselves with such meager paychecks.

The fringe lenders, on the other hand, are only too happy to step in—at an exorbitant price. They defend their practices by pointing out the risks they take. They say they stay open long hours in neighborhoods that banks have abandoned, dealing with people who have credit problems and who may not pay back the money at all.

It seems plausible enough—until you stop to wonder why, if the risk is so great, those businesses are proliferating into empires. Consider just one, ACE Cash Express Inc., the nation's largest check-casher and also a payday lender. In just over 10 years, it has managed to expand to more than 800 stores and, despite that aggressive expansion, already had profits of more than $6 million last year.

Such businesses lure desperate people with a promise of fast cash, just what someone a few dollars away from eviction wants to hear. You can see the lenders' signs littering the roadside: "Need a loan? Have a car?"

But what those greedy sirens know is that people in a financial pinch aren't likely to be helped by a small, payday advance for, say, two weeks or a title loan for 30 days. The lenders know that many of their customers will never quite be able to pay back in full and on time, that they'll always be a few dollars short and a few days late. They know that what was supposed to be a two-week or one-month loan likely will escalate into a burden of a year or more. Meanwhile, the interest will soar into triple digits.

Let the buyer beware, the lenders say. No one is forcing people to borrow. And if they do borrow, they can read the fine print for themselves.

In an ideal world, yes. But the world of people who need those loans is not ideal. They may be single parents. They may be sick or disabled. They may be unemployed, underemployed or unable to read. Many of them don't have the minimum balance needed to open a bank account.

They don't have a lot of options.

The loan sharks are only too happy to invite them in for a swim.

So, what have our lawmakers done?

Well, when they haven't been snoozing, they've been accepting generous campaign contributions from those businesses—and making matters worse.

In 1995, the Legislature passed a law allowing these predatory businesses to charge a monstrous rate of as much as 22 percent a month—that's 264 percent a year—on loans secured by a car title. Most lawmakers say they didn't even realize what they had voted for in the waning days of the session. How could that possibly be?

Whatever the excuse, legalized loan-sharking is disgraceful, ever more so in a prosperous state such as Florida.

The two key players now are Senate President Toni Jennings and House of Representatives Speaker John Thrasher. Today, Ms. Jennings sits by quietly, letting it happen, and Mr. Thrasher looks to be doing all he can to help these lenders stick it to the poor. Yet, together they share a unique responsibility to protect the poor, the powerless and the politically unconnected.

Can they not hear the victims crying out for help? Do they care?

They need to lead the charge to rein in these predatory money-lenders and wrestle their interest rates down from the stratosphere.

These businesses are part of a dangerous slide toward a Florida in which the have-nots are thrust into a minimum-wage, or worse, subculture to be used, abused and tossed aside. It feeds off the low-paying tourism industry, the poorly educated, the new immigrants and those just poor. It is simply wrong and cannot be allowed to happen.

The governor and Florida legislators need to speak up and say "enough," that Florida is better than what these high-interest lenders would make us.

This kind of loan-sharking should be against the law.

# DAVID MOATS

for his even-handed and influential series of editorials commenting on the divisive issues arising from civil unions for same-sex couples

David Moats became editorial page editor of the 22,000-circulation *Rutland Herald* in 1992 after joining the newspaper a decade earlier. So he knew the terrain and the politics of Vermont and understood that he would have major opposition backing a state Supreme Court ruling in December of 1999 that gay couples should share the same benefits as heterosexual couples. He had no idea about the depths to which the controversy would go, however, but knew it was the paper's responsibility to keep the debate moving forward, particularly among state lawmakers in working out specifics of legislation allowing civil unions, which the paper endorsed and which was eventually approved in May 2000. He praised legislators on both sides for wrestling with the contentious and highly emotional issue. Polls showed voters were against approval by a narrow margin. Some advertisers and subscribers grumbled about the paper's stance, and there was some dispute internally among the paper's staff. Moats didn't flinch. He said he was never subjected to any pressure, thanks to the shield of the publisher, John Mitchell, and then-managing editor John Van Hoesen, "who stood by us." Mitchell "figured taking stands was what we should do," a tradition in the family that owned the paper, Moats said. When the Pulitzer Prize was announced, there was an outpouring of public support, even from some politicians who opposed the paper's position. "A lot of people felt vindicated, and that we had done the right thing," Moats said. After House approval of the legislation, as the editorial published here trumpets, the Senate approved, and the bill was signed into law in April of 2000 by Gov. Howard Dean, who later ran for the Democratic Party's nomination for President. The editorial notes how Republicans and Democrats "joined together to respond to a constitutional mandate." Two of the leaders singled out, Rep. Thomas Little, a Republican, and Rep. William Lippert, a Democrat, both survived the debate and its aftermath. They were re-elected in 2000. In 2002, Lippert was re-elected, while Little chose not to run. Moats continues as the *Herald*'s sole editorial writer.

# A Courageous Step

*Rutland (Vt.) Herald* • March 16, 2000

The Vermont House of Representatives took a courageous step Wednesday in giving preliminary approval to a bill providing for civil unions between same-sex couples.

The events of the past two and a half months have been an example of extraordinary lawmaking. Republicans and Democrats joined together to respond to a constitutional mandate. The confidence of their own convictions ought to serve as their best shield against criticism. The swift, sure action they have taken ought to serve as the best protection against the deep division that a protracted conflict would create.

Two people stood out in the debate that preceded the vote Wednesday evening. One was Rep. Thomas Little, the Shelburne Republican who shepherded the bill through the House Judiciary Committee and to the floor of the House. His reasoned, low-key approach to the task kept the debate focused and properly restrained. His conviction in the rightness of his course can only have helped to stiffen the courage of fellow House members.

The other was Rep. William Lippert, a Democrat from Hinesburg, who spoke before a vote was taken, defeating an amendment that would have diluted and weakened the bill.

As Lippert began to speak Wednesday, the House fell silent. Lippert, who is gay, spoke with dignity and with passion. He began by saying it was important for his fellow House members to understand reality.

Gay relationships, he said, are in some ways "miracles" because they manage to take shape within an atmosphere of unremitting prejudice. He asked his fellow House members to imagine how difficult it would be for them to form lasting relationships in such circumstances. He said gay relationships represented a "triumph against discrimination and prejudice."

Lippert said that until two and a half months ago he believed Vermont had made great progress in guaranteeing gay rights. But in the last two and half months, he said, "I have been called names in this chamber and in this building the likes of which I have never seen in my life." He understood that his fellow House members had been subjected to a similar barrage of hate. "I wouldn't have wished this on any of them," he said.

He said he felt, in these circumstances, it was strange to ask, "Should we get our rights now, or should we wait a little longer, or should we ask all the people whether we should get our rights."

He spoke of the burden that the AIDS epidemic had placed on gays. "Don't tell me what a committed relationship is and isn't," he said. The emotional power of Lippert's message combined with Little's reasoned approach to the task were hard for the House to resist.

The House turned aside amendments that would have delayed their decision, either by calling for a constitutional convention or an advisory referendum. Opponents said the people wanted a say on the issue.

But House members already know that a majority probably opposes the action they have taken. Two extraordinary public hearings allowed the public an unprecedented opportunity to express its views, and the volume of mail to the Legislature and to the press has provided the Legislature with a full spectrum of opinion. Votes on Town Meeting Day showed continuing opposition to same-sex marriage or civil unions.

What the House required was not more finely calibrated gauges of public opinion, but the power to weigh the opinion it heard against the requirements of the law. In the end, that is what the House did.

It is likely that, if this bill becomes law, Vermonters will recognize they have lost nothing by extending fair treatment to neighbors who have had to conduct their personal lives in a shadow of discrimination. Vermonters, in the end, will appreciate the leadership shown by the House on Wednesday.

# ALEX RAKSIN and BOB SIPCHEN

for their comprehensive and powerfully-written editorials exploring the issues and dilemmas provoked by mentally ill people dwelling on the streets

It's not often that editorial writers receive words of endearment for their work. But Alex Raksin and Bob Sipchen of the *Los Angeles Times* did. The California Treatment Advocacy Coalition, a group that seeks to improve the lives of people with severe mental illness, congratulated them for their Pulitzer Prize as "our two editorial angels." In a press release, the coalition noted that in protecting the rights and liberties of the mentally ill "we have granted some genuinely helpless individuals the liberty to harm themselves, and others, in the never-ending cycles. Free people should always hesitate to diminish anyone's civil liberties, but in this instance there's good reason." The specific editorial that it mentioned is reprinted here. The editorial was illuminated by a clear, direct headline that signaled the startling and potentially controversial point of view. It was one of ten editorials in a series titled "Helping People off the Streets" that ran from April 23, 2001, to November 22, 2001, with the last five in a daily series. To conduct their research, Raksin and Sipchen prowled the streets and alleys to interview street people and their families. Then they went to the courts, police stations, judges and social service workers. The editorials, said a *Times* press release, helped to pass laws that had been stalled and to keep other legislation moving forward. *Times* editor John Carroll said the editorials were noteworthy because "they were not ivory tower productions. Alex and Bob went to the worst parts of the city . . . and combined sheer reporting with clarity of thought to produce them." Sipchen, who had shared a Pulitzer with other *Times* reporters for spot news reporting in 1993, declared, "This is one of the most conspicuous problems our country faces, and it's shameful that we haven't solved it yet. These editorials came from our hearts, and I think that's why we were successful."

# A Case Against Liberty

*Los Angeles Times* • May 7,2001

Forty years of good intentions have left California's mentally ill in desperate—sometimes tragic—circumstances. You can see the desperate ones on the streets every day. If you haven't seen the tragic ones, consider the case of Scott Harlan Thorpe.

Thorpe, a former janitor, thought the FBI was ordering cooks to poison his meat and forcing him to see an incompetent psychiatrist.

If there had been a way for the state to compel him to take his medications and accept therapy, Thorpe might be living a relatively normal life. Instead, on Jan. 10 he marched into the only public mental health clinic in the Northern California town of Nevada City and, according to eyewitnesses, opened fire. The fusillade killed two clinic employees, including 19-year-old Laura Wilcox, a high school valedictorian who was working at the clinic during college break.

Boasting that he was "the toughest man the FBI had ever tried to break," Thorpe, 41, drove to a nearby restaurant, where he allegedly shot to death its 24-year-old manager.

Thorpe's rampage, which left three other people seriously wounded, offers an extreme but pertinent illustration of why legislators must pass AB 1421, a sensible mental health bill that is working its way through Sacramento this week.

Thorpe's family saw his paranoia deepening and sought help for him. But no one could force Thorpe to accept treatment and stick with it, so the deck was stacked against his relatives. The bill is aimed at such cases, getting treatment to people when their actions suggest that they pose a threat to themselves or others. The legislation would give judges power to force people like Thorpe to take medications to modify their behavior or face confinement.

For two generations, California has been applying what now seems an extreme emphasis on the civil liberties of unfortunate people who cannot refrain from harming themselves and, occasionally, others. Thorpe's is an extreme case, but you'll find less violent (though still troubling) examples on the streets of every city in the state.

It's time to stop averting our eyes, because there's something we can do about it. But doing something means a reduction in the civil liberties of some of the mentally ill and a corresponding increase in the authority of the state. As a general rule, we like to see things go the other way. In this rare instance, Californians should proceed with eyes open and calibrate the adjustment very carefully.

If the Legislature and Gov. Gray Davis approve the bill—and provide enough money to make it work—AB 1421 would be a good first step toward a more balanced public policy.

With that goal in mind, the measure now needs fine-tuning. We commend the bill's author, Assemblywoman Helen Thomson (D-Davis), for persevering against civil liberty absolutists whose well-meaning resistance to the measure works against positive change.

We must not pretend, however, that what Thomson proposes is anything less than a significant widening of the state's authority. As such, it deserves the closest scrutiny. This week, Thomson should listen closely to mental health advocates who contend that the bill, as worded, is too broad in defining those on whom a judge could impose treatment. We encourage her to once again take full measure of the bill's civil rights protections. Then, with reasonable protections adopted, the bill should go forward. California owes it to Amanda and Nick Wilcox, Laura's mom and dad.

They saw in Laura an energetic and compassionate young woman. She was running for student body president at Haverford College and planned to work for a Quaker group after graduation. She might still be rushing toward that promising future had Thorpe's family been able to compel him to get help.

"Amanda and I understand that our daughter was a random victim in this tragedy," Nick Wilcox said. "We also believe that the events of that day were predictable and preventable."

Therein lies a revolting twist: Now, three deaths later, Scott Thorpe is locked up awaiting trial and the state can finally force him to take his medications. There is a better way, and Sacramento must make the start.

# CORNELIA GRUMMAN

for her freshly challenging editorials urging reform of the death penalty

On April 7, 2003, the day the Pulitzers were announced in the afternoon, the *Chicago Tribune*, a morning newspaper, had run an editorial by Cornelia Grumman that praised "a remarkable week for justice" in the wake of former Gov. George Ryan's stunning and controversial blanket commutation of Death Row prisoners. Ryan had declared a moratorium on capital punishment three and one-half years earlier and challenged the legislature to examine the system. The most contentious of the measures approved by the legislature in slightly different versions that would require reconciliation concerned mandating that all homicide interrogations and confessions be videotaped, which passed without a negative vote. That is the subject of the editorial published here that was at the heart of her winning series of editorials. Grumman wrote that "what happened last week was little short of astonishing. A sweeping array of criminal justice reforms zipped through" the legislature. Grumman joined the *Tribune*'s editorial board in 2000 after covering Illinois state government. During that time, she had witnessed a double execution and reported on many of the issues she wrote about in editorials concerning the death penalty and the need for reform. "After a while, it did sort of become a crusade," she told colleagues when the Pulitzer award was announced. The examination of capital punishment has been a longtime pursuit of the *Tribune*, and editors paid tribute to reporters Steve Mills and Maurice Possley and former staff writer Ken Armstrong, all of whom were involved in the effort. Grumman noted the emphasis placed on reporting when it comes to editorial writing. Their reporting helped fuel many of her editorials. "I feel like my work," she said, "has been a footnote to the book they wrote . . . just the last chapter calling for reform for all the problems they detailed. They are my heroes."

# No More Excuses. Go to the Tape

*Chicago Tribune* • April 21, 2002

In one of the Kankakee County sheriff's first attempts at videotaping an interrogation, suspect Christopher Connery was led into a small room. It was bare but for two chairs, a table and a wall thermostat the size of a cigarette pack.

Detectives listened intently to Connery's repeated denials that he had raped and stabbed Melissa Osman to death. By the time investigators left the room to interview another witness, though, Connery appeared to have forgotten something—he had agreed that his interview could be videotaped. A tiny camera was perched behind the thermostat.

Alone in the room, Connery started singing, "Ding, dong, the wicked witch is dead. . . ."

Connery has now taken up lifetime residence at the Pontiac Correctional Center.

For a sheriff's department full of cynics, that marked a conversion to the value of videotaping. Today their basement offices in downtown Kankakee are teeming with converts.

Detectives assert that their community reputation has improved since they started videotaping felony interrogations and confessions in 1996. Serious police brutality challenges have become almost non-existent. Prosecutors rarely lose on a motion to suppress a confession before trial. The police have learned new techniques by watching each other on tape.

Undersheriff Bradley O'Keefe notes another unexpected bonus: The valuable information they learn when the suspect thinks he's alone in the room.

• • •

Videotaping interrogations and confessions stood among the major recommendations issued last week by the Governor's Commission on Capital Punishment. The respected panel spent two years meticulously examining the system and issued 85 suggestions to make it better. Videotaping is one of the more controversial proposals, even though the idea has also been endorsed by a state Supreme Court committee that issued an earlier set of reforms.

The states of Minnesota and Alaska require videotaped interrogations and confessions. An increasing number of police departments around the country have adopted it on their own.

So why is it that so many law enforcement officials in Illinois still regard videotaping as a neutron bomb to effective policing? Why do places like Kankakee remain lonely islands of reason in a combative sea?

Mere hours after Monday's press conference to announce the commission's report, spitballs started flying. Why? Because too many cops want to serve and protect the status quo. Because they see it as a knock to their credibility rather than as a tool to help build strong cases while protecting the rights of the accused.

Law enforcement folks have plenty of reasons to worry about credibility, but this isn't one of them. The reasons they should be focused on include Ronald Jones, Corethian Bell, Rolando Cruz and Alejandro Hernandez—not to mention the 7- and 8-year-old boys who were wrongly accused of murdering 11-year-old Ryan Harris.

All were Death Row inmates or murder defendants who eventually were released because police took bad confessions from them. That means DNA or someone else's confession exonerated them from the crime they "confessed" to police. Had their interrogations been videotaped, that might have been discovered weeks, rather than months or years, later.

Ronald Jones confessed to murder. But he later claimed at trial that he had been interrogated for eight hours and brought to the crime scene to enhance the detail and accuracy of his statement. A videotape, with a date and time stamp on it, would have resolved that issue years ago.

A Tribune series published in December illustrated that it's not hard to extract a false confession from someone who, like Jones, has a low IQ or who is an alcoholic or a drug addict.

So taping only murder confessions, as is the practice in Cook County, doesn't go far enough. Corethian Bell confessed on videotape that he murdered his mother. But DNA tests later linked someone else to the crime. After 17 months in jail, Bell was released in January. A video of his interrogation leading up to the false confession would have shed light on what happened here.

Another Death Row inmate, Aaron Patterson, for years has maintained he confessed to a crime he did not commit because he was subjected to police torture. Given that he was interrogated by officers working under notorious Chicago Police Commander Jon Burge, his claims may have credibility. A videotape would have resolved the issue years ago.

Dozens of excuses, from the picayune to the far-fetched, have been thrown out by police departments terrified by the idea of pulling back the curtain to the interrogation room.

**Excuse No. 1:** All that fancy equipment costs too much.

Video cameras cost a few hundred bucks. Sony sells digital video cameras starting at $500 retail. The entire setup, including cassettes, could reach $1,000. That's cheaper than the alternative financial burden, shelling out millions in civil liabilities for false confessions. DuPage County paid $3.5 million to exonerated Death Row inmates Rolando Cruz and Alejandro Hernandez; Cook County paid $38.5 million to the four released Death Row inmates known as thé Ford Heights Four. Cook taxpayers are destined to shell out millions more in legal fees and settlements for mishandling interrogations and confessions of four men wrongfully convicted of murdering medical student Lori Roscetti. Then there are the two young boys initially charged in the Ryan Harris case after their questionable confessions.

**Excuse No. 2:** Who has room to store all those cassettes?

In the Kankakee sheriff's evidence room is one small bookshelf on which sits all of last year's 157 videotapes, and there's plenty of room for more. Now with digital video technology, interviews could be stored on computers instead of shelves.

**Excuse No. 3:** This is one more technicality that will let murderers and rapists to go free.

Many prosecutors and police who use videotapes say just the opposite is true: Videotape helps win their cases or leads to faster plea bargains. "I would describe it as a big improvement," said Kankakee County Judge Clark Erickson. "We're spending a lot less time on pre-trial motions. It just narrows the issues."

In Minnesota, Hennepin County Prosecutor Amy Klobuchar said there are two major advantages to videotaped interrogations. They squelch virtually all police brutality claims because judges and jurors are able to see for themselves whether brutality occurred. And jurors are able to see what a defendant's demeanor was after the crime, rather than have to rely on someone else's descriptions and memories. "We had a guy who claimed he was blind," Klobuchar said. "When police left the room, he picked up a paper and started reading. The camera was on the whole time."

**Excuse No. 4:** Things can go wrong with the tape.

True. Kankakee Chief Investigator Ken McCabe said he has a case now where no audio was recorded on a tape. But this is the first time that has happened after handling more than 500 videotapes. Exceptions can be written into the law to allow confessions to be admitted when there was a technical breakdown or practical problem with videotaping. The commission recommends just such an exception.

**Excuse No. 5:** Sometimes a suspect will start confessing in the squad car or in the field before he can be taken to the station for interrogation.

Minnesota has provided the answer. Have cops carry small tape recorders for instances when a confession occurs outside of the police station.

**Excuse No. 6:** Suspects will clam up if they know a camera is on.

That was the same argument made before Miranda warnings were imposed, and it turned out not to be true. Kankakee Police Chief Michael Kinkade said about 55 percent of last year's felony suspects agreed to be videotaped. At the sheriff's office, more than 95 percent of felony suspects have assented to videotaping, O'Keefe said. Cameras can be positioned to be unobtrusive.

**Excuse No. 7:** Juries won't understand the kinds of tactics police use, which can involve legally protected lies or misleading statements.

To that, Kankakee Circuit Judge Kathy Bradshaw-Elliott said juries have gotten increasingly sophisticated about police questioning tactics by, believe it or not, watching television crime shows like NYPD Blue and Law & Order. Beyond that, people simply have the ability to understand the sometimes tough interrogation techniques used by police when they're carefully explained in court.

Some authorities suggest videotaping should be voluntary. Videotaping already is voluntary. Mandating it statewide is good, sensible policy. And for all the election year Nervous Nellies, this has nothing to do with being soft on crime. Videotaping interrogations helps further the search for the truth.

No one craves truth more than victims. Ask Dorothe Ernest of Hinsdale, whose daughter Kimberly was murdered while jogging in Philadelphia in 1995. The suspects claimed their confessions were coerced; the jury believed them. A videotape, Ernest believes, would have proved otherwise.

Illinois' criminal justice system is flawed. The 13 men who have been wrongly sentenced to die since 1977 stand as stark evidence of that. It is time to substantially improve that system, and videotaping interrogations and confessions will be an important step toward that.

A videotaping bill has sat in the House Judiciary committee for years. It is a fine bill. Some committee members have said the recommendation of the governor's commission will prompt them to take fresh look at it.

Great. Do it now. The Illinois legislature has proved it can respond quickly and forcefully when it is faced with a crisis, as it did nearly a decade ago in reforming the state's child welfare system.

Well, here is an issue that is no less one of life and death. The governor's commission on capital punishment has offered dozens of ways to improve on Illinois' capital punishment system. Move on them. No one craves truth more than victims.

# Afterword

In the introduction, we concluded that more than a few of the editorials published here are of uneven quality and suffer from the twin problems of dull writing and lack of unity. We also pointed out the growing concern of some critics of editorial writing today that many current pieces lack "passion," however that is defined, and hunker down into a safe, rambling dialogue that fails utterly to bring the point of view and the reader to full boil. You will be the final judge of these perspectives.

As you judge, perhaps the most important part to consider in each editorial is its date.

This anthology amply reflects the refinements in the craft of editorial writing and the intellectual and professional development of editorial writers over the 86-year time span of the Pulitzer Prizes. The fiery, sermon-like length and tone of some of the earlier editorials when newspapers were the nation's primary medium of communication now seem ill-suited to the mass media of print and electronic communication of today and the technology that has revolutionized the presentation of news and opinion. The early writing, like the issues they address, may seem antiquated, but both can be fully enjoyed if the reader appreciates historical perspective and, as with luxuriating in good poetry, has the patience to devote time to a reflective read.

Fortunately, history and opinion writing have a way of progressing together for the sake of mutual accommodation so that many of the later editorials shed some of the writing problems and create genuine sparkle that makes the reading and appreciation of the argumentation and point of view more enjoyable.

Whatever your conclusions in judging the worth of these Pulitzer Prize editorials, we trust that you will think on the historical framework in which they were written.

# *About the Editors*

WM. DAVID SLOAN, a professor of journalism at the University of Alabama, is the author of more than twenty other books and numerous articles on journalism history and writing. Among his books are *Great Editorials* and *Masterpieces of Reporting*. He is also the author of the series "Great American Editorials," which appeared for ten years in *The Masthead*, the journal of the National Conference of Editorial Writers. He is the founder of the American Journalism Historians Association and served a five-year term as editor of its research journal, *American Journalism*. The AJHA recognizes him with its annual "Sloan Outstanding Faculty Research Paper" award. In 1998 he received the AJHA's Kobre Award for lifetime achievements. He has served as national president (1998–2000) of Kappa Tau Alpha, the mass communication honor society. On its ninetieth anniversary, KTA selected him as one of the five most important members in its history. Professor Sloan has taught at the University of Arkansas and has worked as reporter, columnist and editor on five newspapers.

LAIRD B. ANDERSON is professor emeritus of journalism at the American University School of Communication in Washington, D.C. He is also an experienced journalist, having worked at the beginning of his career as a reporter, editorial writer, and columnist for *The Times* (Gainesville, Ga.), as bureau chief and capital correspondent in Tallahassee, Fla., for the *Miami News*, and as a reporter in Chicago and Washington for the *Wall Street Journal* covering economic affairs. He frequently lectures and conducts workshops for international journalists in the United States and abroad, primarily in South Asia, Eastern Europe, Africa and Central America. He is the author of many articles on the economics of the media, opinion writing, and, in his capacity as a retired U.S. Army Reserve infantry and special forces officer, the conduct of military operations and media-military relations. Professor Anderson is a co-editor or contributor to four books. The latest is *Beyond Argument: A Handbook for Editorial Writers* published by the Scripps Howard Foundation and the National Conference of Editorial Writers Foundation.